Don't sweat the Aubergine

Don't sweat the Aubergine

What works in the kitchen and why

Nicholas Clee

✳ SHORT BOOKS

First published in 2005 by
Short Books
15 Highbury Terrace
London N5 1UP

10 9 8 7 6 5 4 3 2 1

A CIP catalogue record for this book
is available from the British Library.

ISBN 1-904977-27-8
Printed in Germany by
GGP Media GmbH, Poessneck

Illustration copyright © Emily Fox

JACKET DESIGN: GEORGIA VAUX

For Nicolette, Rebecca and Laura

CONTENTS

INTRODUCTION

The most stressful event in your life, I have read, is moving house. Giving a speech is up there too. Weddings can cause a good degree of anxiety. Here's another scenario to get you in a sweat: there are eight people coming to dinner, you're attempting a dish you haven't prepared before, and it's not going well.

Why did you buy a whole leg of lamb? Boning it might have taken Gordon Ramsay five minutes, but took you 45. You have spent a further half an hour inserting little bits of rosemary and garlic, which stuck to your fingers, into the flesh. The cannellini beans to go with it were supposed to be cooked by now, but the one you've just tasted had the consistency of a pebble. Lacking a "gratin dish, preferably earthenware" for the gratin dauphinois, you made do with your old Pyrex, and you stuck to the quantity of milk and cream specified in the recipe even though the liquid came only halfway up the potatoes. Now the liquid has evaporated, and the potatoes are still crunchy. Then there's the pudding:

did you allow some yolk to seep into the whites when you separated the eggs? After 10 minutes of beating, the whites have barely turned white, let alone risen to what the book describes as "soft, snowy peaks". Meanwhile your flatmate/boyfriend/girlfriend/husband/wife, having promised to lay the table and clean the glasses, is still in the bloody bathroom.

I think that we get into these flaps because food experts, and our own insecurities, have led us to think of cookery as the fulfilment of recipes. The recipe sets the standard to which we aspire. If the dish doesn't work as the cookery writers suggested it would, we must have done something wrong. We have all felt those moments of panicked helplessness when natural processes have refused to conform to our hopes.

The recipe said, "Heat 200 ml of cream and 50 ml of milk, and pour over; the liquid should be level with the top of the potatoes." But the liquid wasn't level with the top; it came only halfway up. I must have sliced the potatoes too thin, you conjecture. Or too thick. Or used the wrong kind of dish. But the recipe specified that amount of liquid, so I'd better not add any more, or something else will go wrong. Oh, no: the dish has dried up and the potatoes are uncooked. I'm a failure.

Let me illustrate the drawbacks of adhering rigidly to recipes with a couple of examples. Both dishes contain lamb, and both sound as if they should be straightforward, flavourful and unfussy.

The first appeared in my Sunday colour supplement. It's lamb cutlets with Mediterranean vegetables. You cut plum tomatoes lengthways, sprinkle with olive oil, sea salt and icing sugar, and bake for about two hours. You colour halved onions and whole shallots, sprinkle them with oil, sugar and thyme, and bake them in a foil parcel. You sauté sliced courgettes for two to three minutes; you sauté sliced aubergines for five to eight minutes; you put all the vegetables together. You wash and top some green beans; you slice fennel with a mandolin. Then you season your rack of lamb, colour it for two minutes each side in a frying pan, and put it in the oven for five minutes. Boil the beans, add them to the fennel with some olives, olive oil and basil. Assemble the lamb, bean mixture and courgette mixture on four plates.

There is a place for this kind of recipe. That place is in the kitchen of the Michelin-starred chef who wrote it, or in the homes of enthusiastic amateurs such as those who appear on the television programme *Masterchef*. I am an everyday cook. I am never going to prepare this version of lamb cutlets with Mediterranean vegetables.

The second recipe is typical of the hearty stews you find in books celebrating country cooking:

1 kg shoulder of lamb, cubed
Lard
4 carrots, sliced
3 onions, thinly sliced
4 medium turnips, sliced
1 dstsp flour
1 glass white wine
1 bouquet garni
Salt and pepper

**In a casserole, heat a layer of lard, and brown the
lamb in it. Add the carrots and onions and, when
golden, sprinkle on the flour. Throw in the white
wine, and the turnips. Add the bouquet garni,
and season with salt and pepper. Simmer for two
hours, adding a little water if the stew is in danger
of drying out.**

That looks like something I might be bothered to tackle.
But I have some doubts about the details. Lamb is fatty;
with lard as well, the sauce in the stew is not going to be
easy to digest. Like many stews, this one has vegetables that
flavour the sauce and that are also part of the finished dish.
After two hours, the sauce, not the vegetables, will contain the
flavour. The carrots, as anyone who has eaten overcooked
specimens of this vegetable knows, will be particularly dull.
    The recipe tells you to use ground pepper. But pepper,
if simmered in liquid for some time, becomes acrid.
    The consistency of the sauce might also be a problem.
The recipe tells you to add water if the dish is in danger
of drying out; but you are more likely to find that water
from the vegetables and juices from the meat, with only
a dessertspoon of flour to thicken them, produce more
liquid than you want. Perhaps you're meant to leave the pot
uncovered, to allow the sauce to reduce; but have you
noticed how often recipes omit this important detail?
    Lamb cutlets with Mediterranean vegetables belongs
to the largest genre of recipes in books and magazines: ones
so elaborate that even keen cooks will shy away from them,
except perhaps on special occasions. Yet, in important

12

respects, such recipes are not elaborate enough. They are long on instruction, short on help. Those aubergines with the rack of lamb, for example: you are going to have to fry them in batches, while they absorb a great deal of oil. Will they really cook through in five to eight minutes? I've never managed to get a sliced aubergine tender in that time. (You may wonder, too, why the recipe does not tell you, as most recipes do, to salt the aubergines in advance. We'll come to this controversial topic later.) What about the cooking time, 10 minutes or so, for the lamb? How rare do you want it?

So we resort to a simple recipe, such as the stew. But it turns out to be too simple: again, it ignores the problems that the cook is likely to encounter. A bit of extra work will produce a nicer dish. The sauce would benefit from the removal of the vegetables and of the grease. Then, one might add some freshly cooked, glazed turnips and carrots as garnish.

Here are some annoying things that authors of recipes do:

They tell you to take a piece of roasted meat out of the oven and leave it "in a warm place". Such as where? Your airing cupboard? A warm oven with the heat switched off might suit; but you are likely to have other food cooking in it. Unless you are the happy owner of a double oven. I am not.

They tell you to make a sauce, set it aside and keep it warm while you perform five further stages of the cooking process. See above.

13

They tell you to peel and slice 1 kg of potatoes, and fry them in a pan "large enough to hold them in a single layer". That pan would be the size of a dustbin lid.

They tell you to brown onions, then to add cubed meat or mince and brown that too. You have to turn up the temperature to brown the meat, which you leave undisturbed in order for the browning reactions to take place. Meanwhile, your onions will burn.

They think that you have enough patience to wash rice until the water runs clear.

They continue to base instructions on handed-down, questionable assumptions: you must salt aubergines "to draw out the bitter juices", or fry meat to "seal" it.

Have you ever tried making ratatouille according to a supposedly authentic recipe? It takes *for ever*. You've got to cube aubergines and salt them. Then you've got to rinse and dry them. Then you fry them; even salted, they absorb a lot of oil, they stick to the pan, and they remain determinedly firm. Then you've got to chop and fry, separately, onions, peppers and courgettes. Then you assemble the ingredients with tomatoes, which you have skinned and deseeded. Life is too short to stuff a mushroom, Shirley Conran said. Stuffed mushrooms are convenience food compared to ratatouille.

The point I'm making is that we'd be better off, more relaxed, happier, better read, if we didn't follow recipes so much. What we want for the cooking we do from day to day, and even for the cooking we do when we entertain, is a set of techniques that we know will work. Then we can improvise – as we always have to do, because of the vagaries of the cooking process – without worrying that we are committing solecisms.

Julian Barnes recently published an entertaining book called *The Pedant in the Kitchen*. His approach is the opposite of mine. He worries away at recipes, questioning how precisely to apply the instructions. I am far less diligent. I look at a recipe and think, I can't be bothered to do that. Or, that wouldn't work if I tried it. Like Barnes, though, I am curious about why writers recommend certain methods. They don't often tell you. They can be inconsistent. A writer may instruct you to simmer stock for three to four hours. You buy the writer's next book, and the stock recipe specifies a simmering time of just one hour. Why the change? I'd quite like to know.

I have come to my own conclusions about how long to simmer stock; as well as about how to make a simple stew, about whether you need to treat aubergines with salt before cooking them, and about many other techniques that are the subject of unexplained, inconsistent or baffling assertions in conventional cookbooks. This book explains why I have come to those conclusions. It includes a little science, borrowed from better-informed writers; sometimes the recommendations are a matter of personal taste, with which you might disagree.

It's also about gaining confidence in your own taste. Nigel Slater tells a story about a woman who asked him about the tablespoon of parsley he had specified in one

15

recipe: was it, she needed to know, a heaped tablespoon or a level one? To which the polite answer is, how much do you like parsley? Or perhaps, would you prefer tarragon? Of course, you'd be ill-advised to mess around too much with a cake recipe. But many of the choices you make in cooking are a matter of how much you like certain flavours, whether you prefer sauces to be thick or thin, and so on. I put more chilli in the pasta sauces I cook for myself than you would like, probably, or than an Italian chef would approve of, certainly. But I like chilli, so there.

What follows, then, is advice on cooking methods, as well as a collection of templates – for soups, stews, sauces and more. I have to admit, though, that I have been unable to write a book about cooking without including what you might call recipes. My advice about stock is a recipe of sorts, even though I do not give precise instructions about the quantities of meat, vegetables and water to use. I cannot describe the making of a béchamel without telling you that the proportion of 28 g of butter and one tablespoon of flour (about 28 g again) will make a roux of the correct consistency, and that it will thicken about 280 ml of milk; once you know that, though, I hope you'll make this sauce by taking a knob of butter, adding flour and cooking the mixture until the roux feels like loose, wet sand, and then adding milk gradually until you have the consistency you want. There's no avoiding recipes when it comes to puddings, either, unless you're going to have fruit salad at the end of every meal. Maybe that's why I'm not much of a pudding maker. But I do give a few of my favourite pudding recipes here.

I'm not knocking recipes, or recipe writers. Delia Smith is, deservedly, a national treasure, and she gives instructions that produce the results she promises. All cooks need collections of recipes such as hers. Recipes give us new ideas, help us to expand our repertoires.

However, there is a telling survey suggesting that, on average, people cook no more than two dishes from each cookbook they buy. We read the recipes and think, that looks a bit tricky. Or, where am I supposed to get hold of bream? And we return to our old standbys.

This book is about broadening the range of those standbys. We're eating one of mine this evening: barbecued chops of pork belly. I'll poach the chops very, very gently. I'll make a sauce with tomato ketchup (we'd run out of ketchup last time, so I used purée), honey, sunflower oil, vinegar, mustard and garlic – a delicious mixture of sweet and sour. I'll marinate the chops. I cannot be bothered to get the barbecue going, so I'll cook them in the oven – quickly, at gas mark 6/200°C, hoping that they won't dry out in that time.

I won't measure the ingredients. I should guess I'll use about four tablespoons of ketchup, a dessertspoon of honey, a tablespoon of oil, a tablespoon of vinegar and a teaspoon of mustard, along with two cloves of garlic and some salt (on the advisability of using which in marinades there is disagreement, as we shall see). Possibly, the mustard will prove to be a little strong. But we won't mind that.

I think I know roughly how these ingredients will behave. If the sauce starts to look charred (as, containing honey, it might), I'll turn down the oven. If it doesn't thicken, I'll turn up the oven, or leave it in for longer. I don't expect to get in a flap. Isn't this the way most of us want to cook, most of the time?

P.S. The chops were delicious – and not too mustardy. I turned them over halfway through the cooking. I suspect, though, that I poached them for too long; one hour in barely moving water, rather than one and a half hours, would have sufficed.

WEIGHTS AND MEASURES

Metric	Imperial	Fl oz (UK)
142 ml	¼ pint	5 fl oz
284 ml	½ pint	10 fl oz
568 ml	1 pint	20 fl oz
1 l	2.1 pints	35 fl oz
2 l	4.2 pints	70 fl oz

Metric	Imperial
28 g	1 oz
57 g	2 oz
113 g	4 oz
227 g	8 oz
454 g	1 lb
1 kg	2 lb 3 oz
1.5 kg	3 lb 5 oz
2 kg	4 lb 7 oz

Until I came to write this book, I had no idea how much Parmesan I put into a spaghetti carbonara. About 25 g for two, I discovered (page 112). It seems to be in excess of what most recipes recommend. Perhaps I should be more restrained: my quantity probably unbalances the dish. But I continue to grate the cheese self-indulgently, because I like strong flavours, and I worry that only a couple of tablespoons of Parmesan will fail to make much impression.

"Yes – oh dear, yes – the novel tells a story," E. M. Forster wrote. Oh dear yes, a cookery book must have recipes. You'd be right to complain if I simply told you to use as much Parmesan in your carbonara as you liked. But the precise measurement is a necessary convention of the cookery genre. You need to interpret it – just as, Forster thought, you should look beyond the narrative surface for the most important stuff of a novel. With an outline of what works, you can decide on your own preferences. You might prefer less Parmesan. You might prefer Pecorino. Or Cheddar.

Quantities in recipes fall into three categories: guides to how much people will eat; guides to appropriate flavourings; guides to the chemical behaviour of the dish. The first two tend to be open to interpretation; the last usually has to be followed accurately. To generalise, the instructions in the savoury section of this book – with the exception of the Sauces chapter – mostly fall into the first two categories; in the Puddings chapter, the third category is more prominent.

Imperial measurements, officially discarded, linger in

the compositions of many standard recipes. You'll notice, for example, that the quantities in the **béchamel sauce** (page 50) correspond with more memorable imperial equivalents: 1 oz of butter, 1 oz of flour, ½ pint of milk. The batter (page 218): ½ pint of milk, 4 oz of flour, one egg. Sorry: the metric versions just aren't so neat.

TEMPERATURES

Gas mark	Celsius	Fahrenheit
¼	110	230
½	120	250
1	140	285
2	150	300
3	160	320
4	180	355
5	190	375
6	200	390
7	220	430
8	230	445
9	240	465

An oven thermometer won't cost you very much. If the reading it gives you from the central shelf of your oven corresponds with the reading on your oven dial, you have a rare cooker. A publisher friend, wanting her colleagues to try out recipes in one of the company's books, got them to test their ovens first: there was a 50°C variation between ovens at the same setting. My own oven is hotter than the dial tells me it should be.

If a recipe tells you to cook a soufflé, say, at gas mark 5/190°C, you need to be cautious if your oven will generate a heat of 220°C at that setting.

Different sources give different gas mark/centigrade conversions. Some say that gas mark 4 is not 180°C, as I have asserted, but 175°C; some, that gas mark 7 should be 210°C; and so on. I must admit that I don't know what the correct readings are. I don't trust my own oven to give them.

Put your thermometer on a rack above a pan of steaming water. You'll find that the temperature goes down. But the steam will not cause the thermometer in a 200°C oven to descend to the temperature of boiling water (100°C). In my experience, the dial will drop to about 160°C. I cannot expect steam in the oven significantly to slow the cooking of, say, a joint of meat; indeed, it might speed up the process, because it cooks more efficiently than does radiant heat. For this reason, steam does not, as many cookery writers imply, help to keep meat moist.

Another popular way of trying to keep meat moist is by wrapping it in foil. Steam builds up inside the foil; again, the meat will emerge dryer than it would have done if left uncovered.

According to Harold McGee (*McGee on Food and Cooking*), foil deflects a good deal of heat energy that radiates from the oven walls, ceiling and floor. When I put a loose tent of foil around my thermometer, left it for half an hour, and took a reading, the dial was just as high in the foil as it had been outside it; but perhaps we're talking about the kind of heat rather than the temperature. Foil does give protection to certain foods. Whole garlic cloves, for example, go dry and bitter very easily if placed naked in an oven; surrounded by foil, they become mild and tender (see page 153).

Cookery books use such formulae as: "Put in a gas mark 3/160°C oven for an hour and a half." That's because writers don't have enough room to give, every time, instructions along these lines: "Put in a 3/160°C oven but keep checking to see if the liquid is bubbling too fast or too slowly; if it's bubbling too fast, and the liquid is reducing faster than the potatoes are cooking, turn down the heat; if there's little activity in the dish, turn up the heat; you want a very gentle simmer to allow the potatoes to cook while the liquid slowly reduces and thickens" (see **Gratin dauphinois**, page 183); and, even if they did have the room, they think, with justification, that readers would find such qualifications offputting. Just give us an instruction that will work!

I am sorry to tell you that there are very few dishes that you can just put in the oven and forget about, confident that they will take care of themselves in the time the recipe specifies. (**Roast belly pork** – see page 211 – is one of the exceptions.) Please bear this warning in mind when you read the recipes in this book, or in any other books. My oven may be hotter or cooler than yours. My roasting pan or casserole or gratin dish may be thicker or wider, or made of a different material. The meat in my stew may take longer to tenderise than the meat your butcher sold you.

These factors mean that oven settings and times that work for me may not work when you try them.

It's worse than that: settings and timings that work for me one week let me down the next. I put a gratin dauphinois into the oven at 190°C, leave it for an hour, and come back to find it still swimming in milky liquid. Next time, the same settings and utensils produce a dried-out concoction sitting underneath a burned crust. I have to turn down a stew to 110°C because it's bubbling too vigorously; the next stew, in a 150°C oven, declines to show any activity at all.

You haven't failed if your food doesn't behave in the way the recipe writer tells you it should. Everyone has to improvise. The oven setting is not the point; the point is the result you want to achieve. Don't approach roasting with the notion that you have to start cooking your meat in a 200°C oven for 25 minutes; think about the browning reactions you want to generate. If 25 minutes in a 200°C oven achieves them for you, good. Don't take it as a rule that you should cook a stew in a 140°C oven; the rule is that you want the stew just to blip a little as it simmers. Turn the oven up or down until you get the effect you want. Even then, you need to be watchful. A stew that blips gently after 30 minutes might be boiling furiously an hour later.

Then, to add another layer of complication, there are fan ovens. I don't have one, so I'll quote Jenny Webb, who, as author of *The Fan Oven Book*, should be authoritative. Fan oven owners can set their ovens at 10 to 20 degrees Celsius lower than recipes advise, she told readers in a *Guardian* piece on the subject, and can reduce cooking times by 10 minutes in the hour. My advice (page 211) about roasting belly pork on the floor of an oven is redundant if your oven has a fan, which in theory will make the bottom of the oven just as hot as the top.

The temperature on your hob

Here, too, you have to do a certain amount of fussing. Some foods need fast-boiling or steaming: pasta, rice, green vegetables (see the relevant chapters). Meat that you're cooking quickly (a steak, for example), or that you're browning before stewing, also needs cooking at a high heat; but be watchful. A frying pan with oil can get hotter and hotter, and the heat under it needs to be regulated if the food is not to end up blackened rather than browned.

Stews (see page 222) should cook at a very gentle simmer, with only a few bubbles blipping at the surface: subjected to a pummelling from fiercely boiling liquid, meat dries up in protest. This low heat can be difficult to maintain on a hob, especially in a casserole with the lid on, because the build-up of steam will raise the temperature of the contents. A heat disperser will help, as will leaving the lid off. But the liquid in an open pan will evaporate.

Sometimes, you want evaporation: to thicken a sauce, or to concentrate its flavour. You have to adjust the heat under a pan in order to get the rate of evaporation you want; and remember, if you want less or thicker liquid in a stew, and if the gentle simmer is evaporating the liquid too slowly for your liking, you'll have to take out the meat before you turn up the heat. If the meat endures rapid boiling, it will go tough.

In preparing recipes that involve sauces, the trick is to have the sauce at just the right consistency at the moment you want to serve it. Good luck. If you get it wrong (if, say, your tomato sauce is as thick as you want it before you've started cooking the pasta), you cannot put the lid on the pan to arrest the evaporation, because the sauce will start bubbling more vigorously and will most likely stick to the pan base. You'll just have to turn it off and warm it up again later; or, if the pasta will be ready quite soon, put the pan of sauce (or the sauce decanted into another container), covered, into the bottom of a very low oven.

EQuIPMeNT

This is not a comprehensive list. I don't have very much to say about cheese graters, lemon squeezers or sharp knives, except that if you want to grate cheese, squeeze lemons or cut things up, they are, you know, jolly handy.

Heat disperser

A metal disc – they used to be made of asbestos – for inserting between a pan and the ring on a hob; it tempers the heat, and spreads it more evenly. Cost: £5 each, or less. Buy a couple.

Of course, it's nice to have decent, thick-bottomed saucepans. But for many jobs – boiling or steaming vegetables, boiling pasta – rubbish pans will do. If you need the pans for more delicate tasks, such as warming through mashed potatoes or other cooked vegetables, use a disperser to imitate the task – of imparting heat evenly – that a thick bottom would perform. Making a flour-thickened sauce such as béchamel in a cheap pan can be disastrous, because the pan's base gets too hot, rapidly thickening the liquid in contact with it, and causing that liquid to stick and scorch. With the aid of a heat disperser, the pan imitates a far more expensive item.

Hobs on cookers usually generate more heat, even in solid, expensive pans and casserole dishes, than the simmering of sauces, stocks and stews requires. Use a heat disperser.

Steaming basket

I have a cheap one. It's a kind of perforated trivet, with flaps at the side that enclose the contents when you put it inside a saucepan. The lids of my pans are not efficient: steam pours out of them. Nevertheless, the arrangement works fine: food in my cheap steaming basket inside my inadequately sealed saucepans cooks at least as quickly as it would if immersed in boiling water.

Steaming preserves more nutrients than does boiling. I use my steamer – controversially, some might say – for green vegetables (see page 131) and for fish (page 278).

Roasting pan

You need an expensive one, I'm afraid. Cheap pans will probably do for roast potatoes and other vegetables; but if you roast meat in one, you'll find that the juices from the meat will hit the pan, boil, and burn. These juices should have formed the base of a delicious gravy.

Casserole dish

Again, the price of a good one, such as a Le Creuset, is worth paying. Stews, pot roasts and the like need slow, even cooking, which the thick walls and base of a Le Creuset foster. Also, a good casserole will have a tight-fitting lid, retaining moisture. A cold stew in a heavy casserole will take a long time to get to simmering point in the oven; don't worry about that (see page 231).

Cast-iron frying pan

I have one that I bought for £5. I wish I had several; then, I could use one for omelettes, and the other for heavy-duty frying of meat. As it is, my all-purpose pan makes good omelettes anyway. You "season" the pan by pouring in some oil and leaving it on a low heat for a couple of hours. Then you must remember never to wash it in washing-up liquid, which removes the oily patina; use water, or paper towels, only. The pan develops a slick, non-stick surface, on which omelettes slide like skis on ice.

The drawback of cast iron is the weight – particularly when cooking omelettes, which require a certain amount of manipulation. If you buy a lighter omelette pan, season it before you cook with it the first time, wipe it with paper towels rather than washing it, and use it for omelettes only.

Non-stick saucepan

No matter how well seasoned your cast-iron pan, you cannot use it for making scrambled eggs: the eggs will stick, and will not be enjoyable to wash off. They will stick to metal saucepans too. For scrambled eggs, a non-stick pan is best. If you have one, you might as well cook béchamels in it as well.

Ridged grill pan

Also known as a griddle. One of the most fashionable kitchen accessories. Dark griddle stripes on food are reckoned to be highly desirable.

A grill pan is not ideal for cooking thick pieces of food, the outsides of which will be blackened by the time the centres are hot. I use my pan for lamb cutlets or steaks; for boned chicken legs; for chicken breasts, which I slice into two or three pieces; and for bacon.

Griddling vegetables such as courgettes, asparagus and aubergines is popular; but it leaves courgettes and asparagus too crunchy, I find, and doesn't produce in aubergines the melting consistency I like.

Our enthusiasm for char-grilling, incidentally, may not be good for us. Charred food has been found to contain carcinogens, as has the woodsmoke from outdoor barbecues.

Stockpot

Your largest saucepan probably won't be big enough for stock-making. Invest in a large stockpot, which can have a second function as a pasta pan.

Food mill

Moulinex makes one called a Mouli-légumes. You turn a handle to push food through a metal disk with serrated holes; the mill usually comes with two disks, one with very small holes, one with slightly larger ones. I use it for mashed potato, pushing the potatoes down on to the disk and working the turning device over them; for soup; and for tomato sauce made with whole, chopped-up tomatoes. The mill leaves the unwanted tomato skin on the disk.

I prefer the taste – perhaps I mean the consistency – of food that has been worked manually rather than blitzed in an electric machine. Putting potatoes into a food processor, for example, is disastrous (see page 177). Soup, I think, is more interesting after manual pulping than after electric blending.

Here's what else I don't use food processors or blenders for. Mayonnaise: food-processed mayonnaise does not have the liveliness of flavour of one turned or whisked by hand. Chopping and slicing: the chopping and slicing blades of food processors do much more damage to the cells of vegetables than do carefully wielded knives; you'll find that electrically sliced onions and potatoes, in particular, have moist and slightly slimy surfaces.

However, I do use a food processor to make crumble and pastry. I lack the dexterity and patience to mix fat and flour by hand.

Pestle and mortar

Don't use a garlic crusher. It produces an unpleasantly strong, bitter purée. Instead, cut the garlic into manageable pieces and grind it in a mortar with a little salt. Or you could crush it on a chopping board with the blade of a heavy knife. The salt helps turn it into a creamy pulp.

A mortar is the traditional receptacle in which to turn – you move the pestle constantly in the same direction – **aioli**, or garlic mayonnaise (see page 46). I use it for ordinary mayonnaise, too; it's large enough to contain the mayonnaise that one egg will produce, and because it's heavy it does not wobble about as I turn the pestle.

A pestle can also, as the derivation of the word implies, make **pesto** (page 43). Or you can use the pestle to grind spices – but remember that spices such as cumin will leave their flavour behind, to invade subsequent preparations. You might want to invest instead in the following item.

Herb mill, or coffee grinder

These are electrical devices, of course. Don't use them for chopping herbs, apart from rosemary or curly parsley: they will turn fragile leaves such as basil or tarragon or flat-leaf parsley into flavourless mush. But they are invaluable for dried chillis – have you ever tried to "crumble", as the recipes instruct, a dried chilli? They will also grind whole spices such as cumin and coriander seeds. You may need two mills or grinders: one for spices and chillis, the other for such ingredients as parsley, breadcrumbs and pine kernels.

Balloon whisk

Beating egg whites or cream by hand is quite hard work. But by the time you've got out your electric whisk, plugged it in, whisked your eggs or cream, dismantled the machine, washed it and put it back in the cupboard, you'll certainly have spent more time on the job than if you'd done it manually. Also, hand-beating enables you to feel how your ingredients are progressing: whether your egg whites are approaching the "soft peak" stage, for example. It's too tempting, with an electric whisk, to leave the machine running for just an extra minute, to make sure that the foam is perfect: it will be perfect one moment, and in a state of collapse the next.

Salad whizzer

A plastic bowl with a meshed plastic container inside; you put on the lid and turn the handle to spin the container, the contents of which throw off their water. Dry salad leaves will accept an oil-based dressing; wet ones will repel it.

Purists tell you that this process can damage delicate leaves. Gordon Ramsay advises that you wrap them in a clean dishcloth, hold the ends, and give it a twirl. When I tried this technique, I sprayed bits of salad all over the kitchen. So I rely on my whizzer.

INGREDIENTS

Salt

I hope you aren't too maddened by my vagueness in the following pages about the quantities of salt you should use. We all have different tastes; and, if we've ever sprinkled salt on to a pile of chips, we can probably make a rough guess about how much salt we should add to the contents of a pot. I trust that you won't pour a tablespoon of salt into a stew for six people. Be cautious at first; taste as you go along, and add more seasoning if necessary.

Water evaporates, but salt doesn't. As liquid boils away in an uncovered pan, the proportion of salt in it goes up. The teaspoon of salt that may have seemed a moderate addition to a stew will become excessive if you end up with a reduced, concentrated sauce.

Salt, sprinkled on to something moist, will suck up the water. Many cooks like to sweat vegetables with high water contents such as aubergines, courgettes and cucumbers, sprinkling salt on them and leaving them to drain in a colander, for various reasons: to reduce their sponginess, so that they don't absorb so much oil when frying (aubergines); to prevent their throwing off a lot of liquid in the pan, so that they fry rather than stew (courgettes); and to concentrate their flavour (cucumbers). Sometimes this operation is worthwhile; sometimes, in my view, not (see the **Vegetables** chapter, page 130). A second reason for sweating aubergines – one still advanced from time to time – is that the salt draws out their bitter juices (see page 134).

The water-absorbing quality of salt is responsible for the widely disseminated advice that salting meat before frying or grilling it will cause it to lose its juices. But the effect of the salt is negligible by comparison with that of the high heat of the pan or grill, which drives liquid from the meat at a tremendous rate. That's why a steak sizzles in the pan; that's why it shrinks. If you've salted it, at least it will have a flavoursome crust.

A soaking in brine, a solution of salt in water, will increase the tenderness and moistness of meat when it is cooked. Pork belly, brined for three days and then gently roasted, is meltingly soft and juicy (see page 212).

Salt in cooking water hastens the softening of vegetables and reduces the loss of nutrients. You have to be careful: overcooked members of the cabbage family become rank, and green legumes go grey and flabby if they steam or poach for too long. I omit salt when I boil potatoes, so that their textures do not collapse.

Every cookery writer recommends sea salt (or rock salt) in preference to table salt. However, there have been tests in which experts have failed to distinguish between them. I think that I favour Maldon sea salt as a seasoning, even though I'm not confident that I could back up that recommendation by passing a salt-tasting test; I use table salt in cooking water — for pasta, say, or for poached eggs.

Pepper

I have been even more vague in my advice about pepper than I have about salt. It's up to you. I have to leave it out of a good deal of the food I cook, because my daughters won't touch it. So I add it at the table. I get the fresh pungency of the freshly ground grains; but sometimes I miss the milder, integrated pepperiness that cooking brings.

My one piece of advice is not to add ground pepper to stocks or stews. It turns acrid after long simmering.

Oil

On cooking, extra virgin olive oil loses the fragrance and fruitiness that make it stand out from the ordinary, refined stuff. But it's so cheap these days — can it be genuine? — that I use it as an all-purpose oil anyway. In the text, I've written simply "olive oil". If I had the money, I'd buy a standard brand for cooking and a fancy, estate-bottled one for salads. Sad to say, I don't.

I use olive oil for salads, for pasta sauces, and for any cooking that involves Mediterranean vegetables. For other purposes, I fry with sunflower oil. Vegetable oil is fine too. Cookery writers often recommend groundnut oil, but it's hard to find round our way.

One of the more baffling of the instructions commonly appearing in cookery books is that you should heat oil, for searing meat or for stir-frying vegetables, until it is smoking. If it's smoking, it's degrading, and will have a degraded flavour. It may also be harmful: burnt materials are thought to be carcinogens.

For frying at high temperatures, use vegetable, sunflower or groundnut oils, which have higher smoke points than does olive oil. Heat the pan first, so that the oil has only brief contact with it before you add the ingredients; otherwise, the oil is more likely to burn. When you can feel, by lowering your palm towards the pan surface, that the pan is hot, add the oil, swirl it around quickly, and add your meat or vegetables. Keep them at a lively, but not ferocious, sizzle.

Sesame oil has a low smoke point. Don't fry with it, unless you're going to do so very gently; instead, add it to stir-frys at the end of cooking, as a flavouring.

Wine and other alcohol

An enduring memory from *The Galloping Gourmet*, a hit TV show of the 1960s. Graham Kerr, the GG, is standing before a stewpot, brandishing a bottle. We need a little wine at this stage, he confides; then he starts pouring the bottle into the stew and, leeringly, doesn't stop. Heady days.

It was a time when the notion of alcohol in food seemed daringly sophisticated. Now, when it causes less of a frisson, we're inclined to use alcohol more sparingly, in the knowledge that too much of it can throw the balance of flavours in a dish out of whack.

Wine or other alcoholic drinks in cooked food taste overpoweringly raw and acidic unless they are reduced. Don't add them to a dish just before serving. Typically, you use the drink to "deglaze" – loosen the residues, in order to incorporate them in a sauce – a pan in which you've fried meat and/or vegetables; you let the liquid bubble for a minute or two before adding it, with other liquid, to a stewpot (see page 224), or you use it as the sauce for a **sauté** (page 259). As it cooks, a good deal – though not all – of the alcohol evaporates; so do the volatile acids. The liquid becomes milder, and sweeter. Vinegar may be used in the same way, and also loses its rasping qualities after simmering and evaporation.

(Other acidic foods, such as tomatoes and onions, also become sweeter as they cook. That's one reason why you simmer a tomato sauce until it thickens, and why you soften onions in butter or oil.)

Our idea of a professional kitchen is likely to include chefs wielding spectacularly flaming pans. Setting light to brandy or other spirits is standard practice. But is there any point to it, other than to create an impressive display? My own experiments suggest that boiling is just as efficient in getting rid of the spirity flavour – indeed, that it produces a better-tasting liquid.

SAuCEs

Vinaigrette

For a green salad for 4
1 dstsp white wine or red wine vinegar
Pinch of salt
3 dstsps extra virgin olive oil

In your salad bowl, combine the salt and the vinegar; the salt will dissolve. Add the oil, and stir vigorously to amalgamate.[1] – see WHY YOU DO IT, following

Just before serving,[2] tip in the salad ingredients, which should be dry,[3] and toss thoroughly.

VARIATIONS

Proportion of ingredients. The three parts oil to one part vinegar formula works well with most salad greens, off-setting their flavour with just the right amount of tartness. You may prefer a five-to-one ratio for bitter greens such as

41

endives. The starchiness of potatoes can be offset with a greater proportion of acidity: I use two parts oil to one part vinegar in potato salads.

Oils. You can also use sunflower oil, vegetable oil or groundnut oil – or a combination.

Vinegar. You could use balsamic vinegar – although I'm not so keen on introducing a dark brown ingredient to a green salad. Or lemon juice.

Garlic. A little goes a long way in a vinaigrette. Some people simply rub the bowl with the cut side of a clove. I take a sliver, crush it with a little salt, and add it to the vinegar.

Mustard. I'd use half a teaspoon of Dijon mustard with the ingredients above. Like salt, it combines happily with vinegar, so you should stir it into the vinegar in the bowl before adding the oil. If you try adding it at the end, you'll have trouble amalgamating it. (But if you want grains of salt in your salad, grind them over at the end.)

Anything else. There are all sorts of ingredients you could add. Pepper, obviously. Roquefort or other blue cheese (a dessertspoon, say), crumbled into the vinegar and amalgamated before you add the oil. A dessertspoon of double cream to substitute for the same quantity of oil. A shake of soy sauce. Or Worcester sauce. Make a Thai-flavoured vinaigrette with a small piece of finely chopped lemon grass, finely chopped garlic, finely chopped ginger, rice wine vinegar, sesame oil, a shake of fish sauce, and chopped coriander leaves. I'm not too keen on sweetness in a salad dressing, but some people like to add a little sugar or honey to the vinegar.

Add herbs to the salad: chives, basil, tarragon, marjoram, parsley.

1) *Amalgamation*. Vinaigrette is an emulsion in which vinegar is dispersed in oil. Amalgamating the two is a much more foolproof process than is creating a mayonnaise emulsion (see page 45); but the vinegar will fall away from the oil almost immediately. Give the sauce another stir before tossing the salad in it.

2) *Late dressing*. Oily dressings soon discolour salad leaves and turn them soggy.

3) *Dry leaves*. Water on salad leaves will repel the oil in the vinaigrette.

Pesto

Once you've made your own, you probably won't want to go back to the bottled stuff. Bottled pesto has a stale taste, and isn't reminiscent of basil, or pine nuts, or Parmesan, or olive oil, at all.

HOW TO MAKE IT
30 g pine nuts
Large handful of fresh basil leaves
3 tbsps grated Parmesan
1 clove garlic
Salt
120 ml olive oil

Put the pine nuts in a dry saucepan above a gentle heat until they give a lightly toasted smell. Careful: they burn easily. Grind them: I do it in an electric herb mill, because bashing them up with a pestle is hard work.

Chop the garlic, then put it into a mortar with a little salt, and grind to a paste with the pestle. (Or use a heavy bowl and a wooden spoon.) Wash the basil leaves and pat them dry with paper towels. Add them to the mortar, with the pine nuts, and grind them against the bottom and sides, until you have a green slush. Add the grated cheese, and blend it in. Add the olive oil, stirring it in a little at a time, until you have a thick sauce. You may not need all 120 ml.

Or: throw pine nuts, basil and garlic into a food processor. Blend. Throw in the cheese. Blend briefly. With the motor running, pour in olive oil through the spout until the sauce has the consistency you want.

Check for saltiness. Add pepper if you like.

You can use pesto to dress pasta. Or dollop it into a vegetable soup. I like to stir it into boiled new potatoes. Or try this. Cut an aubergine in two horizontally, and then into vertical slices. Brush with olive oil, season with salt, and bake at gas mark 6/200°C for 25 to 30 minutes, or until soft. Spread pesto on the slices, and put mozzarella cheese on top of that. Put back into the oven for five minutes. Eat hot, lukewarm or cold.

You can also make pesto with parsley or mint.

Mayonnaise

"This classic sauce", Raymond Blanc claims (in *Cooking for Friends*), "is very simple to make." That is an example of the Annoying Things That Chefs Write. Vinaigrette is simple: it cannot go wrong. Mayonnaise, as every cook of experience knows, *can* go wrong: unless you're careful, it will split.

HOW TO MAKE IT
As an accompaniment to a meal for 3 to 4 people
1 egg, at room temperature[1 – see WHY YOU DO IT]
½ tsp Dijon mustard
Pinch of salt
150 ml oil[2]
1 tsp white wine vinegar

Separate the egg, and put the yolk into a bowl; discard the white, or save it for a mousse or a soufflé. I use, instead of a bowl, a mortar, and I turn – I think that is the approved term – the mayonnaise with a pestle. But any bowl will do, and you can also mix the oil and egg with a small whisk. The only requirement is that the receptacle be stable enough to take your whisking or turning, because you cannot hold it with your free hand – you'll need that for the jug of oil. A cushion of dry dishcloth or a paper towel

45

on a chopping board should hold it.

Mix the yolk, mustard and salt.[3] Put the oil into a measuring jug. Pour a drop – no more – on to the egg, and start whisking or turning. When you have incorporated the oil, add another drop,[4] whisking all the while; without letting up your whisking for a moment, continue to add drops of oil, each time waiting for egg and oil to blend before adding the next.

By the time you've added half the oil, the mixture may be very thick; thin it with the vinegar, before adding more oil as before. You should be able now to add a little more oil each time, or to pour it in a slow but steady stream – but you cannot stop whisking.

Judge for yourself when the mayonnaise has the consistency and flavour you want. You may not need all the oil. If you're not eating the mayonnaise immediately, cover the bowl with cling film and put it in the fridge, where it will keep for three days. But it's best on the day.

VARIATIONS

Thin the mayonnaise with lemon juice rather than vinegar.

Leave out the mustard if you like.

Aioli is a garlic mayonnaise that traditionally accompanies salt cod, or perhaps poached chicken. It contains a preposterous quantity of garlic – six or more cloves with the ingredients given above. Chop the garlic finely, put it in a mortar with some salt, and grind it with the pestle until it turns to a creamy pulp. Or grind it on a chopping board with the blade of a heavy knife. Then add the egg, but not the mustard, and proceed as above.

You may prefer to save the tasting of such a powerful concoction until you find yourself on a sun-drenched terrace in Provence. Use only the garlic you want – but you probably shouldn't give the name aioli to the garlic-lite version.

For a tartare sauce, to accompany fish and chips, add to the mayonnaise a teaspoon each of chopped gherkins, capers and shallots.

Rouille is a fiery mayonnaise with **harissa** (see pages 295 and 129).

(see pages 295 and 129)

WHY YOU DO IT

1) *Don't start cold*. Mayonnaise is an emulsion, in which droplets of oil are dispersed – thanks to your whisking or turning – in the liquid of the egg yolk, and in the vinegar or lemon juice. The emulsifiers in the yolks need waking up – they're sluggish when cold, and when brought into contact with other cold ingredients. However, I usually find that I get away with using mustard from the fridge.

I bring the egg to room temperature in lukewarm water.

2) *What oil?* I use ⅓ extra virgin olive oil, and ⅔ sunflower oil. Not everyone likes mayonnaise made entirely with olive oil, finding it too heavy; if you do like it, be aware that, according to Harold McGee, an extra virgin mayonnaise is likely to separate an hour or two after preparation. Groundnut oil is a possible substitute for the sunflower, as is grapeseed – although I am not terribly keen on the latter.

3) *What to add when*. Salt, stirred into the yolks initially, makes them more viscous, aiding the separation of the oil into little droplets. The mustard aids emulsification too. Some recipes tell you to add the vinegar at this stage, but it's easier to incorporate the oil without it. However, you do need to thin the mayonnaise with vinegar or lemon juice once it becomes stiff, because the stiffness indicates that there is not enough liquid left to hold more oil.

4) *Drop by drop*. At first, you can emulsify only a tiny drop of oil. If you add too much, you'll end up with some that has not been emulsified; then you'll add more to it, and that won't emulsify either. You'll produce either a split liquid with oil and water separate, or a sauce in which the water is incorporated in the oil rather than the other way round.

Hollandaise

Hollandaise is scarier than mayonnaise, because you have to worry about heat as well. If the eggs get too hot, they will curdle. You need a double boiler, or a bowl that you can rest inside a pan so that the base of the bowl will not touch the water simmering below. Steam rising from the water heats the eggs gently.

You can try making hollandaise in a saucepan on a direct flame; but it is a lot harder to manage this feat successfully than it is to warm custard in a pan (see page 300). In custard, the eggs are dispersed in milk and cream. With only eggs, butter and a little vinegar or lemon juice in your pan, you'll have to work very carefully to stop the eggs catching on the base and curdling.

This sauce goes wonderfully well with asparagus, and with poached fish. It's not always practical: as you'll see, it requires undivided attention, which you may not be able to spare if you have lots of other things on the go.

HOW TO MAKE IT
Enough for 4 people
3 tbsps vinegar
2 egg yolks
150 g butter, cut into six pieces

In a saucepan on the hob, boil the vinegar until it has reduced by a third. Bring water in a saucepan to a simmer, and turn down the heat so that the water merely shows bubbles rising to the surface. Place a bowl inside the pan, making sure that the base of the bowl does not touch the water. Put in the egg yolks and vinegar,[1 – see WHY YOU DO IT] and start whisking. Add a piece of butter, and whisk it in until it has combined with the eggs; add some more; and so on. Continue whisking until the sauce thickens; turn off the heat immediately when it does. Add salt, and pepper if you like.

Herbs go well with a hollandaise; tarragon, particularly so.

You can hold the sauce for about 20 minutes above the hot water, provided that you whisk it from time to time.

1) *Helpful vinegar.* It's easier to add vinegar or lemon juice to a mayonnaise after you've incorporated a certain amount of oil. But in a hollandaise, the vinegar protects the yolks against the curdling effect of the heat (cf *McGee on Food and Cooking*). You could also add lemon juice to the yolks.

If the sauce separates, you might be able to rescue it by adding an ice cube and beating frantically. Then warm the sauce, very carefully, again.

If the worry about curdling doesn't kill you, the cholesterol in the sauce probably will.

Béchamel

28 g butter
1 tbsp (28 g) plain flour
280 ml milk

Melt the butter over a low heat in a (preferably non-stick) saucepan. Add flour to make a roux[1−] see WHY YOU DO IT and cook very gently, stirring, for one to two minutes; the roux should have the appearance and consistency of golden, wet sand, but should not darken. Turn up the heat a little, add a modest portion of milk,[2] and stir it; when it has formed a thick, smooth paste, add some more milk, stirring until that, too, has been incorporated. If the liquid is bubbling away before the new milk is incorporated, take the pan off the heat and stir until it is. Then return to the heat, and continue adding milk bit by bit until you have a smooth sauce of the consistency you want, and let it bubble for a minute or two;[3] if you're going to put it into a serving bowl, be aware that it will thicken considerably as it cools.

VARIATIONS

Some recipes tell you to flavour the milk first, as you would for a **bread sauce** (see page 53). The extra flavour would be nice; but I cannot be bothered. The béchamel is usually going to be a part of a dish, rather than the main element of it.

The most common addition to this sauce is cheese: mornay sauce is the official title. You use it for a **macaroni cheese** (see page 122), of course, or for **eggs Florentine** (page 83), or perhaps to pour over cooked leeks, which you then bake to make a gratin. Half a teaspoon of mustard brings out the flavour of the cheese; a pinch of nutmeg enhances the sauce too.

Adding chopped parsley makes a sauce to accompany fish or gammon. I like to use **fish stock** (page 62), or the stock made from boiling the gammon (page 257), and finish the sauce with cream; or to use half stock, half milk.

You can add a beaten egg to the sauce made to cover a **moussaka** (page 252). One egg is right for the quantities given above – and you should make the sauce quite thick. The moussaka topping will have a deliciously light, custardy texture.

1) *The roux*. The butter both enriches the sauce and disperses the flour before you add the liquid. Coated in fat, the flour is less likely to clump together to produce a lumpy sauce. Cooking the roux for a short time also softens the raw flavour of the flour; that flavour is less assertive in the Italian flour known as "00".

The derivation of "roux" is "red", suggesting that the flour should be cooked long enough to change colour. In a white sauce, you don't want the colour to change; but in a gravy or other brown sauce, you do – and they involve the same process as making a béchamel. You cook the flour in the fat long enough to let it caramelise, and to contribute to the colour of the sauce, before adding stock. A browned flour, however, is less effective as a thickening agent.

2) *Warm milk or cold?* You can, as various recipes advise, warm the milk first; your sauce will thicken much more quickly. But, provided you amalgamate milk and sauce with care, you are not more likely to get lumps if you start with cold milk. In either case, it's easier to add the milk on the heat, so that the sauce thickens as you go, rather than away from the heat, when you'll have to thicken the whole lot at once.

3) *Simmering*. You may have been told to simmer a béchamel for half an hour or an hour; the instruction sometimes comes with the gloss that simmering gets rid of the floury taste. That is not the point of the simmering; it's the point, as I've said above, of cooking the roux. Chefs simmer a béchamel in order to allow all the starch granules to dissolve, creating a very smooth texture. Home chefs need not be so fussy.

Velouté

A velouté is a roux-based sauce made with stock. See, for example, **Blanquette** on page 245.

Bread sauce

Gordon Ramsay thinks it's horrible. I'm wary of arguing with a three-star chef, and particularly with him; but I love it.

HOW TO MAKE IT
For 4 (though I might eat it all)
Bring 280 ml of milk slowly to the boil with half a peeled onion studded with a couple of cloves, along with a little salt, a bay leaf, a few peppercorns and a pinch of nutmeg; turn off the heat, cover, and leave to infuse for half an hour. Strain into another pan through a sieve, add breadcrumbs, and warm through. I'm afraid that I don't know how many breadcrumbs you'll need. Add some, stir and simmer; the sauce will continue to thicken, so err on the side of too few at first (unless you want an excuse to add more milk and create more sauce – but of course this milk will be

unflavoured). When the sauce has the consistency you want, take it off the heat and stir in a walnut-sized knob of butter. You could add a couple of tablespoons of cream too. You can leave the sauce and warm it up later, by which time it will have become very thick and will need loosening with a little more milk.

STOCKS

There are limits to the efforts to which I'm willing to go to prepare food, but making stock is well within them. It is not difficult; you can use ingredients, such as the remains of a roast chicken, that might otherwise have been wasted; and you will end up with the wherewithal to make delicious sauces, soups and risottos (or risotti, if you like), as well as dishes such as **gratin Savoyard** (page 187). Even the best stock cubes, such as the Just Bouillon brand, will not impart such richness. The worst have the salty, powdery, artificial qualities of crisp flavourings.

"A stockpot is not a rubbish bin," writers admonish. Stop bossing us about! Still, they're right: flabby carrots and discoloured leek leaves will compromise your stock. You won't get much of a stock from a poor chicken, either. A battery bird, with its brittle bones and feeble muscles, will produce little gelatine, less flavour, and a liquid with the consistency of dishwater.

Chicken stock

HOW TO MAKE IT
1 kg chicken wings
Water to cover
Vegetables – some or all of the following,
roughly chopped: 2 onions, 1 carrot,
1 leek (cleaned and minus the rough green leaves),
2 celery sticks

Put the chicken wings into a stockpot, casserole dish or other pan with a capacity to hold all the ingredients with room to spare. Cover with cold water by no more than 5 cm.[1 – see why you do it] Bring the pot slowly to a simmer on a gentle heat. As the liquid begins to bubble, skim off the scum[2] that has risen to the surface with a spoon or slotted spoon, and add the vegetables. Return the pot to the point at which bubbles are rising to the surface, then turn the heat right down and simmer, uncovered, with only a few bubbles giving evidence of the cooking process,[3] for two hours.[4] Strain into another pan through a colander, gently pressing down the meat and vegetables to extract as much juice as possible; then strain again, through a sieve lined with a new, washed J-cloth.[5] Refrigerate immediately.[6]

VARIATIONS

This pale stock is known as fond blanc. To make a darker, more flavoursome variety, roast the wings first. Anoint them with a little oil and put them into a hot oven (gas mark 6/200°C) for about 30 minutes, or until browned.

Your butcher might also give you, or sell you cheaply, bits of chicken carcass. You could roast them first, too.

If you roast the chicken wings first, deglaze[7] the roasting pan with half a cup of water, and add this liquid to the pot.

Don't throw away the remains of a roasted chicken. Gather all the bones and leftover bits from people's plates, and put them into the stockpot with the carcass, as well as vegetables. If you're lucky enough to have bought a chicken that came with giblets, and haven't used them already for the gravy with your roast, add them; but leave out the liver, which gives the stock a bitter taste. Make a simple pâté with it instead (see page 206).

You don't have to peel the onions: there's goodness in the skin, although you might not want it to discolour the fond blanc. Be cautious with the carrots, which add a good deal of sweetness to the liquid. Mushrooms and unpeeled garlic cloves are other possible ingredients. You might add herbs, too: parsley, thyme and bay work well.

If you've used chicken wings, don't throw them away. They are forgiving things, and remain moist and tender after two hours in liquid. Allow them to cool, and cover with a **marinade** (see page 265). Cook them in a gas mark 6/200°C oven for 15 minutes, or under a grill.

WHY YOU DO IT

1) *Don't drown the stock.* You can add more water later, if you have too little. The flavour of a concentrated stock that has been diluted will be better than that of a watery stock that has been boiled down.

You know that you've got the ratio of water to meat right when, after cooling, the stock has turned into a jelly (see point 4, below).

Don't add salt to a stock. You may want to reduce the liquid later; that will increase the concentration of any salt in it. Add whole peppercorns, if you like, but not ground pepper: long simmering will turn it acrid.

2) Scum. It comes from the connective tissue in the meat and from the bones. Gentle heating allows it to rise to the surface. If the pot boils too rapidly, the scum will be drawn back into the liquid, turning it cloudy. Skim it off. The reason you add vegetables later is that they interfere with the skimming process.

3) Simmer gently. Ignore recipes that tell you to cover the pot. The build-up of steam under the lid will raise the temperature of the stock, causing it to bubble more vigorously; boiling liquid will absorb the scummy material and emulsify the fats, and will end up tasting of scummy material and emulsified fats. A heat disperser (see page 28) will help you to keep the temperature down; or you could put the stockpot into the oven, at the lowest possible setting (gas mark ¼/ 110°C). However, the surface of the stock will get hotter than it would if exposed to air in an open pan on a hob.

You may have a nervous feeling that your pot should be showing more obvious evidence of simmering. Don't worry. The liquid does not have to boil to extract flavour from the meat and veg, nor does it have to be at 100°C to break down the collagen (see point 4, below). According to

Peter Barham (*The Science of Cooking*), gelatinisation starts at about 70°C. Don't allow the temperature to drop too much, though: you'll create a happy breeding ground for bacteria.

Heston Blumenthal recommends cooking stock in a pressure cooker, sealing in the flavour. When I tried this method, I produced a murky liquid of the sort I would have got from any other covered pan.

4) *It's possible to overcook stock.* I don't think that any other preparation is the subject of such variations of advice about cooking times. "Eight hours with the water steaming but not bubbling will reward you with a jewel-bright, flavour-packed consommé," Richard Whittington writes in *Home Food*. Other writers do not go quite so far, but agree that long cooking is good: Hugh Fearnley-Whittingstall, in the *River Cottage Meat Book*, suggests "an absolute minimum of three hours – better still, four or five". By contrast, there is Shaun Hill, who in *How to Cook Better* advises a simmering time of 40 minutes.

When you simmer meat and bones with aromatics, you're doing two things, principally: extracting the flavour from the ingredients; and converting collagen – a protein from the bones, skin and connective tissue of the meat – into gelatine. The flavour may leech into the liquid in the time that Shaun Hill suggests, and will certainly be there in an hour. The gelatine, which will give the stock a wonderfully rich and unctuous quality, will take longer to produce. However, I have made satisfyingly gelatinous chicken stocks in two hours.

I have tried an eight-hour stock. It certainly looked

pure, but it had a null flavour. Once all the flavour is in the liquid, further cooking seems to cause it to lose freshness. Michel Roux, who carries some authority in these matters, advises a one-and-a-half-hour simmer. I think you can risk two hours; you'll get a bit more gelatine. Don't cook it for longer than that.

5) *Straining*. I've seen recommendations that you use a sieve lined with a paper towel, but I find that paper towels clog up. I get a clean J-cloth, wash it (I'm not sure what substances adhere to pristine J-cloths), and line the sieve with that. The cloth catches a fair amount of gunge. Just use a colander if you don't mind gunge in your stock – there's no need, other than an aesthetic one, to worry about it.

6) *Storage*. Cool the stock as soon as possible. A hot container will raise the temperature of your fridge; plunge the container instead into another one containing iced water (being careful that the water does not rise up the sides and invade the stock), and then refrigerate. The stock should set, with any fat in it sitting as a layer on the surface, for easy removal.

There is a tradition of keeping stocks indefinitely, with the remains of each one contributing to the preparation of the next. The only stipulation, given in both Richard Olney's *Simple French Food* and in Alastair Little and Richard Whittington's *Keep It Simple*, is that you boil it up every three days or so. Other writers are more likely to advise you to keep stocks for a week; I have done so without any ill effects.

I must tell you, though, that the Food Standards Agency advises that you cool stocks within two hours and consume them within two days; or that you conserve them in the freezer (ice trays are useful containers). Don't reheat stock more than once, the FSA adds. There may be some bacteria that will resist the rise in temperature; and, as the stock cools again, they will multiply.

7) *Deglazing*. This is a term you'll come across a lot in descriptions of the making of gravies and sauces. As meat browns, it undergoes what are known as Maillard reactions – chemical changes that produce a great deal of flavour. The flavoursome residues of those reactions stick to the bottom of pans in which you have roasted or fried meat. You can incorporate that flavour in sauces by reheating the pan and adding liquid – water, wine or other alcohol, cream: the liquid will release the residue, which will dissolve as you stir. In the case of your roasted chicken wings, remove them to the stockpot, and put the roasting dish on to a medium heat; add water, and scrape and stir with a wooden spoon until you've lifted all the residues. Pour the liquid into the stockpot. If there are still bits of chicken left in the roasting dish, repeat the process.

A note about nutritional value, because you'd think that stock would be good for you: it isn't, much. "It has no food value apart from some minerals," Good Housekeeping (*The New Cookery Encyclopedia*) asserts. I'm not sure what happens to the protein from the meat and the vitamins from the vegetables, but they don't hang around, apparently. The point of stock is flavour.

Veal stock

Good butchers will sell you veal bones. Ask for them to be chopped up. Brown them in the oven, then follow the procedures above. The gelatinisation process from these bones takes longer, so you need to simmer this stock for about three hours.

You can also make a stock with lamb bones. It is insistently lamby, and "can only ever really be used with lamb dishes", Alastair Little and Richard Whittington (*Keep It Simple*) advise. I make lamb braises, or gravies for lamb roasts, with chicken stock.

Fish stock

HOW TO MAKE IT
Trimmings and bones from white fish[1 – see WHY YOU DO IT]
Water to cover
1 onion
1 leek
1 stick of celery
Parsley

Chop the vegetables finely, and soften them for 10 to 15 minutes in butter.[2] Add the fish, parsley and water to cover – as in the chicken stock, by no more than a few centimetres. Bring to a gentle simmer, and continue to simmer for 30 minutes.[3] Strain as above. You'll probably need to use it within 24 hours.

Fennel, with its aniseed edge, is a nice flavour in fish stock. You could include wine or vinegar; add to the sautéed vegetables and let the liquid reduce by about half. The reduction will reduce the acidity, which might otherwise inhibit the cooking of the vegetables.

WHY YOU DO IT

1) *Use white fish*. Oily fish, such as mackerel and herrings, will not make a digestible liquid. But you can use for a stock the shells from shellfish, bashing them up first (Fergus Henderson in *Nose to Tail Eating* suggests you might use a hammer for this job). They will be salty.

2) *Softening*. For advice on this procedure, see page 160. It sweetens the vegetables; a less harsh edge to their flavour is welcome in a fish stock.

3) *Half an hour is enough*. Overcook meat stock, and you'll produce something that is not as nice as it might have been. Overcook fish stock, and you'll produce something unpleasant. Bones cooked for longer than half an hour are in danger of breaking up and adding bitterness to the liquid.

Vegetable stock

This is not, officially, a stock — it's not recognised in classical French cuisine. But it's very handy as a standby on all those occasions when you might use a meat or fish stock but, for reasons of culinary or ethical inclination, cannot. Use it in soups to give more depth of flavour than water would provide; try it in a vegetarian risotto.

There's no point in giving a recipe. Use onions, carrots, leeks and celery; fennel bulb, garlic (left whole – chopped, it will be too dominant a part of the stock) and mushrooms are optional. Add, too, the herbs recommended for the stocks above.

Cut the vegetables up small. Soften them in butter or oil (see page 160) for 10 to 15 minutes, then add the herbs and water to cover. You can cover the pan; the reasons given above for leaving a pan uncovered do not apply here. Simmer for no more than 30 minutes. All the flavour will be in the liquid by then; you will only dull the flavour by cooking the stock for any longer. Strain in a sieve.

SOUPS

Symphony orchestras cannot make their reputations playing Brahms, it is said; you might also say that chefs do not make their reputations cooking soups. Of course, there are soups that are gastronomic marvels. If you want to be gastronomically marvellous, you'll probably find a recipe from Gordon or Jamie or Nigella to suit. But the essence of soup seems more humble. Precise instructions are beside the point; this is food that you improvise, making use of ingredients to hand.

The first is a broth: stock (which might also be vegetable or fish stock) is heated, flavoured, and added to a starchy ingredient. In the second, vegetables are cooked together, sometimes after an initial softening in butter or oil; the soup is usually blended. In the third, involving dried legumes such as beans or lentils, some of the ingredients have different cooking times, and are therefore cooked apart and assembled just before serving.

For **fish soup**, see page 293.

A very simple soup

For 4

Make a dark chicken stock (see page 56). Heat four bowlfuls of it – or more, if you want second helpings – in a saucepan, with salt to taste. In 2 tbsps of olive oil, fry two cloves of finely chopped garlic until it starts to turn brown; be careful, because the stage between browning and burning is brief. When it's cooked, add a whizzed, dried chilli if you like. Toast four pieces of white bread, and put each, torn up as necessary, into a soup bowl. Pour some oil and garlic over the toast in each bowl, and pour the hot stock over that.

VARIATIONS

When the stock is simmering, cook 350 g of spinach in it: cram the spinach into the pan, and wait for it to start to collapse; then stir it into the liquid – it should be tender in no more than a couple of minutes. Divide the stock and the spinach between the four bowls with their bread, garlic and oil.

Add four ladlefuls of stock to the garlic and oil; then pour in two tins of tomatoes with their juice. Simmer for 10 minutes or so. Pass through a food mill. Warm the soup again; pour it over the toast in the bowls.

Skin four plump tomatoes (see page 190), cut them up, and add them to the browned garlic and oil; cook until the tomatoes go mushy; add a portion of stewed tomato to the bread before pouring hot stock over them.

Spread a little olive oil over each side of the crustless bread, and bake in the oven until brown; or grill on a ridged pan.

Pasta or noodles are an alternative starchy ingredient to the bread. Heat the stock and throw in (for four) 150 g of small pasta shapes; divide between each bowl a tomato stew made as above; pour over the broth and cooked pasta.

Flavour the stock with chopped chillis (as many as you like, with the seeds removed if you don't want the soup to be too fiery), a teaspoon of minced ginger, a couple of bashed-up stalks of lemon grass, and a couple of cloves of crushed garlic; add 200 g to 250 g of cooked and drained noodles (see page 124) to warm through. (They'll make the soup very starchy if you cook them in the stock.)

The deliciousness of these soups lies in the distinctive deliciousness of the ingredients. In leek and potato and related preparations, a bit more blending takes place.

Leek and potato soup

HOW TO MAKE IT

For 4

1 onion, chopped
2 leeks, green parts removed, sliced and washed
3 medium-sized potatoes, peeled and cut up
Stock or water
30 g butter

Heat the stock or water.[1] – see WHY YOU DO IT **Melt the**

butter in a saucepan and soften the onion in it (thin it with a little olive or sunflower oil if it shows signs of catching, or add a little water to the pan – see page 160). Cook until the onion starts to turn golden: about 10 to 15 minutes. Add the leek, and stew until it softens: about five more minutes.[2] Add the potatoes, and pour in the hot stock or water to come to the level of the vegetables at the top. Add salt to taste,[3] and simmer, uncovered,[4] until the potatoes are soft: about 15 to 20 minutes. Blend the soup by pushing it through a food mill, or use a hand-held blender or an ordinary blender.[5] Or, for a rougher texture, mash up the soup with a potato masher. For a richer finish, swirl in a little butter away from the heat (in the hope that it won't split – see page 262), or some double cream (1 tbsp, say), or some sour cream.

VARIATIONS

An even simpler version of this soup has the leeks and potatoes thrown into boiling, salted water, cooked, blended and enriched with butter. I prefer the aromatic base of butter-softened onion – a base that may underlie any number of vegetable soups.

Soften an onion or two, and add whatever vegetables you like, with as much liquid as you like (I prefer thick soups). Add garlic to the onion base; I usually soften it for a minute in the butter or oil before adding the chopped onion (see page 153).

Spices go with most vegetables, and in soup they

complement the root vegetables particularly well, as Jane Grigson famously showed with her spiced parsnip soup (from her *Vegetable Book*). Carrot and coriander has become a ubiquitous combination: for a soup with four carrots, warm a teaspoon of coriander seeds in a dry saucepan until they give off a toasted aroma, grind them in an electric mill or with a pestle, and cook with the softened onion (and garlic) for a minute or two before adding the carrots and stock or water. A potato would give the soup a little more body. After blending, and just before serving, enrich the soup with a little cream, and add some fresh coriander leaves.

WHY YOU DO IT

1) *Add hot liquid.* It's in order to keep the simmering time short. As do stocks (see page 55), soups lose freshness of flavour if their ingredients are overcooked. Take the pan off the heat as soon as the vegetables are tender.

2) *Sweating the alliums.* It removes their harsh notes, sweetening them. You don't have to sweat the leek, which is far less sulphurous than the onion; it will retain more of its raw character if you skip that phase. Some recipes insist that you turn the potatoes with the other vegetables, coating them in fat, before adding the liquid; I doubt if that procedure has any effect on the finished dish.

3) *Salt and pepper.* Add salt when you start simmering: it will season the soup, and hasten the softening of the vegetables. But pepper can turn bitter in simmering liquid. Add it at the table, if you want.

4) *Uncovered*. I don't have full confidence in this instruction, but I have gained the impression that vegetable soups from lidless pans have fresher flavours than do those from covered ones. Perhaps you're more likely to overcook covered soups; or perhaps the volatile acids, which would otherwise escape but which now condense on the lid and fall back into the liquid, are an unwelcome presence. I don't know. Your own experience may make you think that I'm talking rubbish.

5) *Blending is not compulsory* – a minestrone being a famous example of an unblended soup. But the ingredients have given up their flavours to the liquid, and are themselves dull, I find. I like to blend them, but to leave the soup containing hints of its ingredients; mostly I prefer the slightly course texture a food mill produces to the blitzed one from a blender.

However, a food mill is not always ideal. It has a bit of trouble with spinach, and struggles too with legumes such as peas, lentils and beans, trapping their skins. I sometimes use a hand blender, though I do find that it over-processes some portions of the soup as I push it around the pan in the search for unblended bits.

Pumpkin or squash soup

You could peel the squash, cut it up, and cook it as you would in the soups described above. But it's even nicer if you concentrate the flavour. Baking the chunks is one solution; but, because peeling squashes is tricky and wastes a lot of good vegetable, I prefer to cut them in half, anoint them with oil and seasonings (I like cumin seeds in addition to salt), and bake them for about 45 minutes at gas mark 6/200°C, or until tender. Then it's easy to scoop out the flesh, add it to a base of sweated onion and garlic with enough water or stock to make a thick soup, blend, and warm through. Fresh coriander and cream are nice last-minute additions.

Lentil soup

A good many recipes for lentil and bean soups are dictated by the cooking time of the most resilient ingredient. In other words, you overcook the carrots while you're waiting for the dried legumes to soften. It's a mistake to think that the flavours are blending and maturing; they're getting tired, as they do in an overcooked stock (see page 59, or *Add hot liquid*, page 69). The way to get the flavours to blend and mature is not to boil the ingredients for hours, but to leave the cooked soup, as you might a stew, overnight.

For the best-tasting soup, cook each ingredient for only as long as it needs to become tender. If you have ingredients with big differentials in their optimum cooking times, cook them apart, combining them at the end.

For 4
Version 1
250 g lentils
2 onions, chopped
2 cloves of garlic, finely sliced
1½ tbsps olive or sunflower oil
1 tsp cumin seeds
1 tsp coriander seeds
½ tsp turmeric

Some varieties of lentil cook quickly: red ones take about 20 minutes, and green ones such as Puy are usually ready in half an hour. Make an onion and garlic base (see "Leek and potato soup" and variations, page 67); for a spicy soup, add to this base the cumin and coriander, toasted and ground (see page 247), and cook them for a couple of minutes. Wash the lentils, add them to the spicy onion base with a little salt, and cover with water or stock; cook until the lentils collapse, and blend. (For advice on cooking lentils, see page 165.) Add chilli powder or cayenne pepper with the turmeric if you like. Don't blend the soup if you don't want to.

Version 2
Or you could keep the flavours distinct: wash the lentils, and cook them in water or stock with a little salt, ½ tsp of turmeric, and cayenne pepper if you like; in a separate pan, fry the onions and garlic in oil until both are golden (this may take

25 minutes or more – see page 160); add the toasted and ground spices and cook for a couple of minutes longer; stir this mixture into the lentils a minute before you take the soup from the heat. You could mash up or blend the lentils before adding the spicy onions, or blend the entire soup after adding them. Either way, their flavour will be more apparent in this version than in version 1.

VARIATIONS

Carrots add sweetness, but lose character if they spend too long in simmering liquid. The answer is to chop up a carrot into dice (cut a carrot into three or four pieces horizontally, cut these pieces vertically into fine slices, cut more fine vertical slices at right angles to the first ones, then cut fine horizontal slices), and add them to the onion/garlic/spice mixture, cooking until the dice are soft – that may take 20 minutes or more. Then stir into the soup, and blend or not as you wish.

Spinach is a lovely complement to spiced lentils. The most economical way to cook it would be to add it to the soup when the lentils are nearly ready, wait for it to collapse a little, then stir it into the liquid below. Unfortunately, spinach throws off a terrific quantity of water, and can turn a thick soup into a thin one. So, although the method is wasteful of whatever nutrients disappear with the water that the leaves disgorge, I cook spinach apart (see page 188), drain it, squeeze out the excess liquid, and then add it to the soup.

Pep up the soup with some lemon juice: ½ lemon,

added just before serving, for the quantities above. Garnish with coriander leaves or parsley. Stir in, away from the heat (to avoid splitting), a tablespoon of thick yoghurt.

Bean soup

HOW TO MAKE IT
For 6
250 g dried beans (kidney, haricot, cannellini,
or borlotti), soaked overnight
2 onions: 1 whole, 1 chopped
2 sticks celery, chopped
3 cloves garlic: 2 unpeeled, one finely chopped
2 dried chillis (optional)
½ savoy cabbage, cut in half again,
white stalk removed, cut into strips,
then into shreds
Olive oil
Chicken stock

Drain the beans, cover by about 4 cm with fresh water in a saucepan, bring to the boil, and skim off the albuminous scum; add the whole onion and the two whole, unpeeled garlic cloves, the chillis if you're using them, and salt. Simmer, with the pot partly covered, until the beans are tender. It may take one hour; it may take three, or more.[1 – see why you do it] Top up the water if necessary, but don't drown the beans; you want to be left with a concentrated liquid.

Warm a layer of olive oil in a saucepan, and gently fry in it the chopped onion, celery and garlic, adding more oil if the vegetables show signs of catching on the pan; give them 15 to 20 minutes, until they turn golden and sweet.

When the beans are soft, remove half of them with a slotted spoon. Remove, too, the onion and chillis, and throw them away; but keep the garlic cloves, slipping them from their skins and adding them to the beans you have lifted from the pan. Push the beans and garlic through a food mill; or, if you want a simpler task and are happy with a coarser result, mash them with a potato masher.

If your whole beans are not sitting in more liquid than you want in your soup, return the mashed beans and garlic to them, along with the softened onion, celery and garlic. Return to a simmer. You're about to cook the cabbage in this soup; do you need more liquid? If so, and if you're not vegetarian, add some hot chicken stock.[2] Shove the cabbage into the simmering pot, turning up the heat and pushing down with a wooden spoon to get it into the liquid. Once the soup is simmering again, the cabbage should need no more than a couple of minutes to cook. Check the seasoning, and serve.

Going back a stage: if the whole beans, once cooked, are sitting in too much liquid, drain them, but reserve the liquid. Allow the beany sludge to settle at the bottom, then remove the thinner liquid from the top – but keep that too. Mix the mashed beans and garlic with the

drained, whole beans, and return the liquid to them – first the sludgy, tastier stuff, then the thinner stuff if you need it – until you have the consistency you want.

WHY YOU DO IT

1) *I could go on.* For more – quite a lot more, if you can take it – about cooking **dried beans**, see page 138.

2) *Hot stock.* It's safer to heat the stock before adding it to the soup. Food hygienists say that reserved stock should be brought to the boil and simmered for a few minutes before use (see page 60).

"Call that a bean soup?" – or words to that effect – a Tuscan would scoff. A Tuscan ribollita might also contain cavolo nero (the Italian dark-leafed cabbage), carrots, potatoes, tomatoes and leeks, and be served on toasted bread rubbed with garlic. The soup I describe above is much humbler; but, with a little trepidation, I would say that it has the advantage over many more authentic recipes of not containing vegetables that have been boiled for hours on end. If you want carrots in the soup, don't simmer them for longer than they take to cook (take them out of the simmering liquid if you need to). Stew tomatoes with a little olive oil, and add them in the final, warming-through phase. Add chopped leeks with the cabbage; or sauté them, adding them when the onion, celery and garlic have been in the oil for 10 to 15 minutes.

This could be a meaty soup. Simmer a ham hock or piece of gammon with the beans, removing it when the meat is tender. Then cut up the meat and add it to the soup at the end, to warm through. Or use a piece of bacon or pancetta: simmer the rind with the beans, for flavour; cube the meat, and brown it in oil, adding the onion, celery and garlic to the same pan to soften. A simpler version: cook the beans in the usual way, puréeing half, all or none of them as you see fit; then fry lardons and garlic, add them to the soup, and warm through.

Simpler still: cook the beans as above, with an onion and two unpeeled garlic cloves; discard the onion and the skins of the garlic, liquidise the beans and garlic pulp with enough liquid to make a creamy soup; warm through, check the seasoning, and serve with extra virgin olive oil to drizzle on the soup at the table.

If you're using tinned beans: they don't need cooking, of course, so they get treated as would any other cooked vegetable in a soup – added at the end, and warmed through. One possibility: simmer a ham hock or piece of gammon with a clove-studded onion, a carrot and a stick of celery. When the meat is tender, throw away the vegetables. Soften onion, celery and garlic, as in the bean soup above. Liquidise these vegetables with two 400 g tins of beans, drained, and enough ham cooking liquor to make a thick soup. Put in a pan, warm through, and cook savoy cabbage in the soup as above. Add cut-up ham or bacon, warm through, check seasoning, and serve. If you prefer: don't blend the soup, or blend only half the beans to thicken the liquid a little.

Pasta and chickpeas

As I've described lentil and bean soups, I feel that it would be odd to leave out a version of this Italian classic.

HOW TO MAKE IT
For 4
200 g chickpeas
1 onion, peeled
2 whole, unpeeled cloves garlic
2 dried chillis (optional)
2 sprigs of rosemary (optional)
Ham hock or 150 g chunk of pancetta (optional)
Tomatoes from a 400 g tin, drained of their juice
150 g ditalini, or other small pasta shape

Soak the chickpeas overnight, drain them and cook them in fresh water (see page 163) with the onion, garlic and dried chillis. The rosemary shouldn't really be optional; but as you have to find a muslin bag or some other arrangement for tying it up (so that the sprigs don't invade the soup and get in your way when you're eating), let's say that it is. Add the rosemary and the ham hock, or the rind from the pancetta. Remove the ham when it is tender; the chickpeas may take some time longer to cook. If you've used pancetta, cube it, and cook it separately in a little olive oil, frying it gently until it starts to get brown and crispy.

When the chickpeas are ready, they should be

sitting in enough water to contain and cook the pasta as well; keep checking on the water level as the chickpeas simmer, topping it up if necessary with hot water from the kettle. Throw away the onion and chillis; lift out the garlic, remove the pulp from the skins, and return it to the soup. Chop up the drained tomatoes, and add them to the pot; when the soup is simmering again, throw in the pasta, and turn up the heat to cook it; stop when it still has plenty of bite, because it will carry on cooking in the liquid. Stir in the fried cubes of pancetta, if using, or the ham, shredded from the bone; check the seasoning, and cover the pot for a few minutes away from the heat, to allow the pasta to finish cooking and the meat to warm through. Put extra virgin olive oil and Parmesan cheese on the table, for each person to add to the soup in his or her bowl.

If you're using tinned chickpeas: add them to a mixture of stock – perhaps one made with a ham hock and vegetables (see the bean soup variation, above) – and stew made with garlic and drained tomatoes (soften a couple of finely chopped cloves of garlic in olive oil; add the drained, chopped tomatoes and cook them, with chopped dried chilli if you like, until they thicken). Then cook the pasta in this soup, and serve as above.

Eggs

The best eggs I have ever eaten came from a Normandy farm, now in disuse, next to the place where we spend our holidays. The chickens would roam about the neighbourhood, and would lay eggs that were glorious reflections of their liberated lifestyles: vividly yellow, rich and creamy.

After eating such eggs, you cannot help but make the connection between paler, feebler battery offerings and the sad lives of the animals that produce them. Free range or, even better, organic eggs may be a good deal more expensive; but, if you calculate the cost in ratio to nutritional value, they are still among the cheapest foodstuffs on the market.

The proteins in eggs toughen, as they do in meat, if cooked for too long or with excessive vigour. When you're boiling, poaching, scrambling or frying eggs, do it gently.

There is a school of thought that eggs benefit from being kept in a cool place, or even at room temperature. However, Howard McGee (*McGee On Food and Cooking*) warns that the salmonella bacterium enjoys the warmth, and that eggs deteriorate four times faster at room temperature than they do in the fridge. The Food Standards Agency also advises refrigeration. Try to remember to take eggs out of the fridge an hour before boiling them, especially if you don't want their shells to shatter as they hit hot water.

This book includes two recipes – for **mayonnaise** (page 45) and for **chocolate mousse** (page 317) – that involve raw eggs. According to the most recent (March 2004) survey by the Food Standards Agency, one in 290 boxes of eggs on sale in the UK may be contaminated with salmonella. You don't have to worry about that when you cook eggs, because salmonella is destroyed by heat; but a raw contaminated egg will poison you. So the question you have to ask yourself, when making mayonnaise or chocolate mousse, is: do you feel lucky?

Free range and organic eggs are just as likely to be contaminated as battery ones, apparently. Nevertheless, I'm confident in the Martin Pitt eggs I'm lucky enough to be able to buy at a couple of my local shops. The eggs come from farms where the poultry, poultry houses and feed are checked regularly to ensure that they are salmonella-free.

Boiled eggs

I'm sorry: you probably know how to boil an egg. I just have a few pieces of advice, if you won't feel too patronised.

Bring the water to the boil, then turn the heat on your hob right down before lowering in the egg or eggs. You're less likely to crack the shells that way (as you are if you've taken the eggs out of the fridge some time beforehand), and the eggs will benefit from slow cooking. Keep the heat at a level below simmering or boiling point; just let it show a few rising bubbles.

It's impossible to give reliable timings. I'd say that, cooked at this very gentle rate, a medium egg will be soft boiled, with a runny yolk, at five minutes; after seven minutes, the yolk will be part-squidgy, part runny (that's how I like it); at 10 to 12 minutes, it will be hard boiled, but still moist. After that, it starts to get dry and powdery. If you're hard boiling eggs, put them into cold water for a while when they're ready; otherwise, their residual heat will carry on cooking them, and they will develop an unappetising grey-greenish layer around their yolks.

Poached eggs

HOW TO MAKE THEM

Four is usually the most you can poach at once. Crack them into separate cups.[1] – see why you do it
Bring a frying pan or broad saucepan of water – you need only an egg's depth – to the boil,[2] turn down to a simmer, and add 1 dstsp of vinegar and 1 tsp of salt.[3] Gently slip the eggs into the water; maintain a low heat under the pan, as when boiling eggs (see above). Cook for three to four minutes, and lift out with a draining spoon.

I used to put them to dry on paper towels,

but found it hard to prise them cleanly from the soggy paper. So now I put them for a few seconds on to a wooden board, before lifting them on to plates.

1) *Cracking it*. Cracking eggs is one of many simple kitchen skills at which I'm incompetent. I don't trust myself to do it efficiently above simmering water. This two-stage operation is far less stressful.

2) *Cooking in water*. Purists turn up their noses at egg-poaching pans. A poached egg, they insist, is cooked in water; in poachers, the eggs rest in trays, and are steamed by simmering water in the pans below. I can't see, or taste, what's so unacceptable about steamed eggs; and the whites certainly come out neater.

3) *Salt and vinegar*. They help the egg white to set, and also give it a tender texture.

Eggs Florentine

HOW TO MAKE IT
For 2
Cook and drain 500 g of spinach (see page 188); squeeze out the water through the holes in a sieve or colander with the back of a wooden spoon, and arrange the spinach, seasoned, in an ovenproof

83

dish large enough to hold four poached eggs. Make four wells in the spinach. Put the dish into a low oven to keep warm. Heat water in a pan for the eggs. While it is coming to a simmer, make about 250 ml of béchamel sauce (see page 50). Keep the sauce warm on a heat disperser above the lowest possible flame. Poach the eggs and drain them; take the spinach out of the oven, and arrange the eggs in the wells you made. Stir 2 heaped tbsps of grated cheese (Pecorino or Parmesan, perhaps; but you could use Cheddar) into the sauce (the cheese will retain its character best given the briefest possible cooking); check the seasoning of the sauce, pour it over the eggs and spinach, and sprinkle finely grated Parmesan on top. Put the dish under the grill until the surface has browned.

Fried eggs

Here are two possible methods:

Warm a frying pan; add enough butter to give a generous covering of the pan's surface; when it is foaming, crack the eggs over it (or crack them into cups first, and slip them in from there). Cook for a couple of minutes, until the white is set.

Nigel Slater's method: crack eggs into separate cups; heat a generous quantity (a finger's depth, he says) of good olive oil in a frying pan, until a small piece of bread sizzles energetically in it. Tilt the pan, and slip the eggs (no more than two in a pan) into the oil where it is deepest, so that you get hot oil to run over the yolk. Level the pan, and fry the eggs for a couple of minutes, until the white is set; lift out of the oil with a draining spoon.

If you don't like runny yolks, a fried egg is not for you. In the time it takes a yolk to set, a frying white turns to rubber.

Scrambled eggs

HOW TO MAKE THEM

Again, the secret is slow cooking. That, and knowing when to stop: the egg will carry on setting when removed from the heat. If I haven't made scrambled eggs for a while, I often find that I get my timing wrong.

Crack two or three eggs for each person into a bowl. Stir with a fork to blend the yolks and the whites.[1 – see WHY YOU DO IT] Allow 10 g of butter or more (I use more) for every two eggs. Melt half of it over a medium to low heat in a non-stick sauce-pan (use another kind only if you enjoy cleaning off stuck egg – I'd rather clean the Augean stables). When the butter foams, pour in the egg, and continue to cook, over a low heat and stirring constantly, until the egg is set but moist.[2] Take the pan off the heat, add the rest of the butter, stir until it's melted, and tip the scrambled eggs on to warm plates. Add pepper if you like.[3]

Any of the herbs and vegetables that go well with an **omelette** (see page 88) will make a happy alliance with scrambled eggs. You must make sure that the vegetables have disgorged their water, and won't spoil the rich creaminess of the dish. Simply adding grated cheese to the beaten eggs and cooking them together is fine, or you could try a fancier option, reducing a small glass of wine to a couple of tablespoons of liquid in a saucepan, and adding it, with seasonings and herbs if you like, to a mixture of eggs and cheese (Gruyère complements eggs particularly well).

Piperade is an onion, pepper and tomato stew with a bonding of creamy egg. For two: four eggs, lightly beaten; one onion, sliced; two red peppers, deseeded and sliced; one clove of garlic, finely chopped; one 400 g can of tomatoes, or four plump fresh ones; two tablespoons of olive oil. Fry the onion, pepper and garlic in the oil until soft – about 10 to 15 minutes. (Or skin the pepper first – see page 168.) Now, here is one of the rare times when it's important to deseed and de-juice the tomatoes (see page 191): if using canned ones, drain them and squeeze out their juice. You need a dry stew that doesn't water down the egg. Chop the tomatoes, add them to the onion and pepper mix, and cook them until their moisture has evaporated. Add the eggs, seasoned, and cook until lightly scrambled.

Or make them spicy: (for two) fry a sliced onion and chopped garlic in butter or butter and oil; add a teaspoon of toasted and ground cumin (see page 247), a teaspoon of minced garlic, and a chopped green chilli, with the seeds removed if you don't want the heat; cook for a couple of minutes longer, and add four beaten, seasoned eggs; cook gently, stirring, until scrambled. This dish is better with fresh chilli than with dry chilli or chilli powder, I think; and it's also nice with the addition, at the end of cooking, of some chopped coriander leaves.

WHY YOU DO IT

1) *Don't overbeat*. Blend the whites and the yokes, but leave a globby texture. If you beat the eggs until they become runny, they will be tougher when cooked. This rule applies to omelettes as well.

2) *Warm butter, slow cooking*. You get the pan and the butter hot first because you want the eggs to start cooking as soon as you pour them in. However, you have to heat them gently; cook them on a high heat, and you produce pale eggy chunks with the consistency of foam insoles.

Don't wait until the eggs look ready; take them off the heat just before then, and carry on stirring. They will continue to set; if you leave them on the heat, you'll find that they move from readiness to dryness before you can react. The second helping of butter, because it melts rather than cooks, will give a more luxurious butteriness to the eggs, and it will help to arrest the cooking just at the point of perfection.

Your eggs are creamily curdled; but you can still ruin them by tipping them on to scorching hot plates, which will cook them some more.

For an even softer result, add 1 tbsp of milk or cream for every two eggs.

3) *Seasoning*. If you want pepper, add it at the end; it discolours the eggs if cooked with them. Salt breaks down egg proteins. Whether the action has a deleterious effect on the taste of scrambled eggs, I'm not sure; but, to be on the safe side, I don't add salt until the eggs are warming in the pan.

Omelette

HOW TO MAKE IT

You need a seasoned frying pan (see page 30), with a slick surface. A medium-sized pan (24 cm) is about the right size for a two- to three-egg omelette. Blend the whites and yolks of the eggs lightly in a bowl (see "Scrambled eggs", above). Season with a little salt. Warm the pan over a medium flame; add a walnut-sized knob of butter, and twist the pan so that the butter lubricates it thoroughly. The butter should foam, but not turn brown. With the flame still at medium, pour in the eggs, and give them a quick stir with a fork to distribute the heat. The edges of the omelette will set immediately; with a fork or a spatula, pull these edges from the side of the pan, tilting it to allow the runny egg to take their place.[1 – see WHY YOU]

^{DO IT} **When the omelette is set, but the surface still moist, tilt the pan away from you and roll the omelette over towards the far edge;[2] tip it on to a warm plate.**

Herbs: parsley, chives and tarragon are among the possibilities. Add them to the beaten egg before cooking.

Cheese: blue cheese might be a little overwhelming in an omelette, but almost any other kind will be good. Grate it and sprinkle it over the omelette just before rolling, and don't use too much: you want a lightly melted filling, not a sticky wodge.

Vegetables: onions, shallots, mushrooms, peppers, courgettes, asparagus. Cook them apart (see the **Vegetables** chapter, page 130), make sure all their liquid has evaporated, and stir them into the eggs before making the omelette. If you simplified the process by sautéing, say, mushrooms, and then pouring the eggs over them, the browning that has taken place in the pan would discolour the omelette; also, omelettes made in that way seem to be tougher.

WHY YOU DO IT

1) *Quick-setting.* The process, from pouring in the eggs to tilting the omelette on to the plate, should take about a minute. If you left the omelette undisturbed, the egg layer that hit the pan first would be tough before the runny egg above it had set. By pulling in the edges, you allow the runny egg to flow on to the hot surface, and to set as quickly as possible.

2) *Slick surface.* These manipulations will not work unless you have a well-seasoned or non-stick pan: without one, you'll end up with stuck bits of eggy mess. I often do anyway, because I lack skill in rolling an omelette neatly; but the result usually tastes fine.

Frittata

A frittata is an Italian flat omelette, served hot or cold. It's thicker than a rolled omelette, and cooked very gently, so that it doesn't toughen up before it's set all the way through. The medium-sized pan that makes your two- or three-egg rolled omelette will make a five- or six-egg frittata.

HOW TO MAKE IT

Crack six eggs into a bowl, beat them gently with a fork until the whites and yolks are just blended, and stir in 3 heaped tbsps of cheese – Parmesan, say, or Pecorino, or Gruyère, or Cheddar. Melt butter – be generous, use 30 to 40 g – in the frying pan, turn the heat to its lowest, and pour in the egg mixture. Cook for 10 to 15 minutes, until the base of the frittata is well set; the top will probably still be runny. Now, you could do what the professionals do: set a large plate over the pan; rapidly turn over pan and plate so that the frittata lands on the plate upside down; slide the frittata back into the pan for a few minutes, to set the other side. Or do what I do: put the pan under the grill for a minute. Cut the frittata into wedges.

Variations include all those described above for rolled omelettes. Or add bacon or pancetta: chopped slices or cubes.

Spanish omelette (tortilla)

HOW TO MAKE IT
5 eggs
1 large Spanish onion
400 g potatoes, sliced or cubed
(most kinds will do; new, waxy potatoes
hold their shape better)
250 ml olive oil

That's a lot of olive oil. You're part-frying, part-
braising the vegetables in it. Slice the onions
finely; peel and slice, or cube, the potatoes, drop-
ping them into cold water if you need to keep
them waiting for a while and don't want to discolour them. Warm the olive oil in a sauté pan, or
any kind of heavy pan with a lid. Add the onions
and potatoes, stir and cover, cooking them above
a moderate heat. After five minutes or so, stir
again, as the onions start to collapse. Keep moni-
toring the pan; be careful how you stir once the
potatoes soften, because they find breaking up
easy to do. When the vegetables are cooked, drain
them in a sieve, reserving the oil. Stir the vegetables into the eggs, and add salt to taste. Take a
couple of tablespoons of the oil, warm it in a frying pan, and cook the omelette as you would a
frittata (see above).

91

RICE, PASTA, COUSCOUS

Rice

Of the many aspects of cuisine that can make us feel inadequate, surely the most humiliating is an inability to prepare a palatable dish of a simple, staple foodstuff. Yet who hasn't produced soggy, clumpy and gluey rice? I still do, particularly when I use an unfamiliar brand. But I have two principles that have cut down my error rate: I ignore packet instructions, and I don't, despite the advice of most recipes, subject the rice to a wash and a soak before I cook it.

HOW TO COOK LONG GRAIN RICE
Method 1

Bring a large pan of water to the boil. Add salt. Add rice gradually (about 75 g a person is a decent portion), so that the water does not come off the boil.[1 – see WHY YOU DO IT] **Continue to cook, at a rolling boil, and start tasting the rice at about**

eight minutes. It will probably be ready in 10. Drain it when it is tender but before it goes soft.

Method 2

Put rice, unwashed[2] and unsoaked,[3] into a pan – one in which the rice forms a shallow bed. Add cold water until there is a small gap, of a bit less than half a cm, between the top of the rice and the surface of the water. Add a little salt. Bring the pan to the boil, turn down the heat to its lowest setting, and put a heat disperser between the pan and the ring; then spread a clean J-cloth on top of the pan, and a lid on top of that. Simmer for 12 minutes; then turn off the heat, and leave the pan, undisturbed, for another five. Fluff up the rice with a fork; adding a little oil or butter will help to separate it.[4]

Method 3

Heat some butter or oil – a walnut-sized piece of butter, or 1 dstsp oil, for each 75 g of rice. Tip the rice into the pan, and fry it; you'll see the grains turn a milky colour. Then proceed as in method 2, but cook for 15 minutes before turning off the heat and waiting for a further five.[5]

A simple rice lunch or supper

HOW TO MAKE IT

Fry leftover bits of roast meat in some sunflower

or olive oil. Add some chopped onion and/or garlic, and/or green or red peppers, if you like, and continue cooking until the onions are golden (and the peppers are softened). Stir in cooked rice. Season to taste. Cooked fresh or frozen peas are a nice addition. You might also start by frying lardons of pancetta, or pieces of bacon. I like to have chilli sauce on the table; others might prefer soy, or ketchup.

WHY YOU DO IT

1) *Boiling* – easy, but not ideal. We're often told that the "absorption method" – 2 and 3, above – is the way to guarantee separate, unsticky grains. In my experience, this technique is not easy to get right. Boiling, I find, is much more reliable.

You keep the pot at a rolling boil, as you would a pot of pasta, in order to disperse any sticky starch there might be on the surface of the grains. Rice or pasta cooked at a temperature lower than boiling point is likely to clump together. Drain the rice when it is just ready; overcooked rice will also be sticky.

That's let you off a lot of fiddling about, then. There are just two problems: boiling loses nutrients to the water; and the rice it produces is not as fragrant or tasty as that produced by the absorption method. Unreliable as it is, or as my application of it is, the absorption method is the one I use.

2) *Washing*. The rice you buy in packets is clean. It's harmless. In the US (though not in the UK), most of it is better for you in an unwashed state, because it is coated with vitamins that washing would disperse.

The one reason you might want to wash rice is to get rid of the polishing dust that is sometimes still present, and that turns into gum on cooking. But many brands do not require this treatment: Tilda, for example, tells me that its rice leaves the factory dust-free. A reason you might be *told* to wash rice is to reduce the starch content; this instruction does not make sense (see **Soaking**, below). And definitely don't wash rice as a preliminary to any recipe that calls on you to coat the grains in oil or butter, unless you're going to ensure that, before you do the coating, you get every grain dry again (see **Pre-coating**, page 97).

Have you ever followed advice to wash rice "until the water runs clear"? I have. I put the water in a pan, swirled it about a bit, and drained it. Then I repeated the process. And again. And again. After about half an hour, the water was still turning cloudy, and I gave up. When cooked, the rice was the stickiest I've ever prepared (see **Soaking**).

3) Soaking. Some writers seem to think that you wash or soak rice in order to get rid of starch, thus reducing its stickiness. Starch makes up about 80% of a rice grain. You're not going to get rid of all of that – and you don't want to.

Others tell you that a soaking for half an hour elongates the grain, making it softer and allowing water to penetrate more easily. "This means that the grains don't break up in the pan, and therefore don't stick to each other," Sri Owen writes in *The Rice Book*.

No doubt I am deficient in my rice-cooking technique, but I have always found that soaked rice is much more likely to clump together. The softer grain is also stickier. Perhaps I use too much water, or cook the rice for too long – the cooking time of soaked rice will be shorter. Anyway, now I always leave my rice unwashed and unsoaked.

4) *How much water will my rice absorb?* If you use too much water, you may produce rice that is overcooked and sticky; too little, and the rice will be hard. Recipes that give you a volume of water to use for a quantity of rice are not reliable. The size and quality of your pan, the temperature of your hob, the hardness of your water and, most importantly, the quality of your rice are all factors that will affect the absorption rate. My best advice is, get to know the behaviour of a particular brand, and learn how to judge that you've got right the relationship between the depth of water and the depth of rice in your pan.

You might think that the packet would offer some help, but you'd be wrong. Following the instructions on a packet of basmati rice I bought in France recently, I cooked the rice in three times its volume of water: that proved to be far too much. In *The Cook's Encyclopaedia*, Tom Stobart writes: "I once bought a very costly Saudi Arabian variety of rice from a Bedouin trader and found to my amazement that it absorbed no less than nine times its volume of water and would not cook properly with any less." So, if you're tempted to buy rice from a Bedouin trader rather than from the local supermarket, be warned.

Method 2, above, works for me with Tilda's basmati.

The function of the J-cloth is to absorb the steam, which would otherwise turn back to water on the lid of the pan and drop on to the rice. The resting time at the end of cooking helps the rice to plump up and separate. Don't worry if rice sticks to the bottom of the pan – it always does.

5) *Pre-coating.* This, method 3, is the best way to get the absorption method to work. The impregnated fatty layer seems to keep the grains separate. As I say above, this technique won't work with damp rice, because the water will repel the fat. The rice takes a little longer to cook than it does in method 2.

I've been assuming that you want separate grains of rice. Sometimes, you might want it sticky. Separate grains may be aesthetically pleasing, but they're not easy to manipulate with chopsticks. One way to get them to adhere in more manageable clumps is – though this is not the official approach – to rinse the rice first. Another is to buy a stickier variety: Thai fragrant or jasmine rice is stickier than rices sold as long grain, basmati or patna. You might also try rice sold as sticky rice, sometimes known as "glutenous" rice; I've used the inverted commas because rice contains no gluten, which is formed from the starch granules in wheat flour. Use sticky rice as an accompaniment to oriental dishes, to make rice cakes or sushi, or if you like those rather cloying sweet dishes that feature in Asian cuisine.

Pre-coating leads us to dishes that require an initial turning of rice in fat: risotto, paella and pilaf.

Risotto

HOW TO MAKE IT
Generous quantity for 2
200 g risotto rice [1] – see WHY YOU DO IT
1 l chicken stock
1 small onion, or 2 shallots
30 g butter
25 g to 30 g grated Parmesan

Heat the stock to simmering point, on the ring next to the one on which you'll cook the risotto. Chop the onion finely and, in a heavy pan,[2] soften it in half the butter (see page 160). You want it to be thoroughly mellow, so you may need to cook it for 15 minutes; a shallot will take less. Add the rice and, following the instructions above under *Pre-coating*, turn it with the onion and butter until the grains turn milky. Now add a ladleful of stock; stir the rice and stock, which should be simmering gently, until the rice absorbs the liquid. Then add another ladleful, and wait for that to be absorbed before adding the next.[3] Keep stirring. Some rice will stick to the bottom of the pan; don't worry about prising it loose and stirring it back into the risotto.

You'll be able to tell when the rice is nearly ready: it will plump up. Getting to this stage may take between 18 minutes and half an hour. Start tasting; you want the rice to be al dente (having a slight firmness to the bite), with a chalky quality. When it has got to that stage, turn off the heat (the risotto will continue to cook for a while, so it shouldn't be soft already), and add the rest of the butter, along with the Parmesan. Put a lid on the pan. Leave for two minutes, to allow the butter and Parmesan to melt; stir them in. Taste for salt; you may find that the Parmesan has contributed all the salt you want.

VARIATIONS

That is a very basic risotto; but all others, with the possible exception of seafood ones (see page 101), are cooked in this way. You merely add the ingredients you want, but you need to know when to add them.

Risotto alla milanese, officially, includes beef marrow. Not many people use that nowadays, but they do use saffron – one little sachet, or half a teaspoon of strands dissolved in stock (which, officially, should be beef or veal stock), for four people. Add it towards the end of cooking; longer cooking diminishes its impact. You also include some wine, white or red; it goes in after you've coated the rice, and is cooked until it evaporates or the rice absorbs it (see page 39), before you start ladling in the stock. I recently used a glass of white wine in a risotto for four people; it turned out to be too much. Anna del Conte recommends six tablespoons.

Other alcoholic options are vermouth, sherry and champagne. For an even richer finish, add some cream at the end of cooking instead of the butter.

Bacon or pancetta risotto is good. Fry some cut-up bits of streaky bacon, or some lardons, or cubes of pancetta, until they are turning crispy, before adding the onion (if you put the bacon in second, it won't go brown); some garlic would be nice too. Bacon goes very well with green vegetables, which you should cook apart and add to the risotto at the end of cooking, just to warm through, in order to retain their freshness of flavour. Boil some fresh or frozen peas in the stock (don't drain the stock down the sink when they're ready; pour it back into the stockpot); fry slices or match-sticks of courgettes; steam broccoli or broad beans; roast asparagus. If you've fried the vegetables, you probably don't want the extra knob of butter from the basic recipe.

Mushrooms will stand up to longer cooking, so you can add them to the onions before the rice goes in. Dried porcini mushrooms (see page 159), in addition to or instead of fresh ones, contribute an intense funghal flavour: soak them in warm water for half an hour, then add them to the pot at an early stage too, along with the flavoured liquid in which they've soaked. Try also cubes of squash sautéed with the onions; or roast them and add them at the end.

WHY YOU DO IT

1) *For a risotto, use risotto rice.* It is worth being a purist and buying an Italian rice, such as the widely available arborio, for your risotto. Some aficionados, even more purist, insist on carnaroli. Anne del Conte reports that the Veneti make their seafood and vegetable risotti with vialone nano.

This is a dish in which you protect the grains by coating them in fat, while at the same time generating a starchy consistency with frequent stirring. The Italian varieties will absorb a great deal of liquid, and endure a great deal of stirring, without breaking up.

100

2) *Thick pan.* You need a thick-bottomed pan. It doesn't matter if the risotto sticks a little, and if the stuck bits are stirred back into the rest; but in a thin pan the stuck bits will burn. You might use a thin pan and a heat disperser, but that arrangement will hamper you somewhat as you stir, and will mean that adjustments of heat take a while to be effective.

3) *Ladleful by ladleful.* There are two reasons for this instruction. If you use too much liquid, you risk over-cooking rice that should, in the finished dish, be al dente, with a chalky quality; and the stirring of rice in a little liquid produces the creamy consistency that risotto-lovers prize. Nevertheless, I am in heretical agreement with Richard Ehrlich, who in *The Perfect* . . . makes a case for adding a decent quantity of liquid at first. Then, after stirring it about a bit, you can leave the pot for long enough to allow you to grate some cheese, or prepare a salad, before the stock is absorbed and you need to add more. The important point is to be cautious when adding liquid after a quarter of an hour or so, because you should stop cooking at the point when the rice is plump and at the al dente stage. Keep tasting it.

If you run out of stock, use boiling water from the kettle.

Seafood risotto

Claudia Roden (in *The Food of Italy*) says that in the Veneto, where seafood risotto is a speciality, they cook the rice in plenty of stock, rather than adding liquid gradually. I haven't come across that observation elsewhere, although I can see that the less unctuous consistency that this method produces would suit fish and shellfish well.

HOW TO MAKE IT

You add the rice to a pan of simmering fish stock (see page 62) and simmer it until it is al dente, hoping that the moment of readiness coincides with a reduction of the liquid to your required consistency. If there's too much liquid, drain some off when the rice is ready; if there's too little, add some more hot stock or some boiling water. Meanwhile, you cook some mussels (see page 296): a reduction of the mussel liquor, consisting of wine and juices from the shellfish, goes into the pot with the rice. Soften some onions (see page 160), and fry some prawns with them. (If the prawns are uncooked that is; fry them in their shells, and wait for them to go pink. If the prawns are cooked, simply warm them through in the risotto.) When the rice is ready, you stir in the mussels, prawns and onions.

The best fish for risotto is a firm variety such as monkfish, which won't break up when you stir it into the rice. Add it to the pot about 10 minutes before you think the rice will be ready.

In *Gammon and Spinach*, Simon Hopkinson offers a short cut for those without the wherewithal to make a fish stock: use a bottle or two of fish soup. You could make a very nice, straightforward dish by preparing a risotto as in

102

the basic recipe above, with hot soup substituting for the stock, and by adding towards the end of cooking some thawed frozen prawns.

The one point on which all writers are agreed is that you should never add cheese to a seafood risotto. It is an unpleasant combination. The Italians don't add cheese to seafood pasta dishes, either.

Paella

HOW TO MAKE IT

For 4

400 g rice (a Spanish one if you can find it,
or an Italian risotto rice)
4 chicken thighs or drumsticks
4 chorizos (the uncooked sausages,
not the salami-style stuff)
20 mussels
20 prawns
1 onion, chopped
2 red peppers, deseeded and cut into strips
2 cloves garlic, finely chopped
1 sachet of saffron, or ½ tsp of
saffron threads, dissolved in stock
Handful of parsley, chopped
1.25 l chicken stock

Steam the mussels (see page 296) with a glass of white wine. Remove the opened ones from the pan, and boil the liquor until it has reduced by half.

In a little olive oil and at a moderate heat, fry the chicken pieces, in a wide pan that you can put into the oven (perhaps a wide casserole dish, or a frying pan with a detachable handle).[1 – see WHY YOU DO IT] After cooking for five to eight minutes on each side, they should be nicely browned. Remove them to a plate, and chuck away the oil.[2]

Add a little more oil to the pan, slice the chorizos thickly, and fry them. They should release their own, paprika-flavoured oil. When they have done so, and when they are browned, take them out of the pan and put them with the chicken.

In the same pan, soften the onion, peppers and garlic; add a little more oil if you need it (but there should be enough). The peppers will produce some liquid; let this cook away. Tip in the rice, turn it with the vegetables, and cook it until it turns milky. Pour in the stock, and bring the pan to a simmering point. Cover the pan tightly with foil (or, if you're using a casserole, with its lid), and put it on to the bottom shelf of a gas mark 4/180°C oven. After 30 minutes, take it out of the oven, uncover it, and add the chicken, chorizo, mussels, prawns, saffron and parsley, stirring them in gently. Cover again, and put back in the oven for 15 more minutes.

VARIATIONS

Other meat and fish you might add include ham, snails (you can buy vacuum-packed ones) and clams (you prepare and cook them as you do mussels – see page 296). Other vegetables include deseeded and chopped tomatoes (see page 190), peas, broad beans and green beans. The clams, peas and beans will need cooking before you add them, after 30 minutes.

1) *You don't have to be authentic*. This dish makes me nervous. Clearly, I lack the essential machismo – in Valencia, home of the most famous recipe, making paella is the men's job. (I'm also short of confidence when faced with that other favourite masculine task, barbecuing.)

Here's what gets me worried. A real paella pan – a caldero, which is wide and shallow with handles, or the wide frying pan that you will need as a substitute – is much wider than the hotplates on cookers. The rice in the centre of the pan cooks more quickly than that at the outside, and may well stick and burn. The pan, in most recipes, is uncovered, so the liquid is absorbed into the rice and evaporates as well. After 20 minutes or so, you find that you have some cooked rice and some that has scarcely developed from the state it was in when packeted. You're not supposed to stir it, though; the dish should not resemble a risotto. So you add more water, overcooking the central portion while you try to bring the rest to an edible condition.

My compromise is to use a covered pan, and to put it in the oven. Because you're going to leave it undisturbed, you need to be confident that you've added the right quantity of liquid to cook the rice and be absorbed by it. I hope that my suggestion – 1.25 l of liquid to 400 g of rice – works for you.

2) *Throw away the chicken fat*. Because, by the time you've fried the chorizo, you should have plenty of fat, and it will be nicer than the stuff the chicken exudes. If you fry the chorizo first, and then the chicken, you will probably have too much fat in the pan; and, if you discard any, you will lose some of the chorizo's paprika-flavoured oil. Don't throw the fat down the sink: it will congeal. I pour it into a saucer, then scrape it when cold into the bin.

Pilaf

Basic pilaf. This is method 3 (page 93), with the addition of spices. Alternative spellings, often found in your local Indian restaurant, include pilau and pulao. Before you add water, you turn the rice in oil, butter or ghee (clarified butter), with flavourings that might include cumin, coriander, cardamom, turmeric, allspice or cinnamon. If they're finely ground, the spices will burn easily, so just turn them with the rice briefly.

Fancier. Richard Whittington (*Home Food*) has a recipe for turmeric pilaf with raisins and flaked almonds. Adapting his recipe for four people, I'd recommend 220 g of long grain rice, stock or water to make up one and a half times the volume of the rice (or whatever quantity works with the rice you use), one onion, a pinch of allspice, a cinnamon stick, four cardamom pods, a tablespoon of raisins, a bay leaf, salt and 20 g of toasted flaked almonds.

Slice the onion, soften it in oil or butter, then turn up the heat and add the rice, turning it until it becomes milky; add the spices, turning them quickly without burning. Add the stock or water, cinnamon, raisins, cardamom, bay leaf and salt (a quarter of a teaspoon, perhaps). Bring to a simmer, cover and cook as in the basic recipe (page 93). When the rice is ready, discard the bay leaf and cardamom. Whittington recommends stirring in a knob of butter. Scatter the almonds on top before serving.

Meat pilafs. Sri Owen has an Afghan recipe called Qabili pilaf. You make a basic stew (see page 223) by frying lamb pieces or chicken pieces followed by an onion, then adding salt and water, and covering and simmering for 40 minutes (the chicken will be ready in that time; the lamb may need longer). Drain the liquid, which will become the stock in which you cook the rice. Add some carrots, cut into matchsticks, to the meat and onions, as well as some raisins. Add, too, some cumin and saffron. Put the pan on the heat again, add the rice and turn it with the other ingredients; pour in the stock (again, try it at 1.5:1 in relation to the volume of rice), bring to the boil, turn down the heat, cover and simmer as above. For four to six people, Owen suggests 450 g rice, 800 g lamb or one jointed chicken (or six chicken portions), one onion, two or three carrots, 112 g raisins, 2 tsps of cumin and ¼ tsp saffron.

Pasta

As pasta is now the default, easy, everyday meal of choice in so many households, offering advice on such matters as the size of the cooking vessel, the vigour with which the water should boil and the addition to the water of salt may seem as affected as giving a detailed recipe for fish fingers – or as telling you, as I have already done (page 81), how to boil an egg. Still, I shall risk giving offence.

I should guess that of all the recipes currently finding publication, pasta sauces occupy the largest category. The demand is so great that writers are under constant pressure to come up with new dishes, most of which are variations on ones below or elsewhere in this book.

Fresh pasta

It's fun, and satisfying, to make your own pasta; but it takes quite a lot of fiddly work, and requires you to clear half an acre of space to accommodate the drying pasta sheets. So I'm going to cop out and say that making your own pasta is a more committedly foodie operation than this book is designed to describe. Also, perfectly helpful instructions come in more specialist books (try *Marcella's Kitchen* by Marcella Hazan) or with pasta-making machines.

Dry pasta

What most of us use, at least 95% of the time.

HOW TO COOK IT
Bring a large pot of water to the boil.[1] – see WHY YOU DO IT **Add salt,**[2] **and return to the boil. Tip in the pasta,**[3] **stir it, and cover the pot with a lid until the**

water comes to the boil again. Uncover, stir, and
continue to cook at a rolling boil[4] until the pasta
is al dente (with a slight firmness as you bite it).[5]
Drain, and mix immediately with sauce, or with
oil or butter.[6]

WHY YOU DO IT

1) *Large pot*. Pasta, though not quite as demanding as rice
(see page 92), is not entirely foolproof: it sticks together
easily, and goes soggy and indigestible if overcooked. Giving
it plenty of water to move around in – about a litre for each
100 g of pasta – is the first step in keeping it separate.

The water will come to the boil faster if you cover
the pan.

2) *Salt*. You don't have to add it after the pan boils –
though the water will come to the boil faster if you do,
because salt raises the boiling temperature. You can be
generous, using a teaspoon of salt, say, for each litre of
water. It flavours the pasta and reduces stickiness.

3) *What pasta, and how much?* The best Italian brands
are a lot better than anything else. De Cecco is a particularly
good one. Don't use the quick-cook stuff. About 125 g for
each person is a decent, main course quantity.

4) *Rolling boil*. A misguided pedant once wrote to the
Guardian to tick off Richard Ehrlich, who had instructed
readers to ensure that pasta water boiled rapidly. There was
no difference in temperature between boiling water and

fast-boiling water, the pedant wrote. True: but the temperature is not the point. The point is the water's agitation, which helps to keep the pasta separate.

If you put a lot of pasta into a little water, it will lower the water temperature to one considerably below boiling point, and might cause clumping. Even when you use a lot of water, it's a good idea to give the pasta an initial stir to encourage it to separate. Putting the lid on the pot will get the water back to the boil more quickly.

5) *Al dente*. Packet instructions on cooking times are helpful, but they cannot be precise: kitchen conditions and water qualities vary too much. Appearance is a good guide: pasta turns milky white when it is ready. But it's best to remove a piece with a slotted spoon, stick it under the cold tap for a second, and bite into it. Stop cooking when the pasta has passed the crunchy stage but still has some firmness in the centre. Its residual heat will carry on cooking it for a while after it is drained.

You might think that you'd prefer your pasta to be soft; but if you aim to get it that way, you'll find it has a soggy starchiness that is hard to digest.

6) *Sauce it quickly*. A cooling mound of drained pasta in a colander or bowl will stick together. Lubricate it by stirring in your sauce, or some butter or oil, as quickly as possible. When you drain the pasta, put the pot underneath the colander before all the water has drained through, in order to catch a little of it. You can use this cooking liquid if the pasta, once dressed with sauce, seems a little dry.

Pasta shapes

The ones I use most often are spaghetti, penne (the quills: I usually get the ridged – rigati – ones) and conchiglie (shells). Spaghetti goes well with meat and tomato sauces, as everyone who has been through the cookery rite-of-passage of making a spag bol knows, but not so well with creamy ones, in which it is more likely to stick together. Penne and conchiglie go with anything. I've slightly gone off farfalle (butterflies) and fusilli (spirals), parts of which overcook while others remain hard. I buy macaroni for **macaroni cheese**, that insult to Italian gastronomy (see page 122).

Pasta sauces

Tomato sauce

See page 191. The quantities I've given are inauthentic, I'm afraid: Italians use just enough sauce to provide a coating and flavouring. But then the way we usually eat pasta, as a substantial main course rather than as a primo piatto (first course), is inauthentic too.

Other vegetable sauces

For ideas about dressing pasta with vegetables, see the

Vegetables chapter (page 130), and in particular **asparagus** (page 132), **aubergines** (page 134), **broccoli** (page 142), **cauliflower** (page 148), **courgettes** (page 151), **mushrooms** (page 157), **peppers** (page 168) and **spinach** (page 188). Some of these vegetables – the non-green ones, and courgettes – might be combined with a tomato sauce.

Bolognese sauce
(See page 250)

Carbonara sauce

One of my favourite things. In spite of the advice of Rose Gray and Ruth Rogers (in the first *River Café Cook Book*) that this sauce goes best with penne or a similar shape, and in spite of what I myself say (above) about spaghetti and creamy (eggy, in this case) sauces, I still like this with spaghetti. The egg seems to scramble more satisfactorily, for some reason; with penne, I often end up with pasta in a runny, eggy and somewhat unappetising liquid.

HOW TO MAKE IT
For 2
250 g spaghetti
100 g pancetta, cubed[1] – see WHY YOU DO IT
½ clove garlic, finely chopped[2]
2 eggs
1 tbsp double cream (optional)[3]

4 heaped tbsps (about 25 g) grated Parmesan,
or a combination of Parmesan and Pecorino
Pinch of nutmeg

Put a large pan of water on the heat for the spaghetti. Beat the eggs lightly, as you would for scrambled eggs (see page 87). Add the cream, if you're using it. Season with a little nutmeg, and pepper if you like; you may not need more salt, because of the salty pancetta and cheese. Put the pancetta with no more than 1 dstsp of olive oil in a heavy-bottomed pan, large enough to contain the spaghetti when it's ready.

When the pasta water is boiling, add salt, return to the boil, then add the spaghetti. (Some of it will probably stick out of the water. Allow it 20 seconds or so to soften, then stir it in.) Turn the heat under the pancetta to low/medium, and fry it gently; you're aiming to get it ready when the pasta is cooked, so adjust the temperature accordingly. About three minutes before the pasta is ready, add the garlic to the pancetta, and continue frying on a very low heat, with a heat disperser under the pan if necessary.

When the pasta is al dente (see page 110), drain it, reserving a little of the cooking liquid. Tip the drained pasta into the pan with the pancetta. Turn off the heat under the pan, and pour in the eggs, stirring and tossing thoroughly; they should scramble in contact with the hot ingredients. Now add the cheese, and toss that in thoroughly.[4] If the mixture is too dry and sticky, moisten it

113

**with a little of the cooking liquid. Serve, with
more cheese at the table if you like.**

WHY YOU DO IT

1) *Pancetta beats bacon*. I'm all for making do with
ingredients to hand, but I do think, snobbishly purist as it
sounds, that pancetta, with its sweet taste, works a lot
better in this dish than does streaky bacon. I buy pancetta in
a chunk from my local deli; it's tastier, and less watery, than
pre-packaged lardons. You can use slices, cut up, as well.
(You can also use cut-up slices of streaky bacon.) The
pancetta will release its own fat, so use just enough oil to
get the frying process started.

2) *Garlic*. Fry it for long enough to soften its flavour; but
if you put it in the pan at the same time as you start cooking the pancetta, you might overcook and burn it. If you
want to be a bit more subtle, just let it add garlic notes to
the oil: lightly crush a whole clove with a heavy knife, put
it in the pan with the pancetta, keep stirring it around, and
remove and discard it when it's brown.

3) *Careful with the cream*. A modest portion will add
lubrication to the sauce; but if you use too much, you'll
stop the eggs scrambling. You may find that you prefer to
leave it out, and to use a little cooking liquid if the carbonara looks too dry and clumpy.

4) *Timing*. The pancetta pan should be hot, but not so hot
that it immediately turns whatever egg hits its surfaces into

a large, dry lump. The egg should scramble as it does when you make the best scrambled eggs, becoming creamily curdled. The 10 minutes or so that it takes to cook the pasta should suit, too, the pancetta, the heat underneath which you can turn off as soon as you add the drained spaghetti. Stir the pasta around a little; then add the eggs. I find that they usually scramble perfectly under these conditions. As soon as creamy bits of egg are showing on the strands of spaghetti, throw in the cheese, which, being cool, will help to arrest the cooking.

Sausage sauce

HOW TO MAKE IT

For 2

4 sausages (see "Variations", below)
1 clove garlic, finely chopped
1½ tbsps olive oil
1 400 g tin tomatoes, drained;
or 4 plump tomatoes,
skinned and chopped (see page 190)
142 ml pot double cream

Cut the sausages into discs; don't be too con-cerned about cutting them cleanly. Warm the olive oil on a medium heat in a heavy saucepan, and add the sausages.

You needn't worry if they stick, or if bits of them break off, but you should stir them around if they are in danger of burning.[1] – see WHY YOU DO IT

You just want bits of them to go brown, to add flavour to the sauce.

Add the garlic,[2] and stir it around for a minute or so. Add the tomatoes, drained of the liquid in which they were sitting but not of all the liquid inside them,[3] and the cream.[4] As you stir this sauce, you'll find that the encrusted bits on the bottom of the pan lift off. Simmer, very gently, until the sauce thickens. Check the seasoning – the sausages may already be quite salty.

I like this sauce with conchiglie: bits of sausage nestle invitingly inside the shells. I usually have grated Parmesan cheese at the table.

VARIATIONS

Chunky, sweet Italian sausages (bought from any Italian deli) are particularly delicious here. You could also use cumberlands, or fresh chorizos. Or any decent sausage you like.

You can also buy spicy Italian sausages. Or throw in a whizzed dry chilli or two just before you add the tomatoes.

Leave out the garlic, if you like. When you've browned the sausage, add a chopped onion, and cook it until it softens. Then add the tomato, or just the cream; or leave them both out.

Brown the sausage on a more gentle heat, for long enough to cook it thoroughly; then add the garlic, if you like, and the cream, with a teaspoon of Dijon mustard. The

116

sauce will be ready in another minute or so, when the cream has thickened.

WHY YOU DO IT

1) *Don't worry about shapeliness*. The soft sausage is hard to cut into neat discs, and will probably break up a bit as you stir it around the pan. The irregularity of the chunks, and the stray bits of sausage you find as you bite into a pasta shell, contribute to the appeal of the sauce.

2) *When to add the garlic*. I've seen similar recipes telling you to fry the garlic first. That would be fine if you could keep it away, once you put in the sausage, from the hottest parts of the pan, where it would burn. That's not easy.

3) *Draining the tomatoes*. The whole can, juice and all, plus the cream, would give you an awful lot of sauce. I like to keep the juice that the tomatoes hold, though. If you don't want it, you can wring it out of the drained tomatoes with your hands; or, if you're using fresh tomatoes, cut them in half and scrape out the seeds and juice.

4) *When to add the cream*. You could add it once the sauce has reduced, and then simmer further until the sauce thickens again. But, if you're cooking it anyway, you might as well add it with the tomatoes. It will have a tenderising effect on the meat.

Anchovy, garlic and chilli sauce

HOW TO MAKE IT

For 2

1 small (50 g) tin anchovies, drained
1 clove garlic, very finely chopped
1, 2 or more dried chillis, whizzed in
a coffee grinder or small electric mill
3 tbsps olive oil
2 heaped tbsps breadcrumbs

Put on the water for the pasta (see page 108). Whizz up a couple of slices of bread, crusts removed, in a food processor or small electric mill; mix the breadcrumbs with 1 tbsp of the oil, lay out on a baking tray, and put in a gas mark 4/180°C oven. If they are brown before the pasta is ready, turn off the oven but leave them inside, or turn down the oven to gas mark ¼/110°C and put them on the bottom.

When the water is boiling, throw in the pasta. You can make the sauce in the time it takes the pasta to cook.

I prefer to use my own olive oil, distrusting the stuff in the tin, even though it is infused with anchovy. Put the oil on a gentle heat, and add the anchovies and garlic, stirring the anchovies to break them up. They should melt; once they have done so, add the chilli, and turn off the heat.[1 – see WHY YOU DO IT] Cover the pan if the pasta is not ready yet.

Drain the pasta, and toss it with the sauce. Tip in the breadcrumbs, and toss them gently too.[2]

This sauce is good with spaghetti. I like it even better with spaghettini (the finer stuff), or with linguine (fine, flat pasta ribbons).

If I have it, I like to add parsley (a tablespoon) to this sauce. Basil or mint are other possibilities.

The classic southern dish is pasta aglio e olio e peperoncino (garlic, oil and chilli) – as above, but without the anchovies. Or just aglio e olio – without the chilli. The breadcrumbs are optional – but you're not supposed to serve cheese instead. The dish should be basic, and cheap, and the flavour of the oil, garlic and chilli should be uncorrupted. You definitely should not serve cheese if you're using anchovies, because cheese does not combine happily with fish in either pasta or risotto.

You may find the flavour of a whole tin of anchovies too powerful in a dish for two. Use half a tin; or soften the flavour, and remove some of the salt from the anchovies, by soaking them in milk for half an hour before you cook them.

WHY YOU DO IT

1) *Brief cooking*. You're cooking the garlic just long enough to soften some of its rawness. It will still have a strong flavour. If you eat this dish at lunchtime, be aware that you'll probably be tasting the garlic – and exuding it – for the rest of the afternoon.

2) *Crisp breadcrumbs*. Add them at the end. They will take up some of the sauce, but they shouldn't go soggy.

Lasagne

Lasagne that requires no pre-cooking. It sounds as if it's the best thing since – but then, sliced bread isn't so great, is it? (It goes stale faster than does an uncut loaf.) Pasta sheets that do not need boiling and draining, or to be kept separate so they don't stick together, will in theory save you a good deal of tedious work; but, like so many inventions that are supposed to save you time in the kitchen, they have drawbacks.

They absorb a prodigious quantity of sauce. Packet instructions usually tell you to make sure that your ragu and your béchamel are runny; but how are you going to judge how runny they should be? Err on one side, and you get a dish full of slop; err on the other, and the sheets of lasagne don't cook.

A local deli proprietor gave me this solution: boil the sheets of pasta for a minute. Of course, if you're going to go through the effort of doing that, you might as well buy the normal stuff; but sometimes only the no-pre-cooking variety is available.

The sheets stick together with the slightest encouragement, particularly if you cook a lot of them at once. Put five at a time in a big pan of boiling water, fish them out into a colander with a slotted spoon, and run cold water through them. Lay them out on paper towels. The non-pre-cook pasta will retain its stiffness after a minute's cooking, but will then relax and soften.

I used to think that the advice to put oil in the pasta pot was redundant – surely the oil couldn't be effective in company with so much water? Then I found that Harold McGee (*McGee On Food and Cooking*), who has the best credentials to pronounce on such matters, recommended it, particularly for noodles. I still don't think that it's necessary for most kinds of pasta, but it may help with lasagne, if you lift the sheets while they're cooking through the oil globules.

HOW TO MAKE IT

For 4

350 g lasagne sheets
Bolognese sauce (see page 250)
400 ml béchamel sauce (see page 50),
with a pinch of nutmeg
1 heaped tbsp Parmesan cheese

Spread a layer of béchamel along the bottom and sides of an oven dish, to grease it. Put in a layer of lasagne, then a layer of Bolognese, then pasta, then Bolognese, then pasta, then Bolognese; that should use up the Bolognese. Put a last layer of pasta on top of it (you may not have needed all 350 g), and cover the whole lot with the béchamel.[1 – see WHY YOU DO IT] Sprinkle the Parmesan on top, and bake in a gas mark 6/200°C oven for 20 to 25 minutes, or until the cheese has browned.[2]

WHY YOU DO IT

1) *Layering*. Most recipes tell you to put some béchamel on to each layer of Bolognese, but I prefer to retain more sauce for the topping.

2) *Timing.* The Bolognese sauce is cooked already; it's not going to improve for this extra blast of heat. All you want the baking to do is to tenderise the lasagne sheets and brown the surface of the dish. If the lasagne won't take much cooking, and if you're worried that a high heat might toughen the meat in your sauce (see **Stews**, page 222), try this: put the lasagne in a gas mark 2/150°C oven for half an hour, or until you're sure that it's warmed through; then brown the surface under the grill.

Macaroni cheese

HOW TO MAKE IT
For 2
200 g macaroni
300 ml béchamel (see page 50)
100 g Cheddar, or other melting cheese, grated
Pinch nutmeg
½ tsp Dijon mustard

Cook the pasta (see Dry pasta – HOW TO COOK IT, page 108). Meanwhile, make the béchamel[1 – see WHY YOU DO IT]. When it is ready, stir in half the cheese, the nutmeg and the mustard. Check the seasoning; the cheese may have provided enough salt. When the pasta is ready (leave it al dente), drain it, and mix it with the sauce: either in the pan in which the béchamel cooked or, if that is not big enough, in the pasta pot. Tip the mixture into a warmed, ovenproof dish, and scatter the rest of the cheese on top. **Bake in a gas mark 6/ 200°C oven for 20 minutes, or until the surface of the dish is brown.**[2]

If you don't mind a discoloured sauce, gently fry lardons of pancetta or bacon (100 g, say) in a little oil or butter, then add the flour for the béchamel and cook the sauce in this pan. Or add the fried pancetta (but not its fat – there's enough cholesterol in this dish already) to the cheese sauce when it's ready.

Some people put slices of tomato into a macaroni cheese. I don't like the addition of acidic juices to a creamy dish.

Leave out the nutmeg and the mustard, if you like. If you don't like mustard, you might find it worth trying anyway: you'll be surprised by how it loses its heat in the sauce, and enhances the flavour of the cheese.

WHY YOU DO IT

1) *Pasta and béchamel*. People usually describe macaroni cheese as comfort food, by which they must mean "a wodge of something rich and filling". Of course, Italians do combine pasta and béchamel – a floury paste with a sauce based on a floury paste – in **lasagne** and other baked dishes (see page 120). But they make their cheese sauces for pasta with just cheese, butter and cream – a rich concoction, certainly, but not such a heavy one. Still, sometimes a good, old-fashioned, Anglo-Saxon macaroni cheese is just what you want.

2) *Baking*. When you put the macaroni cheese in the oven, the sauce dries out and the pasta sticks together. If you want to avoid those results, put the dish under the grill to brown instead. But a sticky lump of cheesy pasta represents the spirit of the dish more accurately.

Noodles

Packet instructions on Chinese noodles – the ones that come formed into rectangular shapes – tell you to pour boiling water over them, leave them for three or four minutes, and drain, perhaps rinsing them in cold water. Goodness knows why: it's a disastrous policy. The noodles sit in a sticky clump in the cooling water. No amount of rinsing seems to get rid of the starchiness.

Instead, cook them as you do pasta (see page 108), stirring to separate them as quickly as possible, perhaps with a little oil in the pan (see page 120); most brands cook in three to five minutes. If you need to keep them for later, drain and rinse them, but don't leave the noodles in a lump in the colander. Separate them out on paper towels. That's fiddly, I know: so it's better to cook them just before you need them, adding them to broth, or a stir-fry, as soon as they're drained.

Simple stir-fry

HOW TO MAKE IT
For 2
2 spring onions, tough green leaves

removed, chopped, washed
1 clove garlic, chopped
1 tsp ginger, minced
Large handful of pak choi
or other cabbage, finely chopped
250 g cooked noodles (see above)
1 tbsp groundnut, sunflower or vegetable oil
1 dstsp sesame oil
Soy sauce

Having ignored the instructions on your noodle packet, you need also to disregard the many stir-fry recipes that tell you to heat oil to smoking point before adding your ingredients. Why would you want to eat degraded oil? Add the oil (groundnut, sunflower or a vegetable oil that can withstand high temperatures are best) to a hot pan or wok; then immediately throw in your first ingredients.

A wok will work better than a frying pan; and a good wok, seasoned (see page 30), will work better than a bad one. Put it on a medium to high heat, wait for it to get very hot, pour in the oil, swirl it around, and immediately throw in the spring onions, garlic and ginger. Keep them moving rapidly around the pan; they probably won't need more than 30 seconds. As soon as the onions have wilted and the garlic has started to brown, throw in the cabbage. Continue to move the vegetables around the wok energetically. When the cabbage has wilted, add the noodles. When they are warmed through, take the wok off the heat, and stir in the sesame oil and a few shakes of soy sauce. You can throw some salt into the pan at any point; but remember that oriental sauces are quite salty.

As there are writers who have devoted not just one but several books to wok cookery, I cannot pretend to do justice to the subject here. Here are just a few variations on the theme above.

Other sauces: chilli, oyster, rice wine, fish (nam pla).

Other vegetables: what do you fancy? Cut them all into bite-sized pieces; add one vegetable at a time to the pan. After you've fried the garlic/spring onion/ginger base, put in first the vegetables that will take longest to cook.

Meat: tender cuts (chicken breast, pork medallion and so on), also in small pieces. Add them to the onion/garlic/ginger mixture. Or, use pieces of leftover meat; add these to the pan later, but make sure that you warm them through.

Seafood: shellfish, particularly prawns. Other seafood will probably break up in the pan. But you could cook it apart and serve it on a stir-fry base.

Couscous

Most of the couscous we buy is pre-cooked. You can ignore the recipes that tell you to steam it above a stew for half an hour in a couscoussière (a tall, double-layered stewpot), or to improvise with a muslin-lined sieve. Ignore, too, the packet instructions, adherence to which may give you clumps of sticky grains, and try this.

Put the couscous – 100 g is a hearty plateful for each person – in an oven dish. Boil a kettle, and carefully pour over just enough water to soak the grains – they should be damp, but not swimming. Cover the dish with foil, and put it in the oven – the temperature doesn't matter that much, but gas mark 4/180°C works fine – for five minutes. Remove the dish and uncover it, to reveal a solid mass of couscous grains. Pour over a little olive oil, or add a knob of butter, and stir it through; the grains should separate. Salt to taste.

Why hot water? The grains may be advertised as pre-cooked, but they emerge resembling little pieces of grit if you soak them in cold water. The oven-heating helps them to dry out and separate when you add the oil or butter. You could soak the grains in hot stock.

WHAT TO DO WITH IT

The classic way to serve couscous is with a **meat** or **fish stew** (see pages 222 and 293), made with spices such as cumin and turmeric (see page 248), and with plenty of sauce, which the grains will soak up. Tomatoes often play a part, as does **harissa**, a fiery paste that you can buy in tubes or tins, or that you can make yourself (see page 129); add it to the stew, or moisten it with the cooking liquid and put it on the table, so that guests can add it as they like to their plates.

Bake vegetables such as **aubergines** (page 134),

courgettes (page 151), **peppers** (page 168) and **onions** (page 160), and stir them when cooked into the couscous. Accompany this mixture with a **tomato sauce** (page 191), in which toasted spices – for each 400 g can of tomatoes, a teaspoon in total of cumin and coriander seeds, warmed in a dry pan until giving off a toasted aroma, then ground in a mortar or herb mill – have been added to the garlic and oil base. Serve hot or cold.

Try couscous with root vegetables: baked chunks of sweet potato and onion; turnip and/or celeriac, braised in a covered pan in a couple of centimetres of stock (or water) with, for each 450 g of vegetables, a tablespoon of olive oil and a teaspoon in total of caraway seeds (toasted and ground first, if you like), turmeric and cayenne. Leave enough of this braising liquid to moisten the couscous.

For a couscous salad for four: finely chop half a red onion, and soak it in water for an hour (see page 162). Squeeze it dry in paper towels. Dry-fry a small packet of pine nuts in a small pan (careful, they burn easily). Chop a handful of parsley. Grate the zest from half a lemon. Mix all these with 250 g of couscous, with salt to taste, and a little more extra virgin olive oil, if you like. If the salad needs more sharpening, use a little lemon juice.

Harissa

This recipe is adapted slightly from Tom Stobart's in *The Cook's Encyclopaedia*.

HOW TO MAKE IT

Soak 30 g of dried red chillis in hot water for an hour. Finely chop a clove of garlic. In a dry pan, heat 1 tsp of caraway seeds, with ½ tsp each of cumin and coriander seeds, until lightly toasted; whizz them, with the garlic, in a mill or grinder. Scoop this mixture into a bowl. Drain the chillis, and whizz them too, until thoroughly ground up – you may need to do it in batches. Mix the chillis thoroughly with the spices and garlic, and a little salt, adding some olive oil to make a paste. You can keep the harissa in a clean, covered jar in the fridge, provided that it is protected from the air with a layer of olive oil; it should stay fresh for two to three months. Half of each of these ingredients, though, will produce plenty of harissa to be going on with.

VEGETABLES

Appearances aren't everything. That useful lesson is worth bearing in mind when we buy and cook vegetables; or, if we haven't learned it already, perhaps it's a lesson that buying and cooking vegetables can teach us. The supermarkets and some chefs take advantage of our willingness to believe otherwise.

Of course, fresh vegetables and fruit should have such qualities as firmness and sharp colouring. But those qualities do not guarantee good flavour. The perfectly formed, brightly packaged veg and fruit you find in the supermarket are so often less interesting to taste than the comparatively unprepossessing specimens in the local greengrocer.

Supermarket produce may lose flavour as a result of the amount of refrigeration it undergoes. Certainly, at home, you'll find that there are several items that keep better at room temperature or slightly below than they do in the chilly surroundings of your fridge: among them are aubergines, cucumbers, peppers, potatoes and tomatoes.

Dull, olive-green broccoli looks unappetising on the plate, and has probably spent too long in the pan. But following the advice of chefs on how to preserve bright colours may sacrifice flavours and nutrients. Chefs' recipe books usually advise you to use plenty of boiling water for green vegetables, which you then "refresh" in ice-cold water, to fix the colour; you heat them up again before serving. In my experience, vegetables treated in this way are dull to eat; and they lose more nutrients than they would if cooked in only a little water. Even three-star chefs value taste less than they do the seduction of their customers with appearance – because they know that an enticing colour will convince people that the taste is delicious.

I'm prepared to lose a little colour by steaming vegetables. The key factor to get right is the cooking time: broccoli may need no more than three minutes, for example. (Make sure that the water is boiling before you put the vegetables in your steamer.) Test it with the point of a knife; it should be tender but not soft.

The hardness of your water will affect your vegetables. I have noticed that green vegetables go greyer in soft water areas than they do when I cook them at home, in the hard water that comes out of London taps. It may be that some soft waters have a higher acidity, which draws out greenness, than does the stuff that Thames Water provides. Acidity slows cooking too, as anyone who has tried softening potatoes in tomato sauce will have discovered. Another technique is to put vegetables into just enough water to submerge them, and to cook them, uncovered, until the water has evaporated. It works well with broccoli, cabbage and carrots.

131

Steaming and water reduction are more difficult to manage if you have a large quantity of vegetables. Piled on top of each other in a pan, they will cook at different rates according to their exposure to the steam. If you're attempting the water reduction method and you have a substantial mound of carrots, you will need a lot of water to cover them; by the time it has evaporated, the ones at the bottom will have overcooked.

Salt in boiling water, Harold McGee tells us, speeds the softening of vegetables; it also reduces the loss to the water of salts and sugars.

I abandon best nutritional practice when I cook potatoes. Put in cold water and brought slowly to a gentle simmer, they hold their shape better than they do if steamed. Parboiling potatoes for roasting expels surface starch and helps to rough up the exteriors, which crisp in the fat.

Grilled and baked vegetables are fashionable, in part because we associate them with the Mediterranean, and in part because we assume, not always correctly, that they retain their goodness better than do vegetables cooked in water. In fact, an oven-baked potato loses more vitamin C than does a boiled one. Nutritional considerations apart, baking often works better than grilling, which is not efficient at getting many vegetables tender.

Asparagus

Like most vegetables, it is widely available all year round. Like others, but to an exceptional degree, it is superior as native, seasonal produce. The time to buy asparagus is May or June. Restraining yourself until then has a psychological as well as a culinary benefit: you'll feel that the expense, because indulged rarely, is justified.

HOW TO COOK IT

If there is a big contrast between the tenderness of the asparagus tip and the woodiness of the thick end of the stalk, you probably won't want to eat the thick end. So there's not much point in investing in one of those upright asparagus steamers, designed to cook the spears evenly. Cut off the bits of stalk you're not going to eat and put the asparagus above boiling water in an ordinary steaming basket; check to see if they are tender to the point of a knife after three minutes, even though they may take longer. Eat hot or cold, with vinaigrette (page 41), mayonnaise (page 45), hollandaise (page 48) or simply melted butter.

VARIATIONS

Method two: turn in a little olive oil, season, and bake in a gas mark 6/200°C oven. About 15 minutes.

Method three (from Richard Ehrlich): pour a thin film of olive oil into a saucepan. Lay the asparagus spears on top, in a single layer (you may have to cook several batches). Turn the heat on the hob to low/medium, and wait till you hear the first sizzling. Cover the pan tightly and cook, without disturbance, for six or seven minutes.

Baked asparagus, which has a more intense flavour than does steamed, goes well with pasta, in salads (perhaps with a few other greens, some new potatoes and some lardons) and in risottos.

Aubergines

Nowhere in the literature of cookery is the sway of received ideas more evident than in the treatment of aubergines. Routinely, recipes advise you that aubergines should be salted, rinsed and dried before cooking. You leave them in a colander, perhaps with a plate on top to squeeze them a little, for half an hour or so; or, more rarely, you use the technique given in *Classic Turkish Cookery* by Ghillie Basan, who suggests you soak aubergine cubes or slices in salted water. Recipes may add the gloss that the point of the exercise is "to remove the bitter juices".

Once upon a time, it seems, aubergines were bitter. Some varieties still are, no doubt. But I've never found one. In any event, salting probably does not remove bitterness; it disguises it (cf *McGee on Food and Cooking*).

Supporters of salting who acknowledge the lack of bitterness in modern strains of aubergine advance a second reason for the practice: that pre-salted aubergines do not soak up so much oil. It is true that unsalted aubergines soak up all the oil you give them as soon as they touch it. But salted ones soak up quite a lot too; and, if you have cut the vegetable into cubes and are stirring them around, the flesh soon starts sticking to the pan. Stuck bits apart, the cubes are usually still firm after the 10 minutes that recipes tend to give as cooking time. Aubergine is not nice unless it is soft.

Delia Smith says that pre-salting concentrates the flavour, ensuring that the cooked aubergine won't be watery. I experimented. I pre-salted the cubes of half an aubergine; then I baked it with the cubes of the other half, salted only as I put them in the oven. I tasted each kind. There was no difference between them.

HOW TO COOK THEM

Cut aubergines into cubes. Put them on a baking tray or in a roasting pan, and pour olive oil or sunflower oil over them – about 1 tbsp for each medium-sized aubergine. Add salt, and pepper if you like. Toss with spoons, or with your hands. Cook at gas mark 6/200°C for 20 minutes to half an hour, or until tender.

Recipes such as **Parmigiana di melanzane** (see overleaf) and **moussaka** (page 252) require rounds (cut ½ cm discs horizontally) or slices (cut the aubergine in two horizontally, then cut ½ cm vertical slices), according to your preference. Brush them with olive or sunflower oil (if you don't have a pastry brush, pour some oil into a small saucer, dip a fork into it, and brush the aubergine slices with the backs of the tines), season, and bake as above.

You can brush slices of aubergine with oil and cook them in a frying pan or a ridged grill pan, or on a barbecue. But I like the flesh of my aubergines to have a melting texture; and I find that texture harder to achieve by frying or grilling than by baking. Frying cubes of aubergine is, I find, very unsatisfactory: as I say above, the cubes soak up all the oil, stick to the pan, and take ages to tenderise.

Another way of cooking aubergines is to bake them in their skins, then to mash up the flesh with garlic, oil, lemon, salt and any other flavourings you fancy. Tahini, the sesame paste with the consistency of peanut butter, works well. I like a dash of cayenne or chilli pepper. Cumin, dry roasted in a pan until it gives off a toasty aroma and then ground in a mill or mortar, is also nice. One clove of garlic, finely chopped or mashed (page 153), for each aubergine; 1 tbsp of tahini; 1 tbsp olive oil; 1 tbsp of lemon juice; 1 tsp of cumin seeds.

There's a neat way of baking aubergines in Gordon Ramsay's *Kitchen Heaven*. You slice the aubergine in half, slash the flesh, sprinkle one half with garlic, add oil, seasoning and, in his recipe, a sprig of rosemary, put the halves together and wrap them tightly in foil, bake at 220°C (gas mark 7) for 45 minutes, then at 110°C (gas mark ¼) for a further 25 minutes (the aim is to get the flesh really soft).

You scoop the flesh (discarding the rosemary, which will have imparted its flavour) into a pan. Then, Ramsay says, you heat it to evaporate the liquid and to achieve a thick, creamy consistency. So he clearly doesn't think the juices will be bitter: this technique will *concentrate* them.

My one variation on Ramsay's method is to add the oil at the end of cooking, in order to get its full flavour.

My favourite aubergine dish is Parmigiana di melanzane. You slice and bake the aubergines as in HOW TO COOK

136

THEM above, layer them in a dish with **tomato sauce** (see page 191 – it doesn't matter whether you end up with tomato or aubergines or a mixture on top), put chopped mozzarella on top and grated Parmesan on top of that, then bake at, say, gas mark 4/180°C to blend the flavours and brown the cheese. It's delicious hot, even more delicious at room temperature, and most delicious lukewarm. For a generous amount for four people: two aubergines; two portions of one of the tomato sauces on page 191; two balls of mozzarella; 2 tbsps of Parmesan.

Beans

Green beans

The fine beans that are available all year round, and that usually come from Kenya, taste muddy and stale. As do Kenyan mangetouts. Unfashionable runner beans, with their sandpaper skins and stringy textures, are nevertheless much more vibrant in the mouth. Bobby beans, which may not look promising, can be good. The fine beans to go for, when you can find them, are the French ones.

If you insist on the brightest green beans, throw them into a large pot of salted, boiling water, cook (the pan may be covered or uncovered) at a rolling boil for three minutes (the finest beans should be ready by then, but check – they may take a minute or two longer), drain and plunge into iced water. Reheat by tossing them over heat in butter or olive oil. However, this treatment does compromise flavour and nutritional value. Steaming is better and, provided you don't overcook the beans, shouldn't cause too much loss of colour. Tossing them immediately in oil helps to fix it, too. The acid in a vinaigrette, though, will turn them grey; don't dress the beans until shortly before serving.

Not all the ingredients of a hot meal have to be hot. Green beans are very nice at room temperature.

Dried beans

It's encouraging to hear that dried beans are good for us. But enthusiasm declines when we read warnings that we have to prepare beans properly to remove toxins. It drops further on discovering that writers do not agree on what that proper preparation involves. A publishing friend, whose famously scrupulous firm has brought out a book on bean cookery, tells me that various consultants disagreed to such an extent that the editors had to settle for advising readers to follow packet instructions.

The three areas of controversy in the treatment of cannellini, haricot, kidney beans and others are soaking, fast-boiling and salting.

Soaking. Leaving beans overnight in water speeds the cooking time. You'll notice that the beans can double in size, so cover them by a good few inches. I'll confess to the fussiness of soaking and cooking the beans in filtered or bottled water: our hard tap water seems to take longer to cook them, and to toughen their skins.

Fast-boiling. If we don't mind waiting a bit longer for the beans to cook, why bother with the pre-soaking? Because, according to the Food Standards Agency, it means that a subsequent short period of fast-boiling will get rid of any toxins. Dried beans contain substances called protease inhibitors, which can block the digestion of proteins. The FSA advises that the inhibitors become inactive after 10 minutes of fast-boiling, provided that soaking has made the beans receptive to this treatment.

Red kidney beans contain lectins, which can cause nasty stomach upsets. Soaking (the FSA recommends that you do so for 12 hours), 10 minutes of fast-boiling and proper cooking should disable these toxins.

The reason that the FSA encourages fast-boiling is that the high heat under the pan ensures a water temperature of 100°C. If you bring a pan to simmering point, then turn it down as soon as bubbles appear, the temperature may never reach a toxin-zapping level.

There's another side to the story, of course. Some people stick up for protease inhibitors, which, they say, have anti-cancer properties and prevent the formation of blood clots.

I went to an expert on proteins and legumes. Dr Claire Domoney, of the department of metabolic biology at the John Innes Centre, tells me that she does not believe it to be necessary to attempt to inactivate the protease inhibitors. Their effect on protein digestion may be minimal, and is outweighed by their health benefits. In any event, some of them are too stable to be affected by boiling.

However, Dr Domoney does agree with the advice

about destroying the lectins in red kidney beans.

Salt. "In my experience, once [beans] meet salt, they never give in," writes Fergus Henderson (*Nose to Tail Eating*). My experience is different. I soaked some beans last night, and this morning cooked half of them in salted water, and half in unsalted water. Both batches were ready in just over an hour, the only difference being that the salted ones tasted nicer.

Perhaps salt arrests cooking in different kinds of water. I don't know. What I do know is that it does not have the skin-toughening effect, reported by other cooks, on the beans I prepare; but the hard water from my taps does.

So, here's a synthesis of all this advice.

HOW TO COOK DRIED BEANS

100 g is a substantial portion for each person. Soak the beans – it makes a worthwhile difference to the cooking time – in filtered or bottled water overnight. (If your water is soft, tap water may be fine.) Drain and rinse the beans; cover by about 4 cm with fresh water (filtered if you like). Salt to taste, bring to the boil, and skim the white scum – it comes from the protein albumen, as does the scum on a meat stock. Turn down the heat and simmer, covered or, if the liquid is in danger of boiling over, with the lid of the pan leaving a small gap. To give flavour to the cooking liquid, add a peeled, halved onion and a couple of unpeeled garlic cloves.

If you're cooking red kidney beans, follow the

above procedure, but boil them at full blast for 10 minutes before turning down the heat to simmering point.

It's impossible to predict cooking times. I cooked the cannellini beans on which I carried out the salting experiment (see above) in an hour, but I have known them to take three or more.

Towards the end of the cooking time, uncover the pan to allow the liquid to reduce. It can moisten the beans you're going to serve, or form a stock for a soup. If you're keeping the beans for a day or two, store them in their cooking liquid.

For an accompaniment to sausages or other grills/fries (for 4): chop a clove of garlic, and soften it in 1 tbsp of oil. Add 1 dstsp of tomato paste and a little cooking liquid from the beans; cook this mixture for a minute or so. (Tomato paste can have a slightly metallic taste, which cooking mellows.) Add the beans and enough of their cooking liquid to get the consistency you want: moist but not soupy, I suggest. Simmer for 10 minutes, checking the saltiness and adding pepper if you like. You can serve the beans hot or at room temperature.

For **cassoulet**, see page 240. You could also add drained beans as a garnish to **beef, lamb** or **pork stew** (see pages 223 and 238).

If all this is too much fuss, buy tins. They're not bad. The liquid is very salty, though.

Broccoli

My daughters have rather gone off broccoli. That's my fault. It had become the default green vegetable in our house, because for a while it was the only one they would eat; and it could always be found in the shops. But, while it is easy to find broccoli, it is not easy to find it in bright green, firm condition. Inferior broccoli, with its tendency to become waterlogged when cooked, has the pungent, rank odour and flavour that have alienated so many victims of institutional cooking from other members of the cabbage family.

HOW TO COOK IT

It's not my experience that you have to cook broccoli in boiling water to retain its bright colour. Cut off the florets and put them in a steamer above boiling water; start to test them with the point of a knife after three minutes. Remove the florets when tender, and, if you like, turn them carefully in butter or oil; season.

As do other green vegetables, broccoli goes well with anchovy. For four people, warm a little olive oil in a pan, throw in half a clove of finely chopped garlic and let it soften for a minute, then stir in a small tin of anchovies, drained of their oil. You could add some minced fresh or dry chillis too. Keep stirring; the anchovies will melt. Turn the steamed broccoli in this mixture. It makes a very good sauce for pasta. Add a small pot of cream if you like, bubbling it for a minute or so until it thickens.

Purple sprouting broccoli, available in the spring and early summer, is finer tasting than the widely available green (calabrese) variety. Because it is more slender, you can cook it with no water, or very little. Try on it the Ehrlich method of cooking **asparagus** (see page 133); but use a little more oil, and don't bother about getting the florets into a single layer. After a minute, take the lid off, give the florets a gentle stir, and add seasoning. Put the lid back on, and steam until tender.

Or you can stir-fry. Heat a wok or heavy frying pan; then add some oil, swirl it around, and throw in the broccoli. (See **Stir-fry**, page 124.) Keep it moving, and turn down the heat if there's a danger of smoke and scorching. When it's nearly ready, you could add chopped garlic, and/or chilli, and/or ginger. And/or some oyster/soy/chilli sauce.

Cabbage and other greens

Overcooked cabbage is an evocative smell, but not in a good way. It conjures up the grimness of school and hospital corridors; of soggy vegetables sitting in puddles of water beside globs of gristly stew. Members of the cabbage family, sprouts particularly, must be the subjects of more phobias than any other foods.

It's worth exorcising those phobias. These vegetables have bright, crunchy, sometimes sharp, sometimes appealingly bitter flavours. They go superbly with bacon and other

pork products, with anchovy, with cheese, and with oriental flavourings and spices. And they are cheap.

HOW TO COOK CABBAGE

**Though others disagree, I find the taste of savoy
and green cabbage cooked only in oil too
assertive. Strip off the tough outer leaves, trim
the stalk, cut the cabbage in half, then cut each
half in two. Trim off the white heart. Slice the
cabbage, and wash the slices in a bowl of cold
water (it makes them crisper). Put them in a
steamer above boiling water for three minutes.
If they're ready, remove and toss with butter or
oil and seasoning.**

VARIATIONS

Braise the quarters of cabbage in a covered pan with 1 cm
or so of water or stock and some butter. They might
take about 15 minutes to soften. Watch that the cooking
liquid doesn't all evaporate. If there is liquid left at the
end of the cooking time, uncover the pan and turn up
the heat to evaporate it, and stir to coat the cabbage in
the butter.

Heat a wok or heavy frying pan, pour in a couple
of tablespoons of sunflower, groundnut or vegetable oil,
throw in some chopped garlic, then add the steamed cabbage slices, stirring quickly to coat. Add some oyster, soy or
chilli sauce. Or add chopped chillis at the beginning, with
the garlic, and/or finely chopped ginger.

Red cabbage

Red cabbage is one member of the cabbage family that can withstand longer cooking. It is often braised with vinegar and apples, the acidity of which not only complements it in flavour, but also prevents it from losing its colouring.

HOW TO COOK IT
Slice an onion and soften it in butter or sunflower oil, or a mixture, in a heavy casserole. Quarter the cabbage, cut out the white core, and slice it; wash the slices. Add it to the onions; add also 3 tbsps vinegar, 1 tsp brown or white sugar, two cloves, salt, and some nutmeg if you like. If you think that the mixture is too dry and that the cabbage is likely to catch, add a little orange juice, red wine or water. Stir well and warm up the mixture on the hob; then put the casserole into a gas mark 4/180°C oven for half an hour.

Sprouts

HOW TO COOK THEM
Wash them, peel off the loose outer layers, and trim the bases; the popular practice of scoring crosses in the stalks is not necessary. If you have a lot of sprouts, you might find steaming inefficient. So boiling them is the answer; and the most efficient way to do that, even though it loses more nutrients, is with a lot of water. Bring it to the

boil, add salt, then throw in the sprouts. Check with the point of a knife after five minutes; they should be tender but not soft. You could then toss them in a frying pan with oil and garlic, or simply with butter.

Or: slice them and give them, from raw, the stir-fry treatment (see broccoli, page 142, and cabbage, page 143). It's a good way to treat left-over sprouts.

Other greens

They are all delicious if sliced and stir-fried (see the **cabbage** and **broccoli** variations, above). Pak choi has a lot of stalk; separate it from the leaf, chop it into 10p-sized pieces, and put it into the wok or frying pan a minute or so before you add the green bits.

The leaves and stalks of Swiss chard have to be cooked separately, because the stalks can take half an hour to soften. Cut the stalks into fork-sized pieces (in other words, ones of the right size to put in your mouth), and put them into a pan with 1 cm of boiling, lightly salted water and a knob of butter. Cover and simmer. Check after 20 minutes; they may need longer. When nearly ready, uncover the pan and turn up the heat to evaporate the liquid and coat the stalks in butter. Meanwhile, slice and chop the leaves; steam them. They should take about five minutes. Butter a gratin dish. When stalks and leaves are ready, mix them, add more salt if necessary, and pepper and nutmeg if you like; put them in the dish. Pour over enough double cream, or more if you like, to cover. Grate Parmesan on top. (Or cover with Parmesan, or some other grated cheese, only.) Put in a gas mark 6/200°C oven until bubbling, with a cheesy crust: about 15 to 20 minutes.

Brussel tops are my favourite winter greens, although they can taste rather dry. Wash, slice and steam them (about five minutes); toss with plenty of butter, salt and pepper.

Carrots

Sliced carrots soften faster than do batons, for some reason. Boiled and then drained, they lose not only their crunchiness but also their sweetness and colour. They are dreary fare.

I have never looked back since discovering a recipe for carrots in Vichy water, even though I rarely use Vichy water when I follow it. Peel the carrots, then cut them horizontally into three or four pieces; then cut these pieces vertically. You want fork-sized pieces – ones that are single mouthfuls; cut them vertically again if necessary. Put them in a pan large enough to hold them in no more than a double layer. Pour in water to come level with the top of them, or just under – they will emit their own water. Add a knob of butter, but no salt, which might make them too soft. Turn the heat under the pan to maximum, and cook, uncovered, until the water evaporates and the carrots are coated in the butter. (Be careful that the butter doesn't start to burn on the dry pan.) Turn down the heat, and gently stir the carrots in the butter. Add salt; scatter over parsley if you like.

Cauliflower

Choose cauliflowers with white, tightly packed, firm florets. Don't cook them whole: some florets will turn mushy before others get tender. Separate the florets and steam them, checking for tenderness after five minutes. Like its relatives in the cabbage family, cauliflower will give you a powerful reminder of the horrors of institutional food if it's not fresh, or if it's cooked for too long.

I like cauliflower cheese with roast chicken. Make a **cheese sauce** (see page 51 – about 300 ml would be about right for a medium-sized cauli) with plenty of black pepper, and also some nutmeg, to offset the bland qualities of the vegetable; add too ½ tsp Dijon, or ¼ tsp English, mustard. Steam the florets, put into a warm dish, pour over the sauce, scatter grated cheese on top, and brown under the grill. I sometimes prepare cauliflower cheese in advance, cover it with foil, and warm it in the oven (gas mark 4/ 180°C for 20 minutes). In spite of the thickening of the sauce, the skin that forms, and the evaporation that takes place on reheating, it produces a perfectly decent result.

Cauliflower, or cauliflower mixed with broccoli, makes a good sauce for pasta. It needs a bit of dried chilli, I think; and, if you're using cauliflower alone, some colour too. Follow the recipe for **broccoli with anchovy** (see page 142); but, after frying the garlic and melting the tinned anchovies, add 1 dstsp of tomato paste (for a sauce for four), and cook it for a minute before adding the steamed cauliflower. You could also add a little saffron, with the liquid in which it soaked (or a sachet of the

powdered stuff). Other possible additions: sultanas, softened in water for 15 minutes; pine nuts, toasted gently in
a dry saucepan. Crushed tinned sardine could substitute
for the anchovy.

Chicory

The point of chicory, from a culinary angle, is its bitterness.
Careful, slow cooking offsets that quality with sweetness;
but contact with boiling liquid wrecks the bitter-sweet
balance. Try this gratin:

> **Trim the chicory of wilted outer leaves, cut in half
> vertically, sprinkle with salt, and put, cut side
> down, in a buttered gratin dish large enough to
> hold the pieces in a single layer. Cover the dish
> quite tightly with foil – you may need to wrap it
> underneath; put in a gas mark 4/180°C oven.
> After 20 minutes, have a look: if the chicory is in
> danger of sticking and burning, put a little water
> or wine into the dish. Turn the chicory over, and
> cook for another 20 minutes, or until tender (it
> might take up to an hour). Take out of the oven,
> and pour over a small pot (142 ml – for two) of
> double cream. Top with grated Parmesan, and put
> under the grill until bubbling and golden. You
> could add a tsp of mustard and/or a pinch of nut-
> meg to the cream.**

Another way to do it:

Fry some lardons (cubes of pancetta or bacon) in a little oil, until their fat runs. Remove to the gratin dish, leaving behind the fat. Fry the halved chicory in the fat very gently, turning occasionally, for 10 to 15 minutes, until quite tender. Put the chicory in the gratin dish. Make a cheese sauce (see page 51), and pour it over. Put in a gas mark 6/200°C oven for about 15 minutes, or until bubbling. For a substantial dish for two: 100 g lardons, four chicories and 300 ml cheese sauce.

Chillis

They're so often disappointing. Recipes usually advise you to deseed them, because the seeds can be blisteringly hot; but often the flesh that is left behind has no more kick than that of a bell pepper. If mildness is what you're after, look for the larger varieties; small chillis, and the squat ones that might be habaneros or Scotch bonnets, should be more powerful. If you dare, it's worth tasting them before use.

I buy tiny dried red chillis, and use them a lot, particularly in pasta sauces. They're impossible to "crumble", as recipes instruct; I whizz them in a small electric food mill.

The Encona and Cottage Delight brands of chilli sauces are good. You can make a cheat's jerk (West Indian) sauce, as a marinade for grilled meat, by mixing Caribbean chilli sauce with grated ginger, chopped garlic, vegetable or sunflower oil and a little salt. It should have a sweet component too; but, as I say elsewhere (page 266), sugar and honey burn on the grill.

Courgettes

Boiled or steamed, courgettes are mushy and dull; but, if you sauté them, they can disgorge so much water that they boil anyway. So, according to some recipes, they require pre-salting, to draw out this water. An easier solution is to sauté them on a high heat, so that the water vaporises quickly. Buy small courgettes: they usually have more flavour, and they are less likely to flood your frying pan.

If you want a firm, crunchy texture, cook courgette batons, not rounds. Cut a small courgette about three times horizontally; cut these pieces once or twice vertically; at right angles to these cuts, make another vertical cut.

The anchovy/garlic/chilli/cream sauce for pasta (see **broccoli** and **cauliflower**, above) is good with courgettes, too. Or, keep it simple (for two):

> **Soften a chopped clove of garlic in 1 tbsp of olive oil, add batons or rounds of four small courgettes, and sauté over a medium to high heat, stirring constantly, for about five minutes, or until tender. Serve, accompanied by grated Parmesan, with spaghetti or spaghettini. Add a chopped, dried chilli or two to the cooked courgettes if you like. Instead of the Parmesan, try breadcrumbs: whizz up a couple of slices of bread, crusts removed, in a food processor or small electric mill, toss with 1 tbsp of olive oil, put on a baking tray in a gas mark 4/180°C oven for 10 minutes, until brown. Toss gently with the pasta and courgettes.**
>
> **Cut courgettes into pieces of whatever size you**

like, season them and coat with olive oil, put in a roasting pan and cook at gas mark 6/200°C. Stir them around a bit after 15 minutes. They should be tender in about 25 minutes. Cook them with cubed, oiled and salted aubergine, and stir the vegetables into couscous (page 126). Or include them in a ratatouille (page 169). Or toss them with pasta.

Cucumber

Pre-salting, as I've said elsewhere, is usually a bothersome and unnecessary process. But it does do good things to a cucumber. Peel the cucumber, cut it however you like, put the pieces in a colander, and lightly salt the layers. After half an hour, pat the pieces dry with paper towels. Put in a bowl, and stir in a little vinegar (1 dstsp for half a cucumber). You should find that this salad has a lovely balance of sweetness, saltiness and acidity.

Pre-salting is also worthwhile if you're going to make cucumber with yoghurt (tzatziki, or cacik), because it prevents the salad from becoming watery.

For 4
½ cucumber
1 pot (200 g) Greek yoghurt
1 clove garlic, crushed with a little salt
or, for a milder taste, finely chopped (see opposite)
Pepper (you're not likely to need more salt)
4 fresh mint leaves, chopped

Slice or chop the cucumber however you like, and mix with the other ingredients.

Most cucumbers have tough skins, which I prefer to peel.

Fennel

Fennel responds well to the kind of braising you would give to meat – gentle frying followed by cooking in a little liquid. The colouring in oil or butter (or both) and the long cooking sweeten the aniseed notes of the bulbs.

HOW TO COOK IT

Trim off the fronds (which you can use to garnish the dish), as well as any tough layers, and cut the bulbs into halves, quarters or slices – whatever you prefer. Colour them in oil or butter (or both), preferably in a large sauté pan with a lid; or use a heavy casserole or a saucepan. About 10 minutes on each side. Pour in water or stock to about 1 cm deep, bring to a simmer, and cover the pan. Cook gently until the fennel is tender – about 20 minutes to half an hour. Uncover the pan and turn up the heat to evaporate the liquid that remains. Add salt and pepper.

Garlic

Round my way, every other shop has a stall of vegetables

outside. Much of the produce, inhaling the traffic fumes for day after day until finally the proprietor gets rid of it, looks tired; but there's usually something worth buying. If you want garlic, though, you tend to find that all of it, in these shops and elsewhere, is in a sorry state: falling apart, wrinkled, soft and sprouting. Here is one area where the supermarkets have the edge. Tesco's garlic is consistently good.

You can get away, just, with using inferior garlic when you fry it thoroughly and cook it for a long time, in sauces and stews. But it will be bitter in dishes that require long cooking of whole cloves (**chicken with 40 cloves of garlic**, page 236, for example), or in preparations that depend on the pungent zing of raw garlic: **aioli** (page 46), or **garlic vinaigrette** (page 42), or **hummus** (page 164).

Crushed garlic is more pungent than chopped. The violence of a garlic crusher turns garlic acrid and sulphurous – its relative in the allium family, the onion, acquires similar qualities if mashed in a food processor. Halve the garlic down its length, and remove from the interior any green sprouting material, which is bitter. Chop the garlic, sprinkle it with salt, and crush it with the back of a heavy knife; or put it in a mortar and use a pestle. It will become a creamy pulp. Just a speck or two of it, dissolved in the vinegar, will flavour a vinaigrette.

Frying softens and sweetens garlic, as it does onions. That's why recipes often tell you to fry garlic first, before adding other ingredients to the pan; added later, it might not get access to the oil. The drawback is that it burns easily; once you've added the other ingredients, you have to make sure that it moves from the area of highest heat.

Baked, garlic becomes creamy and mild. It's less likely to overcook – you open the skins to find that the pulp has disappeared – if you put whole heads in the oven, anointed with a little olive oil and surrounded with foil. About an hour at gas mark 4/180°C should be right; but I'm afraid that you might find some garlic to be overcooked in that time, and some still to be hard. Or you can toss the garlic in olive oil, scatter in a roasting pan, cover the pan with foil, and then bake – perhaps for half an hour to 45 minutes.

The cloves steam inside the foil. Meat overcooks when treated in this way; but garlic remains more tender than it would if exposed to the radiant heat of the oven.

The cooking time for garlic is similarly hard to predict if it is boiled or steamed. When I put a clove of garlic in the water with potatoes for mashing (page 173), it's usually soft when the potatoes are, but not always.

Leeks

HOW TO COOK THEM

Small, slender leeks: steam them whole. Trim off the tough green bits; slice down through the middle of each leek from the top to about a third of the way down, and make another cut at right angles to the first, so that the layers fan out; wash the leeks in cold water. The reason for the cuts is that bits of grit can penetrate down through the

layers. Put the leeks into a steaming basket above boiling water, and cover; cook for about five minutes, or until tender in their thickest parts to the point of a knife. Drain, and squeeze out excess water with the back of a wooden spoon. Then turn the leeks in butter, and season. You can also serve them lukewarm, with vinaigrette (see page 41); a lovely dish is leeks in vinaigrette with a poached egg (page 82) and fried bacon or lardons. Season with lots of pepper.

I'm not keen on cooking larger leeks whole. They are tough to cut through, and they have a slimy quality. Slice them, wash them, and stew them, lightly salted, in a little butter. They'll be tender in about 10 minutes. You could steam the slices, but they'll be rather watery.

Leeks sit happily in a **béchamel sauce** (page 50), particularly one with cheese; pour the sauce over cooked, small leeks, or stewed, sliced ones, sprinkle cheese on top, and brown under the grill. Leeks also have an affinity with fish (see **fish pie**, page 281).

Lettuce

The pre-bagged, mixed salads you get in supermarkets may be convenient, but they're also tasteless, I find. Further grounds for shunning them may be found in *Not on the Label* by Felicity Lawrence, who describes how these salads are processed. Buy lettuces and other salad greens (avoiding the tasteless icebergs) from the greengrocer; wash them thoroughly (you'll wash the supermarkets' "ready to eat" stuff too, if you've read *Not on the Label*), and dry them in a **salad whizzer** (see page 34). A **vinaigrette** (page 41) won't adhere to wet leaves. Dress green leaves just before you're due to eat them; the oil and vinegar soon cause them to go limp and discoloured.

For a more substantial green salad, try adding chopped-up bits of blue cheese, and/or bits of walnut, and/or fried bits of bacon or pancetta (with their fat – reduce the oil in the dressing accordingly), and/or croutons. Fried croutons take up a lot of oil. Instead, I bake them (for four): three slices of crustless bread cut into squares, tossed with 1 tbsp of olive oil, laid out on a baking tray and put into a gas mark 6/200°C oven for five to 10 minutes, or until golden.

Mushrooms

HOW TO COOK THEM
For 2, as an accompaniment or snack
200 g mushrooms, rinsed,[1 – see why you do it]
woody parts of their stems trimmed, thickly sliced
1½ tbsps olive oil, or about 40 g butter,
or a combination of the two
Salt
1 clove garlic, finely chopped
1 dstsp parsley, chopped
Squeeze of lemon juice

Warm a frying pan, or saucepan with a large base; add the oil or butter. When the oil is warm or the butter is melted, throw in the mushrooms, lightly salt them, and cook, stirring regularly, over a medium heat. They will suck up the oil; keep stirring. After a minute or so they will release their liquid; turn up the heat to let it evaporate.[2] Add the parsley and garlic, and cook for a minute longer. Turn off the heat; add a little lemon juice, and pepper if you like.

VARIATIONS

This recipe will apply to most types of mushrooms. But chanterelles contain a tremendous quantity of water, and, like tender meat, toughen up if allowed to stew. Rinse them, salt them, and put them in a saucepan, with the lid on, over a high flame. Shake the pan to prevent sticking and burning. After a minute or two, they should be swimming in liquid. Drain them in a sieve, and sauté them quickly as above.

Alternatively, you could sieve the liquid into another saucepan, boil it over a high heat until it has reduced to a syrup, and add it to the cooked mushrooms.

The garlic and parsley – a Provençal theme, sometimes including breadcrumbs – are not compulsory. They are added at the end of cooking to preserve their freshness of flavour. Tarragon and basil are also particularly good complements. Or cook the mushrooms with spices (see page 248).

Another possibility: add a small pot (142 ml) of cream

to the cooked mushrooms, and allow it to bubble until it has thickened slightly. That, on toast, makes a nice lunch; as does the same recipe but with sour cream and paprika. You could soften a chopped shallot or two before sautéing the mushrooms.

Baking enriches mushrooms. Turn them, whole, in olive oil, sprinkle with salt, and bake in a gas mark 6/200°C oven for 20 minutes to half an hour, depending on their size.

Funghal qualities are at their most intense in dried mushrooms. You soak them for about half an hour in tepid water, drain, then stew them in butter for about 10 minutes. Or simply add them to a stew or risotto, along with their flavoursome soaking liquid.

All these mushroom recipes might be used as pasta sauces.

WHY YOU DO IT

1) *Washing them*. Mushrooms are mostly water, so warnings that washing them will ruin their texture are wide of the mark. I put them in a colander and give them a quick rinse under a running tap, scraping off bits of earth with a knife.

2) *Absorbing oil, disgorging water*. Mushrooms have the spongy qualities of aubergines. They are similarly greedy: if you add more oil, they'll absorb that too. Be patient. The heat will force them to give up the water they contain; and, once that has evaporated, a coating of oil will reappear on their surfaces.

Onions

Why do cookery writers claim that you can soften onions in five minutes, and brown them in 15? They're like the people who move out to the country and insist that they can get to their London offices in less time than it took them from Shepherd's Bush. It's the need to make something sound better than it is, I suppose.

You cook onions in oil or butter to make them milder and to bring out their sweetness. If you're using them in a stew, when they will cook for a good while longer, you may find that 10 minutes of softening is enough. But if you're making a risotto, you'll find that any raw qualities in the onions will be apparent in the finished dish unless you soften them thoroughly, until golden; it will probably take about 20 minutes. Covering the pan hastens the process, but you need to lift the lid regularly to make sure that the onions are not catching and burning. Even small traces of burned onion will cause a dish to taste bitter.

Sautéing onions in butter can cause problems, because the onions absorb the fat, and catch on the base of the pan; both the onions and the butter can burn. You can thin the butter with a little oil; or (Anna del Conte's tip), keep the mixture moist with a little water.

Browning onions, to add further Maillard flavours to a **stew** (page 222) or to create a tasty accompaniment for grills, can take 40 minutes. If you try to speed up the process, onion pieces that your stirring fails to move for a while get burned. Cook slices of onion on a moderate heat, stirring regularly; make sure there's always a layer of oil in the pan, because onion in a dry pan will catch and burn. Encouraging caramelisation with the addition of a little sugar might help, but it has never made much difference when I've tried it. Browning onion slices in the oven is easier, and works well (gas mark 6/200°C); spread out the slices (or they won't colour), and make sure that there's a layer of oil between them and the roasting pan.

I slice a section of onion at the stem and root ends, peel them and discard any tough layers, cut them in half from tops to roots, and slice those halves. If I'm baking them, perhaps with other vegetables such as aubergines and courgettes, I don't trim the root, and I make sure that the chunks are all connected to it – it holds them together.

Onions for a Venetian-style liver and onions should be cooked very slowly, in a covered pan. Restaurants some-times pretentiously describe this preparation as an onion confit. (A confit implies preservation, and is properly used of jams, or of duck that is cooked, salted and stored in its own fat.) Slice onions thinly, and put them, lightly salted, in a heavy pan with a layer of oil or butter. Cover the pan, and cook over the lowest possible heat, perhaps above a heat disperser. Have a look after 15 minutes or so, and stir if the onions are starting to collapse. Stir again every so often. The onions may take an hour or longer to become soft and sweet. If there's a lot of liquid in the pan at the end of cooking, turn up the heat to evaporate it. To offset the sweetness, you could add a little vinegar at the end of cooking; add parsley and pepper too, if you like. This recipe works particularly well with red onions. (Cook the liver separately. Slice it thinly, removing the stringy bits, and sauté it quickly in butter or oil over a medium heat – just a few minutes.)

Even red onions, sweeter than the normal kind, can be harsh if served raw in a salad. Soak them first, for an hour or so, in cold water, to wash away some of their sulphur; at the end of that time, squeeze them gently, drain them, and dry them with paper towels.

Peas

Asparagus takes less time to cook than most cookery writers allow; fresh peas take more, I have found. Maybe I've been buying inferior peas. Far from being ready in 10 minutes, they're often still like bullets at 15. So I'm a little wary of recipes that tell you to braise peas gently in a little wine or water.

Still, braising is the best method, if your peas are small and fresh enough. Heat 1 cm of water, olive oil or butter and salt in a pan, with some fresh mint if you like; when the liquid is simmering, add the peas and cover. If there's liquid left when the peas are nearly ready, boil it hard, with the lid off, to evaporate, coating the peas in the oil.

Once picked, peas convert their sugars into starch. Frozen peas, having been refrigerated soon after removal from their pods, are exceptionally sweet. Their sweetness is a bit one-dimensional; there is more depth of flavour in a good fresh pea, and the slight starchiness has its own appeal.

Nevertheless, frozen peas are the best frozen vegetables. Try them puréed or mushy: add them to boiling water, bring back to the boil and simmer for a couple of minutes, drain, and mash roughly with a potato masher. Over a very low heat, above a heat disperser, stir in butter and salt. (Sorry to be vague about the quantities, but I do feel that you should use your own judgement here.)

Chickpeas

See **dried beans** (page 138). You'll certainly find it a lot easier to cook chickpeas if you soak them overnight; even after that, some can take four hours to soften. Drain them, bring to the boil in fresh, salted water, and simmer; a peeled and halved onion and a couple of cloves of unpeeled garlic in the liquid will do no harm, particularly if you're going to use this liquid later, perhaps to thin some **hummus** (see overleaf). Cover the pan or, if the boil is too fast and the liquid is in danger of boiling over, leave the lid slightly ajar. The chickpeas are unlikely to be ready in less than two hours.

Bicarbonate of soda in the soaking water and/or in the cooking water will reduce the time it takes to soften the chickpeas – quite dramatically, if you use enough of it. But there is a price to be paid, in loss of nutrients, texture and flavour.

If I'm in a hurry, I open a can. Canned chickpeas may not have the earthy nuttiness of the dried variety, but are worth eating nonetheless, and make a decent hummus.

Hummus

HOW YOU MAKE IT
For 4, as a starter
1 400 g can chickpeas, or 150 g dried ones, cooked as above
1½ tbsps tahini paste
1 clove garlic, chopped and crushed with some salt
Juice of 1 lemon
2 tbsps olive oil
Pinch of cayenne pepper or chilli powder
Salt

I have come to prefer mashing the chickpeas with a potato masher to blitzing them in a food processor; the purée may be rough, but it has more chickpea flavour. Drain the chickpeas; if using canned ones, rinse them of their briny liquid. Put in a saucepan, and mash. Stir in the other ingredients. Have a taste: you might want more lemon, or salt. If the mixture is too gungy, add some of the liquid in which the chickpeas have cooked; if I'm using canned chickpeas, I pour in a little orange juice as a thinner.

Or: put the ingredients in a food processor, and blitz.

You could flatten the hummus on a plate, drizzle over a little more (extra virgin) olive oil, and dust with paprika.

Vary these ingredients according to taste. Some people prefer more garlic; some, more lemon. The tahini, a sesame seed paste, is optional. There are brands that are rather cloying. A tablespoon or two of yoghurt will lighten the texture.

Chickpeas are a nice accompaniment to lamb, as is spinach; and chickpeas and spinach go well together. Cook the chickpeas, and drain them; cook the spinach (see page 188), drain, and chop it. Fry garlic and cumin seeds in oil. Add the chickpeas and spinach, and stir them around to flavour them. A few saffron threads with their soaking liquid would add attractive colour and fragrance; or you could add a little turmeric. For four: 200 g of chickpeas, 750 g of spinach, one clove of garlic, 1 tsp of cumin.

A more satisfying way to cook this dish would be to add the spinach and the spiced oil to the simmering chickpeas; but, as the chickpeas are sitting in liquid and as the spinach throws out a good deal of water of its own, you'll end up with a soup rather than with a side dish.

Or: drain a can of chickpeas, add them with a little water to the fried garlic and cumin, cover the pan and heat gently to warm through until the liquid evaporates or is absorbed (turn up the heat to boil away the liquid if there's too much once the chickpeas are warmed through); add the cooked, drained and chopped spinach. Because of the salt in the chickpea brine, you may not need more.

Lentils

Like the sausage, a humble food that is a challenge to cook to perfection. The best ones are Puy or other green lentils, followed by brown. The split, disc-like, green-brown ones have a more muddy taste, but are fine for soup. Red and yellow ones turn quickly to mush, and are good for dal.

You can put green lentils into a large pan of boiling water, cooking them for 20 to 30 minutes, after which they should be tender but still holding their shape. Then drain. But the liquid you are pouring away, or perhaps saving to use with soup, contains nutrients and flavour. The alternative is to try to use an amount of liquid that will leave the lentils, when cooked, moist but not drowned.

HOW TO COOK THEM

Because lentils cook quickly, you don't need to soak them. They do need washing, though, and picking through: some packets will contain discoloured and damaged ones, as well as extraneous material including, sometimes, small stones. For 4 people, chop an onion and finely chop a clove of garlic; soften the garlic in 2 tbsps of olive oil for a minute; add the onion and soften for 10 minutes. Add the lentils, cover by about 1 cm with cold water, add salt (for remarks about whether salt will toughen the lentils, see "Dried beans", page 140), and bring to a simmer. Turn down the heat, and cover the pan. Check on progress after 10 minutes or so: lentils absorb a lot of water, and you may need to add more. But don't add more than the topmost layer will need to continue cooking. As the lentils near softness, uncover the pan. What you hope is that most of the liquid will have evaporated at the moment when the lentils have softened but have not broken down.

Alternatively, cover the washed lentils with water and cook as above, but soften the garlic and the onion in a separate pan, perhaps for 20 minutes, until they are golden and sweet. Stir the garlic and onion into the lentils just before serving. It depends what you want: a garlicky, oniony flavour that is integral to the dish; or one that is part of it but distinct.

Stop press: I have to admit that what you might call the "absorption method", above, is hard to get right. I have taken to simmering lentils in salted water so that I can drain them when they're tender but not mushy. For a salad, I add them to a vinaigrette, perhaps with chopped spring onions.

Dal

HOW TO MAKE IT
For 2

Use red or yellow lentils (200 g). Wash them, and remove any grit and extraneous material.

For ideas about spice mixes, see page 248. Or cheat and get out an Indian or Thai curry paste; I use about $1\frac{1}{2}$ times the quantity suggested on the bottle. Soften a clove of chopped garlic in butter, or butter mixed with sunflower oil (or, if you have it, ghee). Add a chopped onion, and cook for 10 minutes or so, until softened. Add spices (toast whole seed such as cumin and coriander in a dry pan, and grind them in a mill or grinder; use 1 tsp of the spices you want to be most prominent, and less of any others), or curry paste, and cook for a further minute. Add lentils, and, for a rich dish, a carton of coconut cream, plus water to cover. Careful with the salt: the paste may be salty.

Cook gently, covered; be careful that the coconut cream (you could also use a tin of coconut milk) does not stick to the bottom of the pan and burn. The lentils usually soften in 20 minutes or less. Uncover the pan, turning up the heat if necessary, to reduce the dal to a thick, gloopy consistency. If you like, add chopped fresh chillis and coriander leaves.

Peppers

Raw slices of pepper in salads are indigestible, I find – the ripe red and yellow ones just as much as the green. The flesh is watery; but it's the skins that are disagreeable. They remain so after cooking in a stew as well. I like to get rid of them.

There are three ways to burn and loosen the skin: on a skewer turned above a gas flame; under a grill; and in the oven (see below). You could follow the usual recommendation of putting the charred peppers in a bowl and stretching some cling film over the top; but I've never found that this steaming makes much difference. Scrape off the skin, cut the peppers, and deseed.

The skin of grilled peppers burns before the flesh has done much cooking. For a softer, sweeter pepper, try baking. Put the peppers on to a lightly oiled (to prevent sticking) baking tray in a gas mark 6/200°C oven for about 40 minutes, turning once; they're ready when the skin is loose and charred in places. Cut the peppers in a sieve above a bowl, to catch the juices, which you can add to a stew or salad. Peeling them and then trying to pick all the seeds out of the juices is a very boring job.

I use these baked peppers in ratatouilles and other stews. Of course, they don't need any more cooking; so if you're putting them into a stew, add them at the end, just to warm through. If you're using unskinned pepper slices in a stew, you don't need to treat them as you do onions, softening them in oil first (though you will end up with slivers of shed skin in the concoction). You soften onions, and garlic, to remove some of their harshness; but peppers are milder at heart, and cook quite happily in liquid.

Ratatouille

HOW TO MAKE IT
For 4
1 large aubergine
3 courgettes
3 red peppers
2 onions
1 400 g tin tomatoes, or 6 medium-sized fresh ones,
skinned and chopped
2 cloves garlic, finely chopped
Olive oil

This is an inauthentic recipe, but it honours in part the principle of ratatouille: that the ingredients be cooked apart, then combined.[1 – see WHY YOU DO IT]

Cut the aubergines and courgettes into fork-size chunks, and put them in a roasting pan. Toss them (with your hands, if you like) with enough olive oil to give them a good coating, and with salt. Put the peppers, whole, in the pan alongside them. Bake at gas mark 6/200°C, turning all the vegetables after 20 minutes. (You could start with the aubergines, and add the courgettes, which take less time to soften, after 15 minutes or so.) Cook for about 40 minutes in total, or until the aubergines and courgettes are tender and the peppers have blackened skin (leave the peppers in the oven for longer, if they need it). Skin and deseed the peppers when they're cool enough to handle, retaining their juice.

Peel the onions, cut them in half, and slice them thinly. Soften them in olive oil over a gentle heat for 20 minutes, or until golden and sweet.

Make a simple tomato sauce with the garlic and tomatoes and a little more oil (see page 191), and simmer until thick.

Combine all the ingredients, including the juice from the peppers, and warm through. Check the seasoning. Serve hot, warm, at room temperature, or cold. I like the middle two options best.

VARIATIONS

A ratatouille is even better with herbs: thyme, basil, bay

and parsley are all good complements.

As I explain on page 134, I prefer to bake aubergine; but sautéing courgettes isn't too tricky, if you want to do that (page 151). You'll need smaller pieces – slices, perhaps. They'll have a fresher flavour than the baked ones.

(page 134) (page 151)

WHY YOU DO IT

1) *A late merger*. It's a vegetable stew: why don't you just cook all the ingredients together? Because they'd turn into a vegetable mush, that's why.

You'd fry the aubergines first, because they take longest to soften. After stirring them around for a bit in a pan from which they'd sucked all the oil, you'd add the onions and the garlic; then the peppers; then the courgettes; then the tomatoes. These vegetables will overcook and break up.

There isn't a short cut (apart from leaving out the sweating of the aubergines, and giving them a hassle-free bake). The ingredients of a ratatouille should retain their distinctive characters, but in the context of a binding of tomato and garlic. Combining the ingredients only for a brief warm-through, and letting them cool together, allows them as long to get to know each other (Fergus Henderson's phrase) as they need.

Potatoes

The general rule, as we have seen, is that if you value nutrition above culinary aesthetics you should cook vegetables quickly, in as little water as possible. But the advantages of boiling potatoes — whether slowly, to eat as they are, or rapidly, before roasting — are worth the loss of a few nutrients, in my opinion.

Boiled potatoes

HOW TO COOK THEM

Peel and cut the potatoes into pieces of the size you want. Put them in cold, unsalted water in a saucepan, and turn the heat under the pan to low/medium.[1] – see WHY YOU DO IT **When the water reaches simmering point, regulate the heat under the pan to retain a gentle simmer until the potatoes are tender.**

Scrape new potatoes to get rid of as much skin, or as many surface blemishes, as you like.[2] Cook them as above.

WHY YOU DO IT

1) *A gentle simmer.* Floury, maincrop potatoes (Maris Piper, King Edward or Desirée, for example) often fall apart when boiled, because the outsides overcook before the heat penetrates the interiors. Steaming in particular causes uneven cooking: when potatoes are piled on top of each other, some get better access to the steam than others. Slowly bringing potatoes to a simmer helps to preserve their textures; their surfaces get less of a bashing if the water is maintained at a gentle simmer rather than at a rolling boil. Don't add salt, which would speed the softening.

A boiled King Edward is an unexciting thing, I know. But sometimes, with a creamy sauce or rich gravy, or with the juices from a roast chicken, it's just what you want. You can always make a mash on your plate with a fork and some butter.

2) *A boring scrape.* Although new potatoes keep their textures better, they still benefit from this slow-boiling treatment. They have more tender skins than do maincrop potatoes; how much of the skin you scrape off is up to you. I'm pretty slack about it, because I find that scraping potatoes is a longer and more boring task than peeling them.

Making potato salad, you can boil the new potatoes in their skins, drain them, wait for them to cool a little, then peel off the skins, before cutting them up and tossing them in **vinaigrette** (see page 41). Lord, I hate doing that: it takes me for ever.

Mashed potato

HOW TO MAKE IT
Method 1 (for perfectionists)[1 – see WHY YOU DO IT]
Heat a pan of unsalted water to 70°C. Peel the potatoes, slice them 20 mm thick, and add them to the water, which you should return to 70°C and keep at that temperature for 40 minutes. Drain the potatoes, and put them in cold water for half an hour. Bring a pan of salted water to boiling point,

add the potatoes and simmer until the point of a knife slips into them easily, then drain. Return them to the hot pan and stir them around, over a low heat if necessary, to dry. Push them back into the same pan – or a clean one if you're fussy about the bits of potato that will have stuck to it – through a food mill or potato ricer. Add warm milk until the potato reaches the required consistency; add butter, and more salt if needed. Put the pan on to a low heat, above a heat disperser, and stir until warmed through. Or spoon the potatoes into a heat-proof serving dish, cover loosely with foil, and put into a low oven (say, gas mark 1/ 140°C) for 10 minutes or so.

Method 2 (for the rest of us)

Peel[2] the potatoes[3] and cut them into slices about 1.5 cm thick.[4] Put them into cold, salted water,[5] bring slowly to a simmer, and cook them at a gentle simmer until the point of a knife slips into them easily.[6] Drain, and follow the mashing instructions above.[7]

VARIATIONS

Simmer an unpeeled garlic clove – or two or three cloves if you like – with the potatoes, and put that through the mill too (it will leave behind its skin). Olive oil can substitute for butter; or, luxuriously, truffle oil.

Aligot – or, if you prefer, cheesy mash – is a delicious variation. Prepare the potatoes as above, with the garlic clove. Drain, mash, and add a melting cheese to the potatoes and butter in the pan (about 350 g of cheese to 900 g of potatoes); Cantal is authentic, because the dish comes from the Auvergne, but Cheddar, Pecorino, Gruyère or anything similar is delicious too. Keep stirring on a low heat, again with a heat disperser below the pan if possible, until the cheese is melted and the mixture is warmed through. Warmed cream or milk will loosen the texture. Pepper and nutmeg would be good seasonings; remember that the cheese is salty.

Turning the dish into something that is not Aligot, I like to add fried lardons, with their fat (instead of the butter). I then have a choice of simmering the garlic with the potatoes or frying it with the lardons; the flavour of the latter is more assertive.

WHY YOU DO IT

1) *How far are you prepared to go to avoid glueyness in your mash?* Method one, with its two stages of cooking, is recommended by Heston Blumenthal and Jeffrey Steingarten. Some day, when my diary is empty, I might try it.

Glueyness comes from starch gel that has leached from broken-down cells. After 40 minutes in 70°C water, the cells expand; when you put the potatoes into cold water, the cells bond, and are less likely to rupture. Then you can cook and mash the potatoes safely.

2) *Peeling.* Jeffrey Steingarten is reassuring on this point. It is not true, he says, that most of the nutrients are in the skin or immediately below it. There are plenty in the rest of the potato.

That is welcome news, because it means that there is no good reason to follow those who tell you to cook the potatoes in their skins. How large are these cooks' saucepans, which can accommodate, say, half a dozen large King Edwards and the water to cover them? Because the potatoes are big, their outsides cook some time before their interiors do. Then there's peeling the hot potatoes, a task that I am not dextrous enough to accomplish without scorching myself and getting little sticky bits of peel all over the place. By the time I've peeled six potatoes, they are almost cold; as you may have noticed, cold potatoes firm up. You have to bash them up harder, breaking the starch cells: result, gluey mash.

3) *What potatoes, and how many?* Select a floury, maincrop variety, such as King Edward and Maris Piper. Some say that Desirée, which may be a little waxier than other maincrop varieties, do not mash so well, but I've had perfectly acceptable results with them.

The term "waxy" is used to describe the firmer consistency of new potatoes. Joel Robuchon, creator of the most celebrated mashed potato in the world, uses a waxy variety. Waxy potatoes contain less starch; but I, lacking Robuchon's skill (and not wanting to use as much butter and cream as he does), have found that they produce a more gluey result, perhaps because mashing them requires greater force.

I use about 900 g of potatoes for four people, with a fairly indulgent 75 g or so of butter.

4) *Slicing the potatoes*. If you leave them whole, the outer part of the potatoes will be overcooked before the inner part has softened; the cells in the overcooked potato will be likely to break. If you cut up the potatoes into tiny pieces, you risk overcooking and waterlogging them; you'll also lose a good many nutrients to the cooking water. Slices should cook more evenly than would chunks.

5) *A cold water start*. See **Boiled potatoes**, page 172.

6) *When they're ready*. The potatoes you're going to mash have to be soft, of course; but you need to catch them at the moment between getting tender and falling apart. As I say above, starchy cells in overcooked potatoes will break, leaking gelatinous stuff into your mash.

7) *How to mash*. Drain the potatoes, then return them to the hot pan for a minute, to allow some water to evaporate. Don't bash them about and break up starch cells. Then mash.

Delia Smith suggests you mash potatoes with a hand-held, electric whisk. I am sure that Delia has never made gluey potatoes in her life, but I do not recommend her technique; again, it risks smashing the starch cells, releasing the gel. Certainly, you must never try putting the potatoes into a food processor. The blades will convert them into wallpaper paste.

A hand-held masher has the drawback of forcing you to mash portions of potato several times as you seek to obliterate all the lumps. Several experts recommend potato ricers; but I don't possess one. I used a **food mill** (page 32), which produces a smooth, unsticky result. Joel Robuchon, apparently, forces his milled mash through a sieve.

Reheating mash needs care: while it will withstand a beating from a wooden spoon, it will turn pasty if you cook it again. Put it on to the lowest heat, with a heat disperser preferably, and stir it regularly; warming it in the oven may be a safer option. Don't reheat for longer than 10 minutes.

Roast potatoes

HOW TO MAKE THEM

Turn on the oven to gas mark 6/200°C, put some fat[1 – see WHY YOU DO IT] into a roasting pan and put the pan on to a high shelf. Bring a saucepan of water to the boil. Meanwhile, peel and cut up your potatoes,[2] into pieces of whatever size and shape you like. Add them, and salt, to the saucepan, bring the water back to the boil, and simmer for five minutes.[3] Drain, put the potatoes back into the warm saucepan, and stir them over a low heat to dry them and rough up their edges.[4]

Take the roasting pan out of the oven and tip in the potatoes, turning them in the sizzling fat.[5] Keep the potatoes separate, so that they roast rather than steam. Put back into the oven. Check them after 20 minutes; if they are browned underneath, turn them. (Using my oven, and my roasting pan, I can leave them for half an hour.) If you want to turn them again on to their remaining pale sides, do; they should be tender in 45 to 50

minutes.[6] Tilting the pan so that the superfluous
fat falls away, remove the potatoes to a colander
lined with kitchen paper. Add salt, toss a little,
and serve.

VARIATIONS

Five minutes before the end of cooking, add some rosemary, stripped from its branches, and stir in. Put some
garlic cloves to roast with the potatoes – but beware of
cooking the garlic for longer than 30 minutes, or you might
find that there's no pulp left. You could also take a whole
bulb, rub a little olive oil over it, wrap it loosely in foil, and
put it in the pan with the potatoes. Roast potatoes are delicious with the creamy garlic you squeeze from the husks.

WHY YOU DO IT

1) *What fat, and how much?* Animal fats – beef dripping,
lard, goose or duck fat – work best, some claim. I think that
olive, sunflower or vegetable oil work fine. Use enough to
provide a thin layer in the pan, and to coat all the potatoes.

2) *What potatoes?* I have assumed that you're using
floury, maincrop potatoes – although roasts made with
Desirées are, I have found, a little dry. You can roast new
potatoes too, of course; but I don't agree with those who
say that you should leave them in their skins, which, in my
experience, go tough. So peel them or, in the case of Jerseys
and the like, scrape them thoroughly; put them straight into
the hot oil. Less starchy than maincrop varieties, they don't
benefit from parboiling.

3) _Parboiling_. Cutting up potatoes releases starch from their cells. Rinsing doesn't appear to get rid of it; if you put the potatoes into fat and roast them, they will emerge from the oven with a slimy, chewy crust. Sometimes, I rather like them like that: one of my favourite dishes is shoulder of lamb, slow-roasted above a bed of sliced potatoes, which have been mixed with garlic and rosemary and covered with water or stock (**lamb boulangère** – see page 215). When the lamb is ready, you remove it from the oven, turning up the heat to brown the potatoes and evaporate most of the liquid. The potatoes are deliciously imbued with fat and juices from the meat.

Nevertheless, crunchiness is the quality to aim for. You get it with three procedures: parboiling the potatoes, drying them, and tipping them into hot fat.

I prefer parboiling to steaming. Steaming does not seem to get rid of all the surface starch, and the potatoes are more likely to stick to the roasting pan. Some writers insist that you simmer the potatoes until they are tender and nearly falling apart. I do not think that they need to spend more than five minutes in the simmering water. It's the surface of the potatoes that concerns you; the insides will cook in the oven, and will be just as fluffy. You don't need to start the potatoes from cold, and you can keep the water at a rolling boil if you like (see **Boiled potatoes**, page 172). The point here is to cook and bash up the surfaces – processes that the salt in the water will hasten.

4) _Rough surfaces_. Stirring the potatoes in the hot pan dries them, so that they do not repel the fat when they hit it; it also roughs up the surfaces, helping them to crisp. Some cooks dust the potatoes in flour to create a crispy surface; I don't think that's necessary.

5) *Hot fat*. I have tried turning the potatoes in cold oil, direct from the bottle; I have also tried roasting cold potatoes. Both options work, but a hot, dry potato tipped into sizzling fat acquires the crunchier surface.

6) *Ready in 50 minutes*. Assuming they're on their own in a gas mark 6/200°C oven, that is. Of course, you are more than likely to be preparing them to accompany some other dish that is cooking there: a roasting meat or a simmering stew. It is likely, too, that you will be cooking these dishes at a lower temperature than gas mark 6/200°C.

If you are cooking a stew, your oven will be (I hope, for the stew's sake) at too low a temperature for the potatoes. Consider transferring the casserole dish to the smallest ring on the hob, and putting a heat disperser underneath it. Your roast may be cooking at gas mark 4/180°C; put it on to a low shelf, with the potatoes on a high one. You'll want to take the meat out of the oven at least 20 minutes before carving; at that point, you can turn up the temperature to get the potatoes good and crisp. If you're slow-roasting some lamb or belly pork, say, at a temperature of gas mark 1/140°C or less, try taking it out of the oven before you put the potatoes in; turn the temperature right up (to gas mark 8/230°C), in order to cook them in 30 to 40 minutes, but keep an eye on them. The meat will still be warm when the potatoes are done; I prefer it at this temperature.

181

Fried potatoes

You can follow the procedure for roast potatoes: peel, cut up, parboil, dry, then fry. You must fry them in a single layer, as the recipe books say. How large are these writers' frying pans? I've got a pretty large one, and I find it hard to get into it enough potatoes to satisfy a family of four. Cooking them requires attention: you need to turn them and move them around, to make sure they cook evenly. Grumble, grumble. Still, they taste good.

Chips

I don't make chips often at home. I used to think that they were best left to restaurants, until I learned that even quite prestigious restaurants rely on oven chips. But I still think that maintaining a chip pan, filled with several bottles of rapidly degrading oil, is a bore for the home cook.

Nevertheless, you can get good chips with any old pan, and without a thermometer. It's quite satisfying.

The two-phase method of cooking chips is commonly accepted as the best. If you have a thermometer, you cook the potatoes first at 140°C, for five to 10 minutes; then at 190°C, until brown. During phase one, you're boiling the chips in the oil; phase two is the browning bit. If you tried to combine these phases, the potatoes would brown before the interiors were cooked; also, the first phase – for reasons I don't fully understand – helps to produce a crunchier chip.

HOW TO MAKE THEM

If you have a proper chip pan or a thermometer, this process will be easier. Half fill a large saucepan with oil (I use a mixture of corn and sunflower, or corn and groundnut). Peel and cut the potatoes: choose a thickness, cut them horizontally, then cut these rounds horizontally or vertically, depending on the size of chip you want. Put them into cold water, to remove some of the surface starch; dry them (if you don't, the oil in the pan will erupt).

Heat the oil. Drop in a small piece of bread: it should sizzle gently. Add the potatoes, and don't crowd the pan; you may need to cook them in several batches. Cook for five to 10 minutes, until nearly tender. Remove the potatoes with a slotted spoon (unless you've used a chip basket). Turn up the heat under the pan; now a small piece of bread should sizzle agitatedly. Return the chips to the oil: again, in batches if necessary. When they're brown, remove to a colander lined with paper towels. Keep batches warm in a low oven. Add salt just before serving.

Gratin dauphinois

HOW TO MAKE IT
For 4
4 medium-sized potatoes[1] – see WHY YOU DO IT
1 pot (284 ml) cream

Milk[2]
½ clove garlic, chopped[3]
Pinch of nutmeg
Salt
Walnut-sized knob of butter

Heat the oven to gas mark 3/160°C.[4] Slice the potatoes no thicker than a pound coin, and as thinly as you like, into a bowl of cold water. Drain them. Elizabeth David says that you should dry them at this point, but that seems unnecessarily fussy. Smear the butter over the insides of a gratin dish. (A Pyrex oven dish is fine.)

Put the cream and some milk (about 150 ml to start with) into a saucepan of roughly the same diameter as the gratin dish; add the garlic, nutmeg and a little salt, and tip in the potatoes. Arrange them as economically as possible, and add more milk, if you need to, until it comes level with the top layer. Heat the pan gently. When it starts to bubble, tip the contents into the gratin dish, tidy up the potatoes, and bake for about one and a half hours, or until the surface is browned and the potatoes are sitting in a reduced, wobbly liquid.

VARIATIONS

Another way to prepare gratin dauphinois is with cream only. Unless you use an artery-blocking quantity of the stuff, you'll probably find that it doesn't cover the potatoes; so, in order to cook the exposed potatoes (by steaming) and to prevent the cream from reducing and thickening too quickly, cover the gratin dish with foil. (Nevertheless, it's probably worth using a little more cream than in the main recipe – 350 ml, say.) After about 50 minutes (at gas mark 3/ 160°C), check on progress: if the potatoes are tender but the cream is still runny, uncover the dish and cook for 10 minutes or so longer. If the potatoes are not tender, you may need to turn up the oven. If the potatoes are not tender and the cream has evaporated, er . . . did you cover the dish tightly enough?

WHY YOU DO IT

1) *What potatoes, and how many?* Waxy potatoes such as Charlottes work best, because they retain their textures. But any will do.

"Small portions please," write Alastair Little and Richard Whittington in their recipe (*Keep It Simple*) for gratin dauphinois. "I'll serve and eat as much of it as I like, thank you very much," is my response to that; but I concede that a portion of dauphinois containing the equivalent of one medium-sized potato for each person is about right.

2) *How much liquid?* One way of cooking gratin dauphinois is to layer the potatoes in a dish, and then pour over hot milk and cream; but it's hard to know how much milk and cream you'll need. That's a reason why I suggest putting the ingredients into a saucepan first: then you can add liquid until you have enough. A second reason is to enable you to heat the ingredients. It might take them half an hour to reach simmering point if placed cold in the oven.

3) *How strong do you want the garlic?* You could flavour the dauphinois with a hint of garlic by rubbing a cut clove over the gratin dish, which, if it's earthenware, will absorb some garlic and give it back to the dauphinois during cooking. Or, for a stronger flavour, cut up the garlic and then crush it (using a mortar and pestle, or with the back of a strong knife on a chopping board) with some salt. Mix it with the butter before smearing the butter over the dish.

4) *Oven heat*. It is impossible to give a recipe that you can guarantee will work every time. Containers will vary in heat conduction and surface areas; potatoes will vary in their propensities to absorb liquid. I can prepare a dauphinois one week and find it in perfect condition after an hour in the oven; the next week, I will follow a similar formula and find that at the same point the potatoes are still swimming in milk and cream.

Most recipes suggest that gas mark 5/190°C for 50 minutes to an hour will work; and, often, it will. I prefer to cook my dauphinois more slowly, at gas mark 3/160°C, for about an hour and a half. Check it after 30 minutes. Is it bubbling gently? Good. Check it after 45 minutes. Has it started to thicken? Not at all? Then turn up the oven. Keep checking. The dauphinois is ready when the surface has browned and the potatoes are sitting in a thick, reduced cream. The one issue you don't need to worry about is whether the potatoes will be tender: the milk and cream are excellent aids to cooking.

Other baked, sliced potato dishes

There's a variation on the cream-only version of gratin dauphinois in Rose Gray and Ruth Rogers' first River Café book. You fry cubes of pancetta (100 g for four, say) and garlic before adding them to the cream and potatoes, with sage as well.

Some gratin dauphinois recipes include egg and/or cheese. I wouldn't use egg, because I prefer, in this context, the consistency of thickened cream to that of custard; and achieving that custard is not straightforward – you're more likely to find bits of scrambled egg among your potatoes. But I do use cheese – Gruyère or Cantal – occasionally, in a cream-only gratin.

Sometimes I fry pancetta and garlic in a casserole, then add sliced Charlotte potatoes (900 g) and a couple of sliced onions (for four people). I bake it in the oven (at gas mark 3/160°C again), giving it a stir every quarter of an hour to merge the onion and potato as the onion softens. The onion provides enough moisture to prevent the potatoes from sticking. The mixture emerges golden and melting. A richer version might include cream and/or cheese as well.

Gratin Savoyard is cooked in stock. You mix sliced potatoes, garlic, Gruyère cheese, salt, pepper and nutmeg, layer them in a dish, pour over hot stock to cover, and bake, uncovered, in a gas mark 5/190°C oven (for four: 900 g of potatoes and 120 g of Gruyère). The potatoes will take longer to cook than they do in milk or cream, and the liquid will not reduce so quickly, because it does not thicken, much. You want a browned surface and just enough liquid to moisten each portion. Sliced onions are an optional, inauthentic variation; thyme would be a nice addition. Potatoes boulangères is similar, but without the cheese.

Root vegetables: celeriac, parsnip, turnip, swede

A celeriac is a pain to peel, and you can risk serious injury attempting to get a knife through a large swede. Try not to let these drawbacks put you off these underrated vegetables. Too often in winter we carry on buying out-of-season aubergines, courgettes and tomatoes, ignoring humbler, cheaper, tastier roots.

All may be cut up, tossed in oil, and baked. Celeriac or parsnip, steamed apart until tender, make superb mash with an equal quantity of potato. Another delicious mash to go with roasts consists of equal quantities of turnip, swede and carrot; steam all three, taking care not to overcook the carrot, blitz in a food processor, and warm through with a little salt and nutmeg, as well as plenty of butter.

Spinach

The greater the quantity of a vegetable, the more difficult it is to cook it efficiently. Unfortunately, you need a huge bagful of spinach just to feed four people.

You could plunge it into a large vat of boiling water; some say that this is the best way, because it's the quickest.

You cook it for a minute or two, drain it, plunge it into cold water, drain again and squeeze out the excess liquid, then warm it through with butter and seasoning. As I've said elsewhere, I'm not a fan of this method, which loses nutrients and, I think, flavour.

So: wash the spinach thoroughly; you may need to do it twice (wash the bagged supermarket spinach too). Shove the wet spinach into a pot, put on the lid, and put the pot on the hob above a maximum heat. After a minute or less the spinach will start to collapse; you can take off the lid and stir the leaves, getting them all into contact with the now boiling liquid. Continue to stir for another minute or two. The leaves won't take long to become tender. Drain, and push down on the spinach in the colander with a wooden spoon to get rid of as much moisture as possible. Return the spinach to a pan with a generous portion of butter; add salt and pepper (nutmeg too, if you like), and stir to coat the leaves and warm them through.

If you're going to cook the spinach and reheat it later, my advice is not to follow injunctions to refresh it in cold water, because that process always seems to stun the flavour; instead, shorten the initial cooking, to allow for the cooking that the spinach will continue to undergo before it cools down.

Here's another way, adapted from a recipe in Richard Olney's *Simple French Food*.

For 4

Wash 1 kg of spinach, grab handfuls of it from the colander, and cut the leaves into shreds (gather the spinach together on a board, cut it into fine strips,

and cut those strips at right angles). Pack the spinach into a gratin or other ovenproof dish, the inside of which you have oiled. When a third of it is in the dish, season with salt and pepper, dust it with 1 tbsp of flour, and drizzle over 1 tbsp of olive oil; do the same when you have added the next third, and the same again to the surface when all the spinach is in the dish. Bake for an hour: 10 minutes at gas mark 8/230°C, and a further 50 at gas mark 4/180°C. Some of the liquid from the spinach evaporates; a good deal of the rest is thickened by the flour. The result is surprisingly scrumptious.

Tomatoes

The term "salad tomatoes", as used by greengrocers, is almost always a lie. Those hard, orange things, acidic but otherwise tasteless, are not happy additions to a cold plate; and they're not worth cooking either. Plumper, vine tomatoes are a better bet, although the message that the vine is meant to convey – that the tomatoes have ripened in the sunshine – is probably also a con. They sometimes have the texture of soggy blotting paper, perhaps because they have been refrigerated; with a boost from other ingredients, they can form the basis of a reasonable sauce.

Deseeding tomatoes is one of the jobs that separates the professional cook from the rest of us. Most recipes involving tomatoes tell you to skin and deseed them. These writers have access to better tomatoes than the ones I get hold of: after I've deseeded one, there's not much left. They are also prepared to discard the acidity of the juice in favour of the sweetness of the flesh; but I like the balance between those tastes. You could scrape the juice and seeds into a sieve, returning the juice to the flesh; are you that fussy about tomato seeds?

Deseeding is worth doing if you don't want the juices to soak other ingredients: when you're making certain salads, for example, or sandwiches. Bring a pan of water to the boil, turn off the heat, and drop in the tomatoes for 20 seconds. Drain, and cool them with cold water. The skins should come away easily. Cut the tomatoes in half, and scrape out the seeds and juice.

However, I like Nigel Slater's throw-it-all-in method of making tomato sauce (from *Appetite*). I have adapted it slightly to include vinegar and sugar: even the best tomatoes benefit from an injection of extra acidity and sweetness. Tomato paste, to give a greater concentration of flavour, is optional: judge for yourself how much your fresh or canned tomatoes need this assistance.

Simmering the sauce thickens it, of course; it also mellows the flavour.

Tomato sauce 1

HOW TO MAKE IT
For 2 to 3
Finely chop a clove of garlic, and soften it for a minute or so in 1 tbsp of olive oil in a heavy

saucepan. Add 1 dstsp of white wine vinegar and 1 dstsp of tomato paste, and cook this mixture for a minute; then throw in six roughly chopped, medium-sized tomatoes, a pinch or two of sugar, and a little salt. Cook gently until the tomatoes have broken down and the sauce is gloopy: maybe 30 minutes or more. The skins are not worth eating. You can remove them by passing the sauce through a food mill or a sieve. Check the seasoning. Add herbs if you like: some torn-up basil, or some oregano.

Tomato sauce 2

HOW TO MAKE IT
For 2 to 3

Follow the procedure for sauce 1, but with a 400 g can of tomatoes and their juice. Pour them into the saucepan and break them up with a wooden spoon as they cook. If you want a smooth texture, put the cooked sauce through the food mill.

Tomato sauce 3

HOW TO MAKE IT
For 2 to 3

Put the roughly chopped tomatoes, or the can of tomatoes and their juice, into a saucepan, and simmer with a pinch of salt until thick. Pass the sauce through a food mill or a sieve if you like. Warm through again, take off the heat, and add 1 tbsp of extra virgin olive oil and a clove of garlic, crushed with some salt. Add any other herbs and seasonings you like.

The fruity olive oil and the fresh garlic will of course be much more prominent in this sauce than in the other two. So you need good olive oil, and good garlic. You also need to be prepared to carry the evidence of what you've been eating on your breath.

VARIATIONS

Soften a chopped onion after you've softened the garlic. Add a whizzed dried chilli or two before adding the tomatoes; or add whole dried chillis to the sauce as it cooks, and remove them before serving.

Gently fry cubes of pancetta first, then add the garlic, and onion as well if you want it.

For a puttanesca sauce for pasta, soften half a small tin of anchovies with the oil and garlic, add dried chilli if you like, and proceed with the tomato sauce as normal. When the sauce is nearly cooked, add a dozen stoned, roughly chopped black olives, as well as 25 g of capers, squeezed of their vinegary juice. Add chopped parsley too, if you like.

Baked tomatoes

Cut the tomatoes in half, horizontally (ie, at right angles to the stem). Place on an oiled baking tray. Insert little slivers of garlic in the compartments holding the juice and the seeds, drizzle olive oil on top, and sprinkle with salt. I like to cook these tomatoes slowly, in a gas mark 1 / 140°C oven; it usually takes a couple of hours for their flavour to concentrate. But I can't give you a reason why cooking them at gas mark 6 / 200°C for 20 minutes to half an hour shouldn't serve just as well. You could cook some spaghetti, toss it in butter or oil, and serve these tomatoes on top. Or push the tomatoes through a food mill, add a little more olive oil, and toss the pasta with this purée.

Or: bake the tomatoes with just the salt, and serve as a warm salad with a **vinaigrette** (page 41).

MₑAT

We may justify to ourselves the killing of animals for food, but we surely cannot feel comfortable about treating them with abominable cruelty. That's one argument for buying free range or organic meat; another, more self-interested, reason is that it tastes better. A third is that we can feel more confident about the provenance of what we're taking home. A fourth is that we can feel more confident that the meat hasn't been pumped full of substances we'd rather not ingest.

You can buy a battery chicken for £3. An organic one may cost four times that amount. The price of the battery chicken, the pathetic victim of abuse in the name of cheap food, seems to me to be obscene. That may be easy for me to say: I can afford to pay more. I make sure, though, that I get my money's worth from the chicken I buy. The meat from a 2 kg bird will provide two meals for my family; from the carcass, I make a stock, and get another meal from that. The £12 is good value.

Lean meat is very expensive. Less glamorous cuts, however, are reasonably priced, and are often more interesting. I'd rather eat the steak the French call onglet, and that we call skirt, than fillet. Shoulder of lamb can be more characterful than leg. Nothing is better than slow-roasted belly pork (page 211).

A large bird or joint of meat going straight from fridge to oven will take longer to cook than would one starting off at room temperature. As Richard Ehrlich has shown, instructions to take the meat out of the fridge an hour before cooking are useless: the rise in temperature in that time will be insignificant. To reduce the cooking time, you'll need to get your Christmas turkey out of the fridge at least four hours in advance. It's probably worth doing: the less time the tender breast meat spends in the oven, the better.

Roasts

A roast requires very little preparation, and would provide the most foolproof of all meals if only we had the luxury of a set of unvarying rules about cooking times.

It's not in the interests of cookery writers to advertise that their recipes are fallible. But even they will admit that roasting times and oven settings can be only rough guidelines. You have to keep an eye on the meat, particularly if you're fussy about its level of doneness. If nothing much is happening, turn up the dial – but be wary of drying out the meat by roasting it at a high temperature for too long. If the meat is sizzling too angrily, turn down the dial. You'll learn how to tell when a joint is ready through experience; or, if you want to be punctilious, you could invest in a meat thermometer. If the centre of a piece of lamb or beef is 60°C, the meat is medium done; pork is medium done at 70°C.

The convention is to baste a joint at regular intervals. It may not be necessary. A chicken covered in skin, or a pork joint covered in crackling, or a lamb joint covered in fat, is not going to get extra benefit from having juices poured over it. A lean piece of beef might.

Roast chicken

HOW TO MAKE IT

Wipe the chicken inside and out with paper towels.[1 – see WHY YOU DO IT] Mix 80 g to 100 g of butter with salt, pepper if you like, a chopped garlic clove and herbs – thyme, tarragon or rosemary work well. Rub the butter all over the chicken; you can put some inside the skin covering the breast, too, as well as in the cavity. Put the chicken in a roasting pan in a gas mark 6/200°C oven. After 25 minutes, pour a glass of wine into the pan (not over the breast of the bird), and turn down the oven to gas mark 3/160°C.[2] Cook the chicken for a total of 20 minutes for each 500 g it weighs, plus a further 30 minutes. (A 1.5 kg chicken, therefore, will take one hour and 30 minutes.[3])

Take the chicken out of the oven, and pour the liquid into a saucepan. Leave the chicken to rest in its pan for at least 15 minutes.[4] Just before you

are ready to serve, heat up the sauce, and check for seasoning. The chicken will have exuded some more juices; pour them into the rest of the sauce. Either pour the sauce over the chicken or serve it in a separate jug.[5]

I got the above method from Hugh Fearnley-Whittingstall's *River Cottage Meat Book*, and I love it. I think that it's the recipe that best conforms to the ideal of eating a good chicken: simple, because you don't have to do any fiddling with the sauce, yet also luxurious, because of all that butter. It wants only the simplest of accompaniments: some boiled potatoes or rice, with a salad to follow. The chicken and its sauce are, quite properly, the centre of attention.

You could put the giblets (but not the liver, which, as I said when discussing stocks, makes sauces bitter) into the roasting pan at the start, as well as a chopped onion and carrot, some unpeeled garlic cloves, and perhaps a few extra chicken wings – all to add flavour to the sauce.

Stuff the chicken with unpeeled garlic cloves, and eat the meat with the pulp, squeezed from their husks. Be aware, though, that it's quite hard to predict how much cooking a garlic clove will need before the garlic achieves that soft, sweet quality. You could put a whole head of garlic, cut in half, with the chicken, and at the end push out the pulp into the sauce with a wooden spoon.

Lemon goes very well with chicken. Put a whole lemon inside the cavity, or lemon halves or quarters; or do that, but squeeze the juice over the chicken first.

Or: don't pour the wine into the pan while the chicken is cooking. (But check that the buttery juices aren't in danger of burning on your roasting pan; if they are, add just enough wine, stock or water to keep them liquid.) Wait until the end, remove the chicken from the pan, tip the juices into a saucepan, put the pan on to a medium heat on the hob, and throw in your wine. The advantage of this method is that there will be tasty, caramelised residues in the pan to incorporate into your sauce. Stir them in, bubble the wine to evaporate its alcohol and to lose some of its acidity, and add this sauce to the other juices in the saucepan.

This is a gravy – one with a high fat content. But gravies are more commonly prepared as below.

Gravy

Of course, there are many other ways of preparing a chicken. You might want to accompany it with a proper gravy. Rub a walnut-sized knob of butter, or the equivalent quantity of olive oil, over the chicken before you cook it, and season the bird. At the end of cooking, remove the chicken to a warm plate. Pour the juices in the pan into a bowl. Put the pan on to a ring of your hob, turn the heat to medium, and add some liquid – it might be water, or chicken stock, or a small glass of white wine, or a small glass of cider, or a table-spoon of vinegar. Bubble the liquid, stirring and scraping any residues from the pan into it. (This process is "deglazing" – see page 61). Pour this sauce into another bowl.

Do you want to thicken your gravy? If you do, take a

dessertspoon of the fat that will have risen to the top of the first bowl (the one into which you poured the first lot of pan juices), and put it in a small saucepan.[6] Carefully spoon the rest of the fat into the bin, or into a saucer for scraping into the bin later.[7] Add a dessertspoon of flour – or enough to make a roux the consistency of wet sand – to the fat in the saucepan, and heat gently until the mixture browns a little. Then turn up the heat to medium. You have two bowls, one with the degreased pan juices, the second with the liquid you produced by deglazing the roasting pan. Pour their contents, little by little, into the roux. You add a bit, stir vigorously until it's incorporated, then repeat the process until you get the consistency you want. It's just like making a **béchamel** (page 50).

I suggest that you want a gravy of about the consistency of single cream; or perhaps, since you need to bear in mind that it will thicken as it cools, slightly thinner. Having used 1 dstsp of flour, you'll probably need 150 ml to 200 ml of liquid to reach that consistency – that should be enough sauce for four to six people. So you may need some more stock. Don't add more alcohol at this stage – it will taste raw. If you don't have enough stock, revise your expectations downwards, and use just a teaspoon of flour, which should cope with the liquid in the bowls.

You could make a little stock while the chicken is cooking. One way, as in the HOW TO MAKE IT recipe above, would be to put giblets and vegetables, along with wine or water or both, with the chicken in the roasting pan; the disadvantage of this method is that the bottom of the pan won't give you any tasty, crusty residues. Or you could put

200

the giblets (if you're lucky enough to have them) with some vegetables in a pan and make a simple **stock** (see page 56). If you don't have giblets, buy a few wings; or chop the wings from your chicken and use them. Or you could chop off just the wing tips, using them to add some chickeny flavour to a **vegetable stock** (page 63).

By this time, you might be starting to see why I have come to like the version under HOW TO MAKE IT on page 197 so much. And there is more work to do, if you want your gravy to taste as refined as possible. Put the pan on one side of a ring, and continue to simmer very gently. On the cooler side of the gravy, away from the heat, you'll get some skin, which you can lift off. You can continue with this process until your impatience overcomes your fussiness. Check the seasoning, and serve, in a warm sauce boat.

I used to like getting plenty of thick, dark gravy to cover my food. It seemed to me to be unsatisfactory to have meat and veg sitting on a thin puddle. But my taste has changed: I've come to recognise that the disadvantage of thickeners is that they inhibit flavour, and that thin sauces may be more satisfying for the taste buds. You can follow the procedure above without the flour stage: throw away as much fat from the meat juices as possible, then combine these juices with the sauce you made by deglazing the pan, and add as much stock as you need to bring your gravy to the required quantity. You could skim this gravy, as above, too.

ACCOMPANIMENTS

Roast chicken with gravy can take more elaborate accompaniments than the HOW TO MAKE IT version. Much as I love roast potatoes, I've come to feel, for some reason, that they don't go particularly well with roast chicken; I'd prefer a **gratin dauphinois** (page 183). As the chicken and the gratin are both pale, serve a green vegetable with them; or carrots, perhaps.

Cauliflower cheese goes well with roast chicken. Again, you've got two pale preparations; so, instead of serving potatoes as well, offer another vegetable.

WHY YOU DO IT

1) *You don't have to wash the chicken.* You may want to dry it, and to get rid of any gubbins inside the bird; but bacteria there will be killed by the high heat of the oven. It won't be killed by cold water. I am indebted to Richard Ehrlich for the information that the Food Standards Agency advises against washing chickens, warning that the procedure is more likely to spread bacteria than to kill them.

2) *Oven temperature.* Roasts benefit from an initial cooking at a high temperature; 25 minutes at 200°C will start off the browning reactions, also known as Maillard reactions, that meat-eaters find most toothsome. (Don't ask me to explain them: even Harold McGee calls them "exceedingly complex".) In the case of chicken, what you're browning is mostly the skin; but that, too, is desirable.

Recipes sometimes instruct you to brown the meat in oil before putting it in the oven. It's a good idea to give small roasts, such as poussins, an initial browning, because

202

the oven alone won't get very far with the process in the short time they take to cook.

The browning, once started, will continue at the lower temperature, which is perfectly adequate to cook the meat. Maintaining the high temperature might cause it to dry out. Your chicken will probably cook perfectly well, after the initial 200°C blast, at gas mark 2/150°C.

3) *Cooking time*. You risk poisoning yourself if you eat chicken that is still bloody. Test by inserting a thin knife or skewer into the meat at the thickest part of the thigh: if the juices run clear, the chicken is safe to eat; if there's any trace of red, you need to cook the bird for longer.

There are recipes that tell you to cook a 1.5 kg chicken at 200°C for 50 minutes to an hour. I have found that the juices are clear after that time, but that the leg meat is still a little unyielding for my taste. I prefer the formula I've given above (20 minutes for each 500 g, plus 30 minutes); by that time, the meat is close to falling off the bone.

There is a problem with my timings, though. The breast meat certainly does not take that long to cook; and, the longer it spends in the oven after it has passed its point of readiness, the drier and tougher it gets.

This is the challenge in all meat cookery. You are heating muscle fibres, which become dry and tough if they are cooked for very long; you are also heating connective tissue, which needs long cooking to become tender. Fat is also part of the mix; it keeps the meat lubricated.

The connective tissue is what harnesses the muscles. The bits of an animal that get most exercise have the most connective tissue; in a raw or undercooked state, they are tough. The tender cuts, such as fillet steak, have little connective tissue.

When roasting a chicken, you're cooking tender breast meat and tough leg meat at the same time: it's as if you were cooking fillet steak alongside chuck. You wouldn't cook fillet steak for an hour and a half; and that timing is not ideal for chicken breast, either.

I have found, nevertheless, that the HOW TO MAKE IT method above produces perfectly acceptable results. Perhaps the butter helps to keep the breast meat tender; certainly, fat in "marbled" cuts of meat performs this function.

I don't believe that the sauce in the roasting pan helps to maintain tenderness. Some writers seem to think that surrounding meat with moisture will keep the meat itself moist; but anyone who has eaten an unsuccessful stew will know that it's perfectly possible for meat to emerge from liquid in a dried-out state. The wine or stock in the pan will lower the oven temperature; but that effect will be cancelled out by the qualities of the steam, which is a more efficient heating medium than air. Liquid will "actually increase the fluid loss", Harold McGee writes. The net effect in the basic recipe above – lower oven temperature, but increased heating efficiency – is probably neutral.

As I explain on page 23, I do not believe that surrounding a roast or any part of it with foil is a good idea.

There is a solution that Gordon Ramsay and other chefs prefer: you separate legs and wings from the breast, and start cooking them first.

4) *Resting*. On removal from the oven, a roast has a lot of juice close to the surface. Start carving, and the juice will spurt out. As the meat rests, the hotter, outer meat transfers its heat to the centre, continuing to cook it and transferring juices to it as well; also, the outer layer, as it cools, retains its moisture better. So a rested chicken, or joint of beef or whatever, will be a moister one. Some juices will leak out; you can add those to your gravy.

I've already commented on writers' annoying habit of telling you to keep things "in a warm place". I've got a grill, above my oven, with a door that opens frontwards, providing a table. The best I can do is put the resting meat on that; with the oven on, it's warmish. (I warm plates and serving dishes inside the grill – not turned on, of course.)

However, one of the reasons why cooking a roast meal can be so stressful is that we get far too worried about serving every component of it piping hot. A rested roast will retain its heat for some time, but it does not have to be hot to be enjoyable. A lukewarm gravy would be disappointing, though.

5) *Carving*. If your carving technique is as crude as mine, you may prefer to cut up the chicken in the kitchen, put the bits in a serving dish, and then either pour the sauce over them or keep the sauce in a separate jug. But a whole roasted chicken is an inspiring sight; it seems a shame not to show it off to your guests. So, in spite of the humiliation, I prefer to let them watch me wrestle with it. If the sauce is in the same dish, you risk splashing it about; so I usually keep it separate.

6) *Gravy in a saucepan*. You could, as so many recipes instruct, make the gravy in the roasting pan. But it's tricky to work a roux, and then to stir in liquid and keep it lump-free, over such a wide surface. A small saucepan makes the job much easier; and it also means that the gravy, if simmered for a while, does not evaporate so fast.

7) *De-greasing*. After you've got rid of a spoonful or two of fat, you'll find it hard to get at the rest without spooning up some of the precious juice as well. Try dabbing bits of paper towel on the surface; it will soak up the fat but leave the juice behind. Don't pour the fat down the sink: it will solidify and block your drain.

Here is something you can do with the liver. If you got one with the giblets. Scrape it free of stringy material; don't worry if you turn it into mush. Bubble 2 tbsps of brandy or calvados in a saucepan until it has reduced to 1 dstsp. Chop half a garlic clove and sprinkle with a little salt; reduce it to a pulp with the back of a knife. Melt a walnut-sized knob of butter over a gentle heat in a saucepan; add the garlic, and cook for 30 seconds. Turn up the heat a little, throw in the liver, and stir it around in the butter; it should cook through – going grey – in a minute. Take the pan off the heat, and stir in the brandy or calvados, with more salt if needed. Grind over black pepper, or add a pinch of cayenne. Spoon this pâté into a bowl, and put it in the fridge, where it will set. Spread the pâté thinly on toasted rounds of baguette; there should be enough for four, to go with drinks before the meal.

Roast duck

Duck is tricky to get right. I'm sorry to be pusillanimous, but I'm going to give you three options, and leave it to you to decide which method best suits your taste in cooking – or, if you're adventurous enough to try all three, which works best for you.

In all three cases, you should first prick the skin of the duck all over with a needle – you use such a fine implement because you don't want to penetrate to the flesh, causing it to release its juices. And, in all cases, keep the fat for roasting potatoes; if it pours into a roasting pan, spoon it out every so often; if it joins liquid you've been using for poaching and steaming, put the liquid in the fridge and spoon off the fat when it's settled on the surface.

Method 1 Use the method and timings for **roast chicken**, above. The books say that duck takes less time to cook: that is not my experience.

Method 2 Put the duck, breast side down, on a rack in a roasting tin, and cook it in the centre of your oven for three hours at gas mark ¼/110°C. Turn the duck on to its back, and cook it for a further half an hour at gas mark 7/220°C, or until the skin is crisp. You have to hope that this blast of heat will not dry up the breast meat too much; it may be protected by the fat that remains. But you don't want too much fat still to be there, because its absence will help you to get crispy skin.

Method 3 I don't have the energy fully to explain this version, let alone to follow it very often. Still, it does produce good results. For the complete account see *The Perfect . . .* by Richard Ehrlich (who reports version 2 as well, only with an initial temperature of 120°C – it's possible that the gas mark ¼ setting works for me because I have a hot oven), who has adapted his recipe from Julia Child's *The Way to Cook*. First you steam the duck, over water and on the hob, for 30 minutes; steaming helps to render a good deal of fat. Then, to continue the cooking, you braise the duck, breast down, in the poaching liquid plus more and with some vegetables, in a covered pan and in a gas mark 5/190°C oven, for a further 30 minutes. Then you turn up the oven by one setting to gas mark 6/200°C, uncover the pan, turn over the duck, and roast it for 20 minutes or so, until the skin goes crispy. You may find that the skin crisps more easily with the braising liquid, from which you can make a sauce, removed from the oven.

Roast turkey

A cooked turkey with a moist breast is one of the holy grails of cooking. It's hard enough to produce a tender chicken breast at the end of an hour and a half in the oven; a turkey may be in there for three hours or longer. You see all sorts of suggestions: fast cooking, slow cooking, covering the breast or whole bird in foil (forget that one), covering the breast in buttered muslin. The technique I like best, probably because it's the least fussy, is one recommended by Nigella Lawson (*How to Eat*): you roast the bird breast side down, turning it over only for the last half-hour of cooking. That way, the fat in the turkey's back percolates down towards the breast, where it's most needed. Use the temperatures recommended above for roast chicken; but, as turkeys increase in size, the average time it takes to cook each 500 g decreases. Lawson gives two hours for a 4.5 kg turkey, and three and a half hours for a 9 kg one. But do check that the juices from the thickest part of the thigh run clear.

Other poultry and game

The smaller birds need gentle browning in a frying pan first, because they won't have very long in the oven. After browning, a poussin will cook in 20 minutes to half an hour; a pigeon about the same; a pheasant about 40 minutes.

Roast pork

HOW TO MAKE IT
(loin)

Get your butcher to score the rind; or do it yourself, with a stanley knife, cutting vertical lines about a finger's-width apart. Pat the rind dry, and rub a little sunflower or vegetable oil, along with salt (and pepper if you like), into it.[1 – see WHY YOU DO IT] Season the meat as well, and put it in a roasting pan into a gas mark 7/220°C oven for 25 minutes,[2] then turn down the oven to gas mark 3/160°C.[3] Allow 25 minutes for each 500 g of pork, with an extra 25 minutes. Rest the meat for at least 20 minutes before carving.

WHY YOU DO IT

1) *Crackling*. The drying, scoring and salting all help to produce crispy crackling, as does the initial high oven temperature. However, if you have a small joint, you may find that the crisping has not taken place by the time the meat is ready. I don't advise turning up the oven again; while meat tolerates an initial searing, it dries out quickly if subjected to high heat once already cooked. You could remove the crackling and put it back in the oven while the meat rests; or you could start off the crackling process before you roast the meat, by putting the joint rind side up under a hot grill (or rind side down in oil in a frying pan), until the crackling starts to blister.

2) *Searing*. Unless it is a small joint, without much fatty protection, pork will take a higher initial heat than will chicken.

3) *Cooking*. The lean meat from the loin of pork – that includes chops – is hard to cook well. Pork, like chicken, has to be cooked thoroughly before it's safe to eat: and again, as with the lean meat of chicken, there is only a brief interval between the moment when it is ready and the moment when it dries out.

(shoulder, spare rib roast,[1 – see WHY YOU DO IT] belly)
**Treat the rind as above. Then put the joint, rind
side up, under a hot grill, until there is blistering;
or heat a frying pan with a little oil and put the
joint in it rind side down, manoeuvring it until
every bit of it starts to blister.[2] Put the joint in a
roasting pan on to the floor of an oven set at gas
mark ¼ / 110°C, for seven hours (for a 1.5 kg piece
of pork belly) or longer;[3] you can sit it on a bed of
sliced onions, which you discard at the end. Hugh
Fearnley-Whittingstall says that an 8 kg shoulder
will tolerate 24 hours of cooking.**

VARIATIONS

These are forgiving cuts, with plenty of fat and connective
tissue; I like to cook them slowly until the meat is exceptionally soft. But you could use the higher temperatures and
faster timings given above for loin joints, and produce perfectly nice results.

Pork goes well with oriental flavourings. For his 5 kg
to 8 kg shoulder, Hugh Fearnley-Whittingstall gives the
following paste: 1 tbsp of a spice mix consisting of two star
anise, 2 tsps fennel seeds, ½ cinnamon stick, four cloves and
1 tsp black peppercorns, all ground; stirred into a mixture
of five garlic cloves (crushed and made into a paste), a 5 cm
piece of ginger (also made into a paste), 2 tsps dried chilli
flakes, 2 tsps ground ginger, 1 tbsp brown sugar, ½ tbsp salt,
1 tbsp sunflower or groundnut oil, and 1 tbsp soy sauce.
You're most likely to have a smaller joint than the one in his

recipe, so you can revise these quantities accordingly – and anyway, it's the kind of list you can adapt to your own taste.

You're often told that salt draws out the moisture from meat. But brining – immersing in a salt solution – can make tough cuts of meat juicier and more tender. Fergus Henderson has a lovely recipe for brined and roasted pork belly (from *Nose to Tail Eating*).

Henderson's brine includes four litres of water, 400 g caster sugar, 600 g sea salt, 12 juniper berries, 12 cloves, 12 black peppercorns and three bay leaves: put the ingredients in a pot and bring to the boil, in order to get the sugar and the salt to dissolve. Allow to cool. Put the meat into a china, glass or other non-reactive container, cover with brine, put a lid on, then leave it in a cool place for three days (your fridge may not be big enough; I use my cellar). Take the meat out; dry the skin and treat with oil and salt as above; roast in a medium to hot oven (I should guess he means gas mark 6/200°C), allowing one and a half to two hours for a 2 kg joint. Henderson says that you could start or finish the cooking under the grill, in order to crisp the skin.

Henderson's recipe worked very well when I tried it; it worked even better when I started the pork at gas mark 6/ 200°C, and then, after 45 minutes, reduced the temperature to gas mark 1/140°C. I cooked a 2 kg piece of belly for two and a half hours. It was meltingly tender. The only disappointment was that the crackling wasn't crisp, even though I had given it a grilling first. I might have removed it and put it on a baking try into a hot oven (200°C or higher), but I had something else in the oven, at a lower temperature, by then.

I am sure that the brined pork would be beautiful, too, if cooked for seven hours or more, as above. If you're serving it for lunch, though, you might not want to get up at 6am to put it in the oven.

ACCOMPANIMENTS

Mashed potato (page 173) is perfect with pork, I think. And green vegetables: particularly cabbage, greens or spinach. Pork doesn't give you much help in making a gravy, so I prefer to eat it with mustard. For apple sauce: peel, core and slice up apples, putting them into water acidified with lemon juice to prevent discoloration; drain and put them into a pan above a heat disperser on a low heat, and cover; as they cook, judge whether you need to add more liquid (try a little orange juice); cook until you have a rough purée, and add caster sugar to taste. It's up to you whether you serve it hot; it doesn't have to be.

WHY YOU DO IT

1) *Spare rib and spare ribs*. A spare rib cut, from which your butcher might sell spare rib chops, is not the same as the spare ribs commonly used for barbecuing. The former comes from the shoulder; the latter are trimmed from the belly.

2) *The dream ticket*. You don't have to sacrifice crispy skin to slow-roasting. The initial blast of heat starts off the crisping, which continues even in a very low oven.

You could also begin roasting for the first 25 minutes in a gas mark 7/220°C oven (see page 210) – a procedure that has the advantage of causing more browning reactions – but I think that these cuts are perfectly delicious without them. In exchange for the browning, you sacrifice some moisture from the meat. That sacrifice is not worth making with a slow-roasted belly.

3) *Hold the water*. Recipes may tell you to put the joint on a rack above hot water. As I explain on page 23, I think that steam in the oven is more likely to dry out meat than to keep it moist. I experimented with two pieces of pork belly from the same source: I cooked the first on its own, and the second above water. The second was drier.

Roast lamb

HOW TO MAKE IT
(leg or shoulder)

Set the oven at gas mark 8/230°C.[1] – see WHY YOU DO IT Strip as much rosemary or thyme as you like from its branches, and add enough olive oil to make a spreadable marinade. Add salt and pepper, and massage the mixture over your meat.[2] Chop a head of garlic in half, and put the halves under the meat in a roasting pan. Put in the oven; after 25 minutes, turn down the temperature to gas mark 3/160°C. Cooking time: the initial 25 minutes plus 15 minutes for each 500 g meat.[3] When it's done to your liking (some like it pink; others,

grey), remove the meat to a warm plate and leave to rest for at least 20 minutes before carving. Tip the pan juices into a bowl; skim off the fat.[4] Deglaze the roasting pan with wine, vinegar or stock (see under "Roast chicken", above); warm through this sauce with the pan juices to accompany the meat.

VARIATIONS

If you want more, and thicker, gravy, follow the instructions under **Roast chicken** above.

How about caper sauce? Nigella Lawson's recipe (from *How to Eat*) is a kind of **béchamel** (see page 50) with two parts milk to one part lamb stock (chicken stock would be acceptable); you add capers from a jar, without rinsing them of their vinegar.

Lamb boulangère (again, shoulder or leg) is cooked above sliced potatoes. The lamb is often boned; I'm not sure what benefit that brings. Smear the base and sides of a roasting pan with a walnut-sized knob of butter. Peel and finely slice potatoes (maincrop or new) into a bowl of cold water (to prevent discoloration); drain and mix with salt and finely chopped garlic, as well as (optional) thyme or rosemary and chopped onion; tip into the roasting pan, and put the meat on top. Add stock or water; it doesn't need to cover the potatoes, but might come halfway up them. Put in the oven at a low heat (gas mark 2/150°C) for two hours, or until the lamb is ready; remove the lamb to a warm plate to rest, and, in the 20 minutes that it is doing so, cook the potatoes at gas mark 7/220°C to brown them.

As I say elsewhere (page 180), this is the one instance when I like the somewhat slimy texture that roast potatoes have when you don't parboil them first. But, if it isn't to your taste, you could blanche the slices in boiling water for three minutes before putting them in the roasting pan.

Shoulder of lamb, with its high fat content, will respond particularly well to slow-roasting, as in the recipe for belly pork above (gas mark ¼/110°C for seven hours or more). Lamb shanks, too, are delicious when prepared in this way.

ACCOMPANIMENTS

Lamb and **gratin dauphinois** (page 183) are a dream combination. Roast potatoes are almost as good. Lamb goes very well with white beans or chickpeas; if you like, you could mash the chickpeas with some garlic, salt and oil to make a kind of hummus. Spinach is another happy partner.

WHY YOU DO IT

1) *Searing*. For the point of this high heat, see **Roast chicken** above. Lamb, which has more fat than do chicken and pork, can take a 25-minute blast of 220°C without losing too much of this lubrication.

2) *Don't mess about the meat*. I have got fed up with recipes that invite you to make incisions in the lamb and stick slivers of garlic and rosemary, and sometimes anchovy, into them. The garlic sticks to my fingers, and then the rosemary does too; I spend ages faffing around, irritatedly conscious that more dextrous cooks can probably perform

this task in less than half the time I'm taking. Never again. I think I have a culinary justification for giving up preparing lamb in this way: moisture seeps out of the incisions. So the flavourings go on the surface.

The advice about the cut bulb of garlic comes from Nigel Slater (*Appetite*). You can squeeze some of the pulp with a wooden spoon into the sauce. Instead of, or in addition to, garlic, you could put slices of onion under the meat.

3) *Timings*. The books tell you that these timings and temperatures should produce lamb cooked to medium. For pink meat, allow 12 minutes for each 500 g; for well-done, 20 minutes. Again: you cannot guarantee that your oven or joint of meat will conform to the theories. Keep checking.

4) *Skim the fat*. Lamb has a good deal of fat and, except in the case of a **lamb boulangère** (see page 215), I don't like to eat too much of it with my meal.

Roast beef

HOW TO MAKE IT

My best advice, for all cuts, is to follow the timings and temperatures I gave for lamb (page 214). If you keep the temperature high throughout, as some recipes advise, you risk expelling the fat that gives the meat a tender feel in the mouth. Wipe the meat dry with paper towels, then rub a little oil over it (the oily layer cuts down the

evaporation of liquid, but if you were to rub it on to a wet piece of meat it would be less effective), and some salt and pepper, even though they will hardly penetrate.

Beef will be all the better for a rest of half an hour after cooking, and that delay has the advantage of giving you time to bake a Yorkshire pudding. If the batter occupies the top shelf of the oven, though, getting the roast potatoes crisp will be a challenge – unless you have two ovens. Perhaps you could try this: start the potatoes on the top shelf, above the beef; when you take out the beef, turn up the oven to gas mark 7/220°C, put the potatoes on to the middle shelf and the pudding pan with its fat on top; add the batter when the fat is hot (see below). There's a good chance that the potatoes will crisp up.

Yorkshire pudding

HOW TO MAKE IT
For 4 to 6
112 g self-raising flour
1 egg
A little salt
280 ml milk[1] – see WHY YOU DO IT

Put milk, egg and salt into a bowl. Add flour, a tablespoon at a time, whisking gently with a balloon whisk as you do so.[2] The batter should have

the consistency of single cream. Allow to rest for
at least half an hour before using.[3]

Heat the oven to gas mark 7/220°C, and put a
layer of dripping (appropriate if the pudding is to
accompany roast beef), lard or sunflower oil into
a roasting pan; put the pan into the oven for at
least five minutes, to get the fat hot.[4] Add the
batter, and cook for about half an hour. This
should be enough for four to six people.

WHY YOU DO IT

1) *The ingredients*. The quantities I've given used to be
the standard ones. But they've gone right out of fashion.
Now you see recipes involving two or even three eggs, or
two eggs plus two yolks, or two eggs plus two whites. I
think that these batters can be a bit rich, and I prefer, for
Yorkshire pudding and for pancakes, the original version.
Self-raising flour will, obviously, help the batter to rise; for
pancakes, use plain flour.

2) *Gentle mixing*. Recipes often tell you to make a well in
the flour, and break the egg into it. They don't often give
the follow-up instruction that is the point of the procedure:
you add a little milk to the egg, then stir in the nearby flour,
then add some more milk, gradually working your way in a
larger circle around the flour so that you stir in only the
flour that the liquid will accommodate. Otherwise, you
have to stir all the flour when there is only a little liquid in
the bowl.

Adding the flour to the liquid is the easier way round.

Even carefully working your way around the bowl as described above, you're going to have to bash up the flour a bit, and that will develop gluten, which will make the batter rubbery. You might be worried that you'll create a lumpy liquid if you try to merge a little flour with a lot of milk. Don't worry about a few lumps: you won't notice them once the batter's cooked.

It's not worth getting out a piece of electrical equipment to make a batter. An electric whisk will give the flour a more aggressive going over than is good for it.

3) *Resting*. You don't get much chance to relax when you cook a roast meal, but both the meat (after it's cooked) and the batter (before) should. Resting a batter gives the process that will take place during cooking – the swelling of the starch molecules – a head start, and as a result you'll produce a more cohesive batter. Stir the batter a little when you're ready to use it, to disperse any lumps that have settled on the bottom: it may, because the starch has swelled, have thickened slightly.

4) *Hot fat*. To check if it is hot enough, drop in a teaspoon of batter. It should sizzle fiercely, because you want the pudding quickly to form a crusty base. Don't use a thick oven dish: it won't produce a crispy batter.

If, at the end of all this, your beef has been out of the oven for 40 minutes, don't worry. It will be perfect.

Pot-roasting

This works particularly well for poultry and game. Use a heavy casserole, such as a Le Creuset, and brown your chicken or whatever in a little oil. Take it out, throw away the oil (not down the sink), add a little more, and add flavourings for your sauce: chopped onion, celery, carrot, garlic. Soften the vegetables in the oil, then add some wine or vermouth or vinegar, bubble a little, and add half a ladleful of stock or water. Return the bird to the casserole, put on the lid, and cook either on the hob or in the oven. About an hour for a 1.5 kg chicken should be about right; test in the usual way (see page 203) to see whether it's cooked.

These heavy casseroles take a while to heat up. Start the oven at gas mark 6/200°C; if, after 20 minutes, the liquid is bubbling away, you can turn the dial right down to gas mark 1/140°C.

I know that I told you above to be wary of the effect on food of steam. It may not lower the temperature of an oven to steaming point, but will nevertheless cook the food faster than you might like. But in pot-roasting, you're cooking food inside a sealed pot; in theory the temperature in your casserole should not get much higher than boiling point, whatever the temperature outside. Nevertheless, I would not want to test that theory by leaving the oven at 200°C. Once the liquid in the casserole is simmering, an oven temperature of 140°C will continue the cooking process perfectly well.

When the chicken is tender, remove it to a warm

plate, and leave it to rest, as you would a roast, for 15 minutes or so. Sieve the sauce; spoon off some of the fat from the surface, or dab it off with paper towels. Warm it through in a saucepan, check the seasoning, and serve with the chicken. For variations on this sauce, see **Gravy**, page 199.

Stews

We used to call them casseroles. They were 1970s dinner party staples; you could cook them from all-colour recipe paperbacks that Marks & Spencer sold for less than a fiver. But the term "casserole" has come to seem, like prog rock and the bubble perm, rather naff.

They're stews now. "Stew" has a pleasingly unpretentious sound; in the same spirit, we prefer to invite people for "supper" rather than dinner. Not everyone, though, accepts stew as the generic description of meat (or fish) cooked in a bath of liquid. The meat in a stew, Shaun Hill (*How to Cook Better*) asserts, is not browned before simmering; if it were, it would be part of a braise. This is not a distinction that many others make, even though the most famous dish with stew in the title – Irish stew – does not include browned meat. Richard Olney was not aware of a no-browning rule when he wrote *Simple French Food*: "nearly all stews", he advised, "belong to the branch commonly (some say incorrectly) known as sautés" – the meat and vegetables are given an initial colouring in fat.

The difference between a stew and a braise, according to several writers other than Shaun Hill, is that a stew contains more liquid. If you don't brown the meat or vegetables, but cover them instead with water or marinade and cook them in a covered pot, you're preparing a daube. If you follow that procedure, but then make a sauce with a roux and the cooking liquid, and thicken that sauce further with cream and egg yolks, you're making a blanquette. Dishes such as coq au vin and boeuf Bourguignon, as well as carbonnades and navarins, are stews of the sauté type.

Sorry. This theorising won't get the dinner – supper, I should say – ready. I'm going on about the terms because they describe three basic techniques, on which every stew recipe is an improvisation.

HOW TO MAKE IT
Lamb or beef, for 6
1.2 kg cubed meat[1] – see WHY YOU DO IT
Oil for frying
4 onions, chopped
4 carrots, chopped
2 sticks celery, chopped
2 cloves garlic, chopped
Glass white wine
Stock (see page 55)
Herbs (parsley, bay leaf, thyme)
Salt
150 g mushrooms, sliced

Warm the oil in a frying pan, and add the onions, carrots and celery, stirring them over a medium to low heat until they soften and take on some

colour; it may take 20 to 30 minutes. As the vegetables approach readiness, add the garlic and stir
it in, giving it time to soften.[2] Remove them with
a slotted spoon, leaving behind as much oil as
possible, and put them in a heavy casserole.

Pat the meat dry with paper towels, and dust it
with salted flour;[3] turn the heat up under the frying pan, and, adding more oil if necessary, brown
the meat, in batches, transferring it to the casserole when ready.[4] If there is surplus oil at the end,
throw it away. Put the frying pan back on the
heat, and pour in the wine, scraping the sediments at the bottom of the pan to incorporate
them into the sauce.[5] When the wine has reduced
by about half, pour it into the casserole. Now add
cold stock barely to cover the contents of the
casserole,[6] along with herbs and a little more salt.
Put the lid on.

Put the stew into the centre of a gas mark 1/
140°C oven. After an hour, check it; if nothing is
happening, leave it, but check it again every half
an hour. You want the gentlest possible simmer.[7] If
the liquid is bubbling too fast, lower the heat
and/or put the casserole in a lower part of the
oven. Don't cook the stew beyond the point at
which the meat feels tender when you prod it
with a knife or fork. After the pot has come to a
simmer, that point may arrive in an hour (lamb)
or hour and a half (beef). If you have time, leave
the stew to rest for half an hour after taking it out
of the oven.[8]

Strain the sauce through a sieve into a saucepan.

Separate the meat from the vegetables and herbs, return it to the casserole, and put the lid back on; push down gently on the vegetables and herbs to expel the juice into the saucepan, and then discard them.[9] Spoon off the fat that rises to the surface of the sauce, or dab it off with paper towels. Put the saucepan on to a low heat, to one side of it; at the side away from the heat you will get a skin, which you can remove. Repeat this process with the skin as it reforms over 20 minutes or so.[10]

Meanwhile, sauté the mushrooms in some butter (see page 157).

The sauce will probably be more plentiful, and thinner, than you want. Turn up the heat to reduce it. Check the seasoning. Return the sauce, with the mushrooms, to the casserole, and reheat, covered, very gently. When it is thoroughly warmed through, serve.

VARIATIONS

All that effort just to make a stew? As I said in the introduction (page 11 onwards), there are plenty of more abbreviated stew recipes, and they'll turn out fine. But cookery books, which are only too happy to give you complicated sets of instructions for fancy dishes, rarely pay the same attention to detail when it comes to guidance on simple ones. If you can be bothered, you'll appreciate the benefits of degreasing and skimming the sauce.

The first possible variation is to dispense with the flour. There's a trade-off between the thickness of the sauce and flavour, which flour dulls. Leave it out, if you don't mind a runny sauce. A sauce with no flour is easier to degrease. It can be thickened at the end of cooking with cornflour or arrowroot; I think that these agents add a null quality, but in that view I differ with a more prestigious judge, Raymond Blanc.

You could leave out the wine, or use a different alcohol: brandy or calvados, bubbled until they lose their harsh, spirity edge (see page 39); beer or cider.

Add some lardons or chopped-up bits of streaky bacon. Fry them, very gently, first; the vegetables and then the meat will have some bacon fat to fry in.

To the sauce, add tomatoes: either fresh ones, skinned (see page 191) and chopped (almost all recipes tell you to deseed them, but I never bother), or tinned. In carbonnade of beef, the meat is cooked either entirely in beer, or in a mixture of beer and stock; stout works well. Tomato ketchup is a good complement to a rich, fatty cut of beef such as oxtail.

Try Worcester or soy sauce; remember that both are salty. Lamb goes well with lemon and orange – include peelings of zest; and it goes well, too, with spices such as cumin and coriander, which you fry with the vegetables.

Ingredients added towards the end of cooking, as the mushrooms are here, are known as the garnish. Other nice garnishes include baby onions (softened gently in butter), lardons of bacon or pancetta (also fried), and croutons – the easiest way to make which is to toss cubes of bread in olive oil, spread them out on a baking tray, and put them in the oven until golden.

A less la-di-da kind of garnish is the dumpling. Usually

dumplings contain just over two parts self-raising flour to one part suet: Fergus Henderson's recipe (*Nose to Tail Eating*), which makes plenty of dumplings for six, gives 100 g of suet, 225 g of self-raising flour, salt and a beaten egg: you mix them together, adding a little water to bring the mixture to the consistency of a sticky dough, shape them into walnut-sized balls, and cook for about 10 minutes. You could poach or steam them, in a covered pan containing water; or you could ladle into the pan some of the liquid from the stew, put in the dumplings, cover, and simmer.

That kind of dumpling seems to be the right match for a beef stew. Dried beans or chickpeas suit lamb particularly well. Cook them apart (see page 138 and 163), and add them at the same time as you would any other garnish.

Some fresh herbs could go into the stew just before serving: parsley, say, or tarragon, or oregano.

If you don't want a garnish, but have skimmed the sauce, consider adding a knob of butter, away from the heat, just before serving. It will enrich the dish.

Boeuf Bourguignon belongs to the family of stews in which the meat has an initial bath in a marinade. There are many strict and elaborate recipes, so let us take comfort – as we have to do so often – in Elizabeth David's observation that "Such dishes do not, of course, have a rigid formula." You might put your beef into a marinade consisting of a bottle of red wine, a chopped onion, a tablespoon of olive oil, some herbs, and salt. (The wine might be a Burgundy or a Côtes du Rhône. I'm sure you don't want to use an expensive one; but don't use one you would find undrinkable.) Leave it overnight. The next day, remove the meat and pat it dry. Follow the basic recipe as above, using the marinade, sieved, as the cooking liquid, and topping it up with stock if necessary. Try to include bacon in the initial preparation; baby onions are the best garnish.

WHY YOU DO IT

1) *What meat?* The meats for stewing are the "tough" cuts: among them chuck or stewing steak, oxtail, shin of beef; or shanks, shoulder, middle neck and scrag end of lamb. They come from the bits of the animal that get the most exercise, and that have muscles with a strong re-inforcement of connective tissue. This tissue, consisting largely of a protein called collagen, is very difficult to chew; but, subjected to slow cooking, the collagen breaks down into succulent gelatine.

The proteins in muscle fibres toughen up, expelling all their moisture, if cooked for too long. That's why we fry or grill lean cuts such as fillet steak as quickly as possible. If we stewed them for any length of time they would become – in spite of their liquid surroundings – unbearably dry. In tough cuts, the fibres dry out too, of course; but they become looser, and their gelatinous lubrication gives them a tender feel in the mouth.

2) *Veg or meat first?* If you start with the onions and carrots, you're using fresh oil, which you can then use to brown the meat (put the vegetables in a sieve, and drain the oil back into the frying pan). If you start with the meat, you might degrade the oil at the high temperature you need for browning; the flavour of it will then taint the vegetables.

228

A surprising number of writers imply that you can brown meat in a pan that already contains vegetables. To brown, the meat needs close contact with a high heat, so you will have to turn up the heat and push the vegetables aside in order to allow the meat access to the hot oil on the base of the pan. Already cooked, those vegetables will burn. Take out the veg first, making sure that no trace of it remains: any charred material will spoil your sauce.

3) *Dried, floured and salted.* You dry the meat for two reasons: to prevent an explosive reaction as it hits the fat; and to prevent the flour from sticking to it in clumps. Put about three tablespoons of flour into a bowl, and turn the meat in it; lift out the meat and shake off the excess flour before frying.

You may have heard that you shouldn't salt meat before cooking it: unless you don't like salt, ignore that advice (see pages 37 and 264).

4) *The sealing theory is porous.* The notion of frying meat in order to "seal in" the juices is scarcely more up to date in cooking than bloodletting is in medicine; but you still see references to "sealing" in recipe books. That sizzling noise in the pan? It's the water from the meat being vaporised as it reacts with the pan and the hot oil. Have a look at a piece of browned meat. Does its surface appear to you to be water-impermeable?

The high heat required for browning actually causes rapid fluid loss. Cooks usually think that the sacrifice is worthwhile, though, in exchange for the flavours from the

Maillard reactions, the complex and tasty results of the collision at high temperatures of carbohydrates and amino acids in proteins.

If you fry in butter, you risk burning it at the high temperature you need. Olive oil will cope with a higher temperature; vegetable or groundnut or sunflower oil, lard and dripping, higher still. Heat the oil, and drop in a tiny piece of bread; if it sizzles angrily, you're ready to go. Put in a few pieces of meat at a time — too many, and the temperature will drop.

You know that the temperature is too low if water floods the pan: the moisture should have vaporised instantly. The meat should be brown on one side in a minute or less; turn it once, and remove when the other side has browned.

A medium heat should be enough to get the results you want. You may be going to throw away some of this oil and skim off some more; but if it is burned, it will impart some of its burned flavour to the meat. As you proceed, you'll find that the pan becomes more and more efficient at browning, and that you can turn down the temperature.

5) *Deglazing the pan, and reducing the wine*. See **Stocks**, page 61, and **Roast chicken**, page 199. If you're going to reduce the sauce later, reducing the wine may not be so important at this point; but it will comprise a higher proportion of the finished sauce if you don't do it now.

6) *Drowning the meat*. So long as it is submerged in liquid, the meat will not have to endure a temperature much higher than 100°C (although some of the contents of the sauce may raise the boiling point).

7) *Gently does it*. The heat and rollicking motion of the liquid in a rapidly boiling stew will drive out moisture, as well as fat and gelatine, from the meat; you'll be left with lumps of dry fibre. If, at the end of cooking, you need to boil the sauce to reduce it, remove the meat first.

With the surface of the stew showing only the mildest evidence of disturbance, the temperature of the liquid may be several degrees below the 100°C boiling point (if you put it on the hob and turned up the heat, it would take a little while to come to a proper boil). The loss of those few degrees, as well as of a good many agitated bubbles, will give you a much more beguiling result.

I used to bring stews to simmering point on the hob, then put them in the oven. Harold McGee has reformed me. You just have to learn not to be dismayed to find, particularly if you have a heavy casserole, that the stew you put in a 140°C oven an hour ago is showing little evidence of progression.

You needn't worry. There is progress. Meat starts to cook when it reaches about 50°C; its collagen starts to dissolve at 70°C. Even at below 50°C, the gentle heat is weakening the connective tissue, reducing the time the meat will have to spend at temperatures that will dry it out.

As soon as the meat in a stew is tender, stop cooking. It won't get any more tender, but it will get more dry.

8) *Resting*. The meat will reabsorb some liquid as it relaxes in the cooling stew. An overnight rest will do your stew even more good than a half-hour one: the flavours will develop; and fat will rise to the surface and solidify, so that you can remove it easily.

9) *Disposable vegetables*. Keep them if you like. But they have already done their job, imparting flavour to the sauce. I think that carrots from which all the flavour has departed are particularly uninteresting things to put in your mouth.

10) *Skimming sauce*. A skin forms on the cooler part of the surface: it consists of fat and of protein particles, the removal of which will give you a less greasy, purer-tasting sauce.

Allow the skin to thicken a little, then use a teaspoon to pull it to the side of the pan and remove it. More skin will probably form; remove that too, and repeat until your patience runs out.

Chicken stew

You brown the pieces of chicken first, but more gently than you do beef or lamb: chicken is more delicate; also, it doesn't throw out so much water, so you don't need a high heat to ensure that it fries rather than stews.

A chicken stew is not the same as a **chicken sauté** (see page 259).

Here, off the top of my head, is a recipe: it has something in common with chicken Basquaise, plus a goulashy note.

For 4

4 chicken legs[1] – see WHY YOU DO IT
Olive oil
2 onions, chopped
2 red peppers, quartered, deseeded and sliced
2 cloves garlic, chopped
½ glass white wine
400 g can tomatoes, or 6 fresh tomatoes,
skinned and chopped (see page 191)
1 tsp paprika
Salt
2 tbsps sour cream

Pour a layer (1 to 2 tbsps) of oil into a frying pan. Over a gentle heat, soften the onion and garlic for 10 to 15 minutes, until mellow. Remove them with a slotted spoon to a sieve, to allow some oil to drain back into the pan; when drained, transfer them to a casserole.

Making sure there is no trace of onion or garlic left in the pan, heat the oil again, adding more if necessary (the chicken skin will exude some of its own fat), and colour the chicken legs, salted, in it; you are aiming to get them nicely browned with about five minutes' cooking on each side.[2] Remove them to the casserole; pour away the fat.[3]

On a medium heat, pour the wine into the pan, scrape and stir into it any sediments from the browning process you can find, and reduce this liquid by about half; pour it into the casserole,

233

with the tomatoes (you can bash up tinned ones with a wooden spoon as they heat in the pan), peppers (which, not having a harsh flavour, don't need pre-softening), paprika and a little more salt. Bring the contents of the casserole to a gentle simmer, cover, and continue to cook for about 45 minutes on a very low heat; or put the casserole into an oven at gas mark 1/140°C, or at a setting that will maintain a gentle simmer.

At the end of cooking, remove the chicken to a warm plate, pour the sauce into a saucepan, then put the chicken back into the casserole and cover. (You could return it to the oven, turned off.) Put the saucepan on to a high heat to reduce and thicken the sauce, which will need stirring if it is not to catch. When the sauce has the consistency you want, turn off the heat, check the seasoning, and stir in the cream; pour the sauce over the chicken. Rice is the obvious accompaniment; I'd also enjoy this stew with mashed potato.

VARIATIONS

In this recipe, the liquid might not cover the chicken – so perhaps you should call it a braise. As a moistening agent, you could use, instead of tomatoes, some chicken stock, in which case you might want a thickener for the sauce. Dust the chicken with flour before frying it. Or you could braise the chicken in just a little liquid – that provided by the wine, for instance, or even by a tablespoon of vinegar; the chicken will exude juices too. At the end of cooking, finish the sauce with a little butter or cream.

Add dried porcini mushrooms and their soaking liquid to the braise. Add some sautéed fresh mushrooms at the end. Add fresh herbs: thyme and tarragon are particularly good.

Coq au vin was ubiquitous in the days when we referred to stews as casseroles, and, perhaps for that reason, it has fallen out of fashion somewhat. A revival is due. The bird should be a cockerel, but you'll probably have to make do with chicken.

With one, jointed chicken, use a whole bottle of Burgundy or Côtes du Rhône, as well as a double measure of brandy. Follow the basic beef or lamb stew recipe above: fry onion, carrots and garlic; flour, salt and brown the chicken, and put it into the casserole (but leave out the breast portions); pour away excess fat from the frying pan; bubble the brandy in a small saucepan until it reduces and sweetens, and deglaze the frying pan with it; pour the brandy plus the wine into the casserole with the chicken and vegetables. Bring the casserole to a simmer and cook for 30 minutes; add the chicken breasts and cook for a further 15 minutes. Strain the sauce, skim and reduce it as in the basic stew recipe on page 223: you want quite a concentrated reduction.

For a garnish, fry lardons, as well as mushrooms and/or baby onions. Coq au vin is often served with fried bread: one slice, crusts removed, for each person. As you probably know, bread in a frying pan absorbs a heart-stopping quantity of butter; you could lightly butter one side, put the other on a buttered piece of foil, and bake it. It's not the same, though.

Nigella Lawson has a recipe for chicken cooked slowly

with lemon and garlic. You cut the lemons (two) into pieces, mix them with a jointed chicken, a head of garlic cloves, seasoning, 150 ml white wine and some olive oil, and bake everything slowly in a roasting pan covered with foil. Half an hour before the end of cooking, you uncover the pan and turn up the oven temperature, to brown the meat. The drawback of this method, I think, is that browning meat at the end of cooking can expel the last drops of moisture from it; an initial searing expels some juices but leaves behind plenty, some of which, with luck and care, you can retain. So I'd brown the chicken first, in a frying pan; then mix it with the lemon, garlic, salt and a little more oil (having thrown away the first lot) in a roasting pan, cover the pan tightly with foil (or simply use a heavy casserole) and bake at gas mark 1/140°C for about an hour and a half. You might want to strain the sauce into a saucepan and reduce it.

The best of all chicken and garlic dishes, and one quite unlike any other stew or sauté recipe, is chicken with 40 cloves of garlic. My favourite way of cooking it is the simplest. Put a chicken, cut up into pieces (or just buy thighs and drumsticks), in a heavy casserole. Separate, but do not peel, the cloves of four heads of garlic (it has to be good garlic; and, of course, it has to be a good chicken), and add them, along with salt, and thyme if you like. Pour in a generous glug of olive oil – a good 150 ml. Mix everything well with your hands.

It's important that the casserole should have a good seal, so that the juices don't evaporate. Make a paste with flour and a little water, forming it into a thin sausage and placing it around the rim of the casserole; jam the lid on top. Put the casserole in a gas mark 4/180°C oven for an hour and a half; you could turn down the heat to 1/140°C at the point when you guess that the chicken is cooking – but don't break the seal to have a look. As you pull off the lid at the table, you release a fabulous aroma. You can eat the garlic, squeezed out of the hulls, with the chicken, or spread it on bits of toast or on potatoes.

WHY YOU DO IT

1) *Forgiving legs.* The legs and wings of chicken take best to stewing, and are tolerant of most treatments. You don't have to handle them with the kid gloves you need when dealing with beef and lamb (see page 231); slow-heating and complete submergence of the meat are not essential.

If I buy a whole chicken for a stew or a braise (or for grilling), I get my butcher to joint it. The task takes him about a minute; it takes me at least a quarter of an hour of effortful hacking.

For reasons explained above (see **Roast chicken**, page 203, and *What meat?*, page 228), the lean breast meat cooks quickly and then dries out even more quickly; give the breasts just 15 minutes or so in the pot. Because you cannot interrupt the cooking of chicken with 40 cloves of garlic, you might prefer to use thighs and drumsticks only for that dish.

2) *Browning reactions.* What you're browning is mostly skin; but that will contribute to the flavour. The skin pro-tects the flesh, which on contact with high heat dries out and toughens unappetisingly.

3) *Disposable fat.* Regretfully, you're getting rid of fat that has flavour from the chicken and vegetables. Degreasing a stew always loses flavour; on the other hand, it loses grease. Your body will thank you.

Pork stew

Most cuts of pork are too lean to stew or braise successfully. The exceptions include belly and spare rib chops – not to be confused with spare ribs (see page 213).

A belly pork braise

HOW TO MAKE IT
For 4
900 g boneless belly pork, cubed
6 onions
As many garlic cloves as you like
2 lemons
Olive oil

Soften the onion in the oil (1 to 2 tbsps), remove it to a casserole, and sear the meat as in the lamb and beef stew recipe above. Throw away the oil. Add the garlic and the lemon, cut into quarters, to the onion and pork in the casserole. Season. Cook, covered, in a gas mark 1/140°C oven for two hours, or until the meat is meltingly tender. No degreasing and skimming here: the fattiness, cut through with lemon juice, is an important component of the dish. Serve it with something plain: rice and a green salad, perhaps.

A spare rib pork braise

HOW TO MAKE IT
For 2
2 spare rib chops
½ glass white wine
Chicken stock
1 tsp mustard
Small pot (142 ml) double cream
1 tbsp olive oil

Sear the chops, salted, in the olive oil in a frying pan. Transfer to a casserole; throw away the oil. Deglaze the frying pan with the white wine (see lamb and beef stew above), and bubble to reduce the liquid by half. Add to the meat in the casserole, along with a ladleful of stock. Put, covered, in a gas mark 1/140°C oven, or simmer very gently on the hob, for 60 to 90 minutes, or until the meat is tender. (If the pork is not entirely submerged, turn it halfway through cooking.) Remove the meat from the casserole, and pour the liquid into a saucepan; return the meat to the casserole, putting the lid back on. Reduce the liquid over a high heat until it is a little syrupy, then add cream and mustard, and bubble until it thickens. Check the seasoning. Pour back over the meat, and serve.

Cassoulet

Most cassoulet recipes are highly elaborate. Richard Olney in *The French Menu Cookbook* gives 30 ingredients and four stages of cooking. We home cooks, in love with cassoulet but too lazy, or busy, to prepare the restaurant-standard version, call again in our defence what Elizabeth David said about boeuf Bourguignon (page 227): in essence, that individual cooks interpret provincial dishes in their own ways. You're not sullying the spirit of the dish if you simplify it – quite the opposite.

More complicated and, I suppose, authentic recipes include lamb or mutton as well as pork. Three kinds of meat (and meat fat) are one too many for me.

HOW TO MAKE IT
For 6
500 g dried haricot beans
6 slices boneless pork belly, rind removed
2 onions, 1 of them studded with 2 cloves,
the other chopped
4 cloves garlic, 1 of them chopped
6 Toulouse, Cumberland or other coarse sausages
Chicken stock
6 portions of confit of goose, or confit of duck[1 – see WHY YOU DO IT]
1 tbsp or more of the fat from the goose or the duck
3 tomatoes, skinned and chopped (see page 191)
Salt, herbs
Breadcrumbs

Soak the beans in cold water overnight, drain

them, cover them in fresh water to a height about 4 cm above the top of the beans, bring to the boil, skim off the scum that rises, add the clove-studded onion with three unpeeled cloves of garlic and the rind from the pork belly, and simmer, partly covered. It's hard to predict how long the beans will take to soften; start checking after an hour, and top up the water if the topmost beans are in danger of being exposed. When they are nearly cooked, uncover the pan and allow the liquid to reduce and thicken – it will be a little sludgy. There is going to be another cooking stage, so the beans needn't be completely soft.

Tinned beans, as I've said earlier (page 141), are fine, but somewhat duller-tasting than dried ones, and with a more mealy texture. If you use them here, you'll miss out on the flavoured stock that cooking dried beans would have given you, but you'll produce a perfectly nice meal in far less time. Mix them with the pork, tomato and onion stew (see below), before covering with stock.

Meanwhile, heat the goose or duck fat in a heavy casserole, and brown the belly pork as in the basic lamb or beef stew recipe on page 223; a medium heat should do. Set the meat aside on a plate, turn down the heat, and add the sausages, keeping them moving in the casserole until they are browned in various places. Set them aside too. Add the chopped onion until it is softened (use more fat if necessary), then add the clove of chopped garlic. Let the garlic soften, then add the chopped tomatoes.

Drain the beans, reserving the liquid; keep also the garlic and the pork rind, but throw away the onion. Chop the rind into small squares, and add it, with the beans and the garlic (which will probably melt out at some point, leaving people to find the bare husks on their plates), to the onion and tomato mixture in the casserole. Add the belly pork slices, burying them among the beans. Pour in the bean liquid, along with enough stock to come to the level of the topmost beans. Add salt to taste, and herbs if you want them (bay and thyme, perhaps). Cover the surface with breadcrumbs.

Put the casserole, uncovered, in a gas mark 2/ 150°C oven. Check it after an hour: the mixture should be bubbling gently, and have a crusty surface. If it's bubbling too fast, or not at all, adjust the temperature accordingly. If all's going well, push the breadcrumbs into the bean mixture, and add another layer of them to the surface. Check again after another half an hour. Is there another crust? And is the liquid reducing and thickening? If yes to both, slice the sausage, and add it and the pieces of duck or goose to the beans;[2] you don't have to submerge them completely. Cover with another layer of breadcrumbs, and cook until this too has formed a crust. Serve.

That was quite hard work. Still, the only accompaniment a cassoulet needs is a green salad.

1) *The confit*. Advice on making your own is beyond the scope of this book. You can buy goose or duck confit (the latter is easier to find) at smart shops. Do keep all the fat, which makes particularly splendid roast and fried potatoes.

2) *Add the sausages and confit late*. Sausages go flabby and dull if stewed for too long. The duck or goose is already cooked; what it would add to the cassoulet if there from the beginning would not compensate for what it would itself lose.

A lamb daube

This is a simplified version of the Avignon daube that appears in Richard Olney's *Simple French Food*.

HOW TO MAKE IT
For 6
1.5 kg shoulder of lamb, cubed
MARINADE
1 bottle dry white wine
1 onion, chopped
1 carrot, chopped
3 cloves garlic, crushed
1 tbsp olive oil
Salt
Parsley, bay leaf
Zest from half an orange

6 shallots, chopped
3 cloves garlic, chopped
4 tomatoes, skinned and chopped
Salt

Leave the lamb in the marinade, covered, over-night (use as much wine as you need to cover it). The next day, lift out the lamb and put it in a heavy casserole; pour the marinade over it through a sieve, discarding the solid ingredients. Add the chopped shallots, garlic, tomatoes and salt (remember that the marinade contained salt). Mix everything together, and pack it in quite tightly. If the liquid doesn't cover the ingredients, add water or chicken stock. Bring the contents of the casserole, uncovered, very slowly to a simmer on top of the hob; you can allow an hour or more to get to that point.[1 – see WHY YOU DO IT] Skim off the scum as it rises. Cover, and put in a gas mark 1/ 140°C oven, or at a setting that will maintain a very gentle simmer, until the lamb is tender – start checking after another hour. Skim off what fat you can from the surface; or, better, leave overnight (in the fridge), and lift off the solidified fat the next day.[2] If you have kept the stew overnight, warm it up gently, but do not cook it again.

(I should point out that if you leave overnight a stew cooked with stock, then reheat it, you are going against the Food

Standard Agency's advice that you should not reheat a stock twice – see page 61. But I have never poisoned myself, or heard of anyone being poisoned, in this way, and I'm happy to carry on reheating my stews.)

WHY YOU DO IT
1) *Slow-heating*. See *Gently does it* (page 231). Raw meat produces a good deal more scummy material as it heats in liquid than does meat that has been browned. Warming the daube on the hob, and leaving the casserole uncovered, allows you to skim off the scum as it rises. In a covered, simmering pot, the scum would merge with the liquid (see **Stocks**, page 58).

2) *Runny liquid*. Reducing the liquid in a daube would be as beside the point as doing it when you make a Lancashire hotpot or Irish stew. You serve the meat and vegetables moistened with their cooking liquid. Noodles or rice are ideal accompaniments.

Blanquette

Again, adapted from *Simple French Food*:

HOW TO MAKE IT
For 4
4 chicken legs or
1 kg stewing veal or
4 spare rib pork chops

245

Water
1 onion stuck with 2 cloves
Herbs
Salt
Butter
Flour
Small pot (142 ml) double cream
2 egg yolks

Put the meat in a casserole, add water barely to cover, and bring slowly to a simmer, uncovered, on the hob, skimming as you do so (see *Slow-heating* under "Daube", page 245). Add the onion, herbs of choice and salt, and simmer, very gently, on the hob or in a gas mark 1/140°C oven (see *Gently does it* under beef and lamb stew, page 231). When the meat is tender (45 minutes to an hour for the chicken, perhaps 90 minutes for the veal), take it off the heat, leave it to rest for 10 to 15 minutes (see *Resting*, page 231), and remove it to a warm plate.

Sieve the liquid, discarding the onion and the herbs, into a measuring jug, and work out how much flour and butter you'll need to make a velouté – one that remains quite thin, with only a little body (see "Béchamel", page 50). Return the meat to the casserole, and cover. Make a roux, and follow the béchamel procedure. If you've used a fatty cut of veal, you may want to skim the sauce as described in the basic lamb or beef stew recipe. Check the seasoning, and pour the sauce back over the meat. Mix the egg yolks and the cream,

**and season with pepper if you like. Ladle a little of
the hot sauce into this mixture – you're getting
the eggs used to the high temperature they're
about to meet. Pour the eggs and cream into the
stew, stirring carefully and warming gently. Don't
let the sauce boil: you'll end up with a liquid
containing bits of scrambled egg. When the
sauce thickens some more, serve. (Olney's recipe
includes sorrel, which you stew in butter, then
incorporate into the cream and egg mixture.)**

Curry

What I'm getting at in this book is that most home cooks
are not interested in authenticity; they want to acquire
templates of cookery techniques and recipes, so that they
can be confident of putting together, from ingredients to
hand, something that will taste nice. I reiterate that point
here in a probably doomed attempt to mitigate the offen-
siveness of taking a liberal position on the creation of a
spicy stew. That heading, "curry", is ill-advised for a start:
its use as a generic term for spicy food is a British habit, not
an Indian one.

Buy whole spices when possible. Warm them gently in
a dry saucepan, until they give off a toasted aroma. Ground
them with a pestle and mortar, in a herb mill or in a coffee
grinder. They need a little cooking, in fat, to lose their powdery taste; but you have to do it with care, because they
burn easily. Don't fry finely ground spices such as chilli

powder and turmeric: they will certainly burn. Be aware, too, that the aroma from these toasted spices as they stew with the meat will invade your home, and linger there.

I am going to leave the composition of the spice mixture to you. For four people, you could use a 2 tbsp perm of several of the following: cumin, coriander, chilli powder, dried chilli, fresh chilli, black peppercorns, fenugreek, cloves, turmeric, cardamom (use just the seeds, or put whole pods into the stew), ginger (fresh, grated), mustard seeds, mace, nutmeg. If you can find curry leaves, you could add, say, half a dozen to the frying mixture. Stir in coriander leaves, plus more fresh chilli, at the end of cooking.

Start by frying onions – I'd include three or four – in enough oil to keep them well lubricated; or, if you have it, use ghee (Indian clarified butter). Get the onions to brown (see page 160), then add two chopped cloves of garlic, and let that take some colour too. Add your spice mixture, and cook it gently for about a minute.

Remove this mixture to a casserole, and proceed as you would with a **beef**, **lamb** or **chicken stew** (page 223 and 233), searing the meat, adding it to the casserole, and moistening with water or stock. Don't use wheat flour to thicken it – that really would give the curry an inauthentic quality. If you want a thickener, and can find chickpea flour (besan flour), try that. At the end of cooking, reduce the liquid if you want – you might need to concentrate the flavour. But don't skim off the fat. Count the calories elsewhere; this is too flavourful to waste.

For a Thai-style curry, use 2 tbsps of a paste consisting of chopped lemon grass, green chillis, shallots, lime leaves (if you can find them; or use some lime zest), coriander leaves and stems, garlic, and ginger or galangal (the latter, again not easy to find, is preferable).

This is a fresh-tasting mixture that benefits from shorter cooking. One possibility: fry the paste for a minute, add cubed chicken breast, and pour over a tin of coconut milk, or a carton of coconut cream.

Add a little salt. Simmer, uncovered, stirring occasionally; the chicken may be cooked through in 10 minutes. If the liquid is too thin, boil it hard (with the chicken removed) to reduce it, and return the chicken to warm through again. Add coriander leaves at the end.

Mince

Among the most unrealistic of all recipe book instructions are the ones that tell you to fry some onions, then add mince to the pan and brown it. At this medium temperature, water gushes out of beef, pork or lamb mince, but does not vaporise; it floods the pan, stewing rather than frying the meat. You can carry on cooking until the liquid evaporates, after which the temperature of the base of the pan will go up and browning reactions will start; but by this time the mince will be dry and tough. Also, it tends to stick to the pan, along with the onions, bits of which burn.

You may think that the texture of meat that has been minced into little pieces is not worth worrying about; but it does make a difference to the pleasure of the dish. Cook mince as carefully as you do the larger cuts of meat in a lamb or beef stew (see **What meat?**, page 228). Sear it quickly first, if you want to brown it; simmer it slowly.

Even the best pre-prepared mince will be nowhere near as good as mince the butcher prepares for you. Ask for coarsely ground chuck or stewing steak, or shoulder of lamb, or belly pork. Don't stew lean mince; it's no more suitable for long cooking than is fillet or sirloin steak. Use it for hamburgers.

The meat in a ragu alla Bolognese (Bolognese sauce) is usually beef, or a mixture of beef and pork, and is not browned, according to several authorities, Anna del Conte among them. The meat in a shepherd's pie is lamb; make it with beef, or beef and pork, and you've got a cottage pie.

I follow a few other general principles: I use fresh or tinned tomatoes and/or tomato paste in a ragu, but prefer the sweetness of ketchup in a shepherd's pie, off-setting it with the rich saltiness of Worcester or soy sauce; I use no flour in the ragu, which is a sauce that may well accompany pasta (which of course is made of flour); but I do thicken the stew for the pie. But these are not dishes – no stews are – for which the home cook need have a rigid formula.

Ragu alla Bolognese

HOW TO MAKE IT
For 4
350 g beef mince, or mix of beef and pork mince
100 g pancetta or streaky bacon, preferably

unsmoked, finely chopped
Olive oil
1 onion, chopped
1 stick celery, chopped
2 cloves garlic, chopped
½ 400 g tin of tomatoes, or 4 fresh ones,
skinned and chopped
1 dstsp tomato paste
100 ml white or red wine
Chicken stock
Salt

Put a little oil (about 1 dstsp) in a heavy saucepan or casserole, and fry the bacon gently; it will release its own fat. After three minutes or so, add the onion and celery; you probably won't need any more oil. Allow them to soften and go golden for 10 minutes or so, stirring regularly; add the garlic. Turn the heat right down, and add the mince, breaking it up with a wooden spoon. When it has separated (as I say above, you don't need to brown it), pour in the wine; give the alcohol time to simmer and reduce a little before adding the tomatoes and tomato paste, with enough stock to come up to the surface of the meat. Season, and bring the sauce very slowly to a simmer, uncovered, on the hob. Continue to simmer, at the lowest heat possible (with a heat disperser under the pot if necessary) and stirring from time to time, for about two hours, until the sauce has reduced and the meat is tender.

You could include 100 ml of double cream or milk with the liquid you add to the ragu. Many recipes include carrot with the onion, celery and garlic. Carrot undoubtedly adds sweetness to the sauce; but, as I say elsewhere, I don't particularly like finding flavourless bits of it in my meal. If you have no stock, don't use a cube, which would impart a flavour quite unlike anything you want to find in a pasta sauce; try a bought carton or jar of stock, or (used cautiously) a tin of beef consommé.

Use this sauce with spaghetti, tagliatelli or any pasta you like; use it (without cream or milk, which will be in the béchamel) in **lasagne** (page 120). A simpler version, with lamb instead of beef (though of course you can use beef if you want), forms the basis of a moussaka.

Moussaka

HOW TO MAKE IT
For 4
500 g lean minced lamb (or beef)
3 onions, chopped
3 cloves garlic, finely chopped
Olive oil
150 ml white or red wine
1 tbsp tomato paste
4 aubergines, cut in 2 horizontally,
then cut vertically in ½ cm slices
Béchamel sauce (page 50), made with 500 ml milk,
57 g butter, 57 g flour

20 g Parmesan cheese
2 eggs, beaten

Put a layer of olive oil in a frying pan, and soften the onion and garlic in it over a gentle heat, until the onion is golden – 15 to 20 minutes. Remove with a slotted spoon to a sieve, allowing the oil to drain back into the pan; then put the onions into a casserole or heavy saucepan. Form the mince into six hamburger-shaped patties. Turn up the heat under the frying pan, and brown the patties, as if you were frying hamburgers, three at a time, so that the heat of the pan is not lowered (see *The sealing theory is porous*, page 229). Discard the oil, and, on a medium heat, pour the wine into the frying pan, stirring and scraping to incorporate the residues. Pour this liquid over the meat and onions in the casserole, with the tomato paste and a little salt; a pinch or two of cinnamon, if you like it, works well in a moussaka. Heat the contents gently, breaking up the mince patties so that the uncooked meat in the centre gets heated; simmer until there is no liquid left. Test the seasoning.

The last time I made a moussaka, I didn't fry the lamb: I simply added it to the softened onions and garlic, broke it up, poured in wine, added tomato paste with salt and a pinch of cinnamon, and simmered this stew until the liquid had evaporated. It may have been just as good.

Brush the aubergine slices with olive oil, season with salt, and bake in a gas mark 6/200°C oven for 20 minutes to half an hour, or until tender. I'm sorry: I expect you'll have to do this in two batches.

Make quite a thick béchamel. Stir in the parmesan. I think that you should add some nutmeg too. Allow the sauce to cool before stirring in the eggs – so that the eggs don't curdle.

Put a layer of aubergines on to the bottom of an ovenproof dish. Pour all the meat over the top, and cover with the rest of the aubergines. Cover the whole lot with the enriched béchamel.

Bake at gas mark 4/180°C for about 30 minutes, or until the topping has puffed up, thanks to the eggs, and turned golden.

Shepherd's or cottage pie

HOW TO MAKE IT
For 4
*450 g lamb mince, or beef mince,
or beef and pork mince
100 g pancetta or streaky bacon,
preferably unsmoked, finely chopped
Olive oil
1 onion, chopped
1 stick celery, chopped
100 ml white or red wine
Chicken stock
1 tbsp tomato ketchup
1 tsp Worcester or soy sauce
Salt
900 g maincrop potatoes*

(King Edward, Maris Piper or Desirée, for example)
50 g butter

Start as with the ragu, page 251, but using a frying pan to fry the bacon, then adding the onion and celery. Form the mince into six hamburger-shaped patties, and dust them with flour. Remove the vegetables to a casserole (don't leave any specks behind), first sieving the oil back into the frying pan. Turn up the heat under the pan, and brown the mince, in two batches so that the heat of the pan is not lowered (see *The sealing theory is porous*, page 229). Remove the meat to the casserole, and break it up a little with a wooden spoon.

Discard the oil, and, on a medium heat, pour the wine into the frying pan, stirring and scraping to incorporate the residues. Pour this liquid into the casserole, with the ketchup, Worcester or soy sauce, and enough stock (about 250 ml, possibly – remember that it will reduce and thicken) to make a stew with a thick and clinging consistency. It shouldn't resemble soup. Err on the side of caution: you can add more stock later, but to reduce the sauce you'll have to put the whole stew (you can't very well drain the sauce from the mince) on a very gentle heat, uncovered, and wait for the desired reduction to take place. Be careful, too, with the salt, because Worcester and soy sauce are very salty.

Put the casserole, covered, in a gas mark 1/ 140°C oven (see *Gently does it*, page 231). As with any stew, you're aiming to warm it up slowly

255

towards the gentlest possible simmer; check on progress from time to time, and adjust the temperature accordingly. The time in the oven should be two to two and a half hours.

Peel the potatoes, cut them into slices about 1.5 cm thick, cover with cold, salted water, bring to a gentle simmer, and cook until tender. Drain them, and return them to the hot saucepan to dry. Mash them; a smooth purée doesn't seem appropriate for a shepherd's pie, so use a hand-held masher rather than a food mill or a potato ricer (see "Mashed potato", page 173).

Spread the potatoes on top of the mince, in the casserole or, if that seems too big, in some other oven dish, and dot the butter on top. Bake in a gas mark 1/140°C oven for about 20 minutes, then brown the surface under the grill.

VARIATIONS

Garlic isn't really a shepherd's pie kind of vegetable, but do include it if you like. Mushrooms work well, though: add them when the onions and celery have been cooking for 10 minutes or so, and stir them around until their juices have poured out and evaporated. Delia Smith's recipe includes 75 g of swede, chopped up small. She also suggests half a teaspoon of cinnamon (not to my taste), and a tablespoon each of parsley and thyme.

Most recipes for Bolognese sauce and shepherd's pie tell you to use meat stock, but that's not something I have around the house very often. For shepherd's pie, you could use a stock cube; I find, though, that once you get used to the taste of good, home-made stock, you go off the artificial flavour that cubes impart. Try instead, as suggested under the **ragu** recipe (page 250), stock in a carton or bottle, or a tin of consommé. If your stock is good, and if you don't fancy ketchup or Worcester sauce or herbs, you could make a perfectly delicious shepherd's pie with just the mince, the flour, the vegetables and the stock.

A cheese crust on the potato is a nice enhancement. Add a topping of grated Cheddar, or Pecorino, or Parmesan, before putting the pie in the oven.

A boiled dinner

HOW TO MAKE IT

For 6

900 g piece of gammon

3 onions, peeled

1 leek, tough green parts removed, washed (page 155)

2 carrots, peeled

Some gammon is very salty, and may need soaking in several changes of water for about 24 hours. Ask your butcher. I doubt that gammon from the supermarket will need this treatment.

Put the gammon in a stockpot. Cover with cold water. Bring slowly to a simmer; following the same principle that cautions you to heat a stew slowly (see page 231), you can allow a good half an hour for the bubbling to start. Skim off the scum, and throw in the vegetables. Simmer, uncovered and on the lowest possible heat (with just a few bubbles breaking the surface), for a further hour.

Remove the gammon from the stock, carve, and serve with mustard, mashed potato (page 173), and cabbage. You can leave the meat to rest for a while before carving; or allow it to rest in the stock after the heat has been turned off.

The purpose of the onions, leek and carrots is not to be eaten, nor to flavour the gammon (they won't), but to add flavour to the stock. The liquid may look insipid, but it will form the base of delicious soups.

You can also use the stock to make a sauce. Pour a couple of ladlefuls into a saucepan, boil it to reduce it to about half a dozen tablespoons, check that it won't be unbearably salty, and pour in a 284 ml pot of double cream, with 1 tsp of mustard. Allow this sauce to bubble and thicken a little, and serve it with the gammon. You might want boiled potatoes, or rice, instead of the mash.

Or make a béchamel-type sauce with half stock, half milk (see page 50). Say, 150 ml stock, 150 ml milk, 28 g butter, 28 g flour – or a larger quantity of all these ingredients if you like. Throw in a chopped tablespoon of parsley.

Sautés

"When dealing with chickens," Richard Olney writes in *Simple French Food*, "a sauté is not a stew, because a true sauté, it is claimed, never contacts a liquid during the cooking process." (Actually, the book has "a true stew", but that must be a misprint.) Some authors ignore this distinction, or perhaps disagree with it. Anne Willan, in *Classic French Cooking* (an old Sainsbury's book), offers a sauté of chicken with tomato: you brown the jointed chicken, then make a sauce with shallots, garlic and tomatoes; then you put the chicken in the sauce to finish cooking. You might as well call that a stew. On page 233, I did. It's related to such dishes as chicken Basquaise, with tomatoes and peppers, or chicken cacciatore, with tomatoes and olives. What I'm describing here is a dish in which you brown the chicken, remove it from the pan, pour away most of the fat, and make a sauce that accompanies the meat.

Chicken sauté

HOW TO MAKE IT
For 4
4 chicken legs
Olive oil, or butter/oil mix
200 g button mushrooms, sliced
½ clove garlic, chopped
Butter for sautéing the mushrooms
Small glass white wine

Put a small knob of butter and a little oil in a heavy frying pan (large enough to contain the four pieces of chicken) over a low heat. Season the chicken pieces with salt and (if you like) pepper.

Cook gently for 25 minutes, uncovered.[1 – see WHY YOU DO IT] Turn over; the skin should be browned and crisp. Cook for a further 10 minutes.[2] (Rearrange the chicken in the pan if some pieces are cooking faster than others.) While the chicken cooks, sauté the mushrooms and garlic with some butter in a separate pan (see page 157).

Remove the chicken to a warm plate. Pour away the fat from the chicken pan (not down the sink, where it will solidify), and deglaze it (page 61) with the wine, stirring and scraping to get the tasty residues in the pan into the sauce. Bubble the wine until it reduces by half (page 39), add the mushrooms, and check the seasoning. Serve the chicken with this mushroom sauce.

VARIATIONS

Liquids for sauces: red wine, brandy, cider, calvados, sherry, marsala, vermouth . . .; or vinegar (2 tbsps, reduced by half); or chicken stock. You could add cream (a 284 ml pot) to these deglazing liquids, or deglaze the pan with cream alone; let it bubble a little to thicken.[3] If using alcohol or stock alone, enrich it once it is reduced with a small knob of butter, added away from the heat.[4]

Other garnishes: shallots (onions would be too assertive for this dish – although small, sweet ones would be good), also softened in butter with some garlic; dried porcini, soaked in tepid water for half an hour or so and warmed through with the deglazing liquid (and their own flavourful soaking liquid); sliced, sautéed courgettes; roasted asparagus tips.

Herbs: tarragon is particularly good with chicken. Or thyme, or basil. Add them to the sauce when it is ready.

ACCOMPANIMENTS

You shouldn't want fried or roast potatoes with a creamy sauce: that gives you two kinds of mouth-coating fat to eat and digest. It's an indication of the crudity of my taste that I'm sometimes happy to face this combination.

Boiled new potatoes are ideal; if you've got plenty of sauce, boiled maincrop potatoes work well too. **Mash** (page 173) or **gratin dauphinois** (page 183) is nice if the sauce does not include cream.

If you've eaten a starter including starch, you could leave out the potatoes and go simply for a green vegetable, or perhaps a ratatouille.

WHY YOU DO IT

1) *Open pan*. Conscientiously sticking to the Olney "no cooking the sauce with the chicken" rule, how are you going to make sure that the chicken is cooked through, rather than just browned on the exterior? Olney suggests transferring it from the frying pan to a covered casserole, and finishing it in that. Richard Ehrlich recommends a sauté pan with straight sides and a lid. You brown the chicken, then lower the heat and cover the pan.

My method above comes from *Keep It Simple* by Alastair Little and Richard Whittington. It has the advantage of crisping the skin, and seems to retain more juiciness. It also has a satisfyingly pure quality: the chicken is simply sautéed (unless you insist that the term, derived from the French verb meaning to jump, involves moving something around a frying pan), not stewed or steamed.

You could cook the chicken in the oven, and make a sauce in the roasting tin. But that is roast chicken with gravy.

2) *Is it cooked?* If you're not sure, put a skewer into the thickest part of the thigh. Juices will run out. They should be clear. If there's any trace of red in them, carry on cooking.

3) *Curdling cream*. In my experience, good double cream does not curdle in these circumstances. Delia Smith writes somewhere that crème fraîche never curdles; *that* is not my experience. Factory-made crème fraîche curdles when I cook it, without fail. But rich, thick, and much more delicious farm-produced crème fraîche never does.

Cream goes from runny to stiff quite quickly, so keep an eye on it. Having some extra stock, to thin the sauce if necessary, is useful. Don't add any more alcohol: if it is not subjected to a proper reduction, it will impart a horribly raw, acidic flavour.

4) *Splitting butter*. Butter added to boiling liquid will immediately separate into its constituent parts of fat and water.

Let the sauce cool a little, and you have a chance of allowing the butter and liquid to blend into a creamy, rich emulsion. Don't heat it again.

Fried steak with a sauce made in the same frying pan (see page 267) is, of course, a sauté of this kind. You may have had it prepared at your local restaurant by a waiter with a small burner, a bottle of brandy and a smarmy manner. To do it at home, you need a gas cooker, a frying pan that you can manipulate easily, and some of that waiter's confidence. Fry the steak, pour in the brandy, turn up the gas, and tip the pan so that the flame hits the brandy and ignites it. Watch out. When the flame dies down, pour in cream, and remove the steaks immediately, even if you want to bubble the sauce a little longer to thin it – the meat will toughen quickly if it stews.

However, that's if you want to show off. The sauce will work just as well – and may be nicer – if you bubble the brandy in a separate pan to reduce it before adding it to the steak (see page 40).

You can also treat veal steaks and pork tenderloins in this way.

Frying and grilling

Meat fried or grilled is fast food. You cook it at a high heat to get the flavourful Maillard or browning reactions (see *The sealing theory is porous*, page 229); and you cook it briefly, in order to avoid expelling all its juices.

A pork chop is hard to get right. It is thick, and may need a good 15 minutes in the frying pan or under the grill;

but after that length of time, it is invariably dry. (See page 270 for the solution to this problem.)

Meat for frying and grilling comes from the animal's most relaxed bits, which have done the least exercise and which therefore don't have toughened connective tissues. From a cow, those bits include the sirloin and the fillet; from a sheep, the loin and best end of neck; from a pig, the loin again; from poultry, the breast (although every bit of a chicken can be grilled or fried). Browned and cooked to the point at which it is just done (in the cases of steak and lamb, most gourmets prefer some rareness), this meat is firm but juicy; tender too. Cooked beyond that point, it suddenly expels all that juiciness, and becomes shrivelled and leathery.

A ridged grill pan, or a barbecue, is best for grilling meat. Overhead grills do not sear the meat as satisfactorily; they also seem to dry it out more.

Salt

Don't salt meat before you cook it, you're advised: you'll draw out the juices. Meat consists of about 75% water. A dusting of salt on raw meat will not have a significant effect on that percentage; and, as the meat cooks, it undergoes a drastic water-reduction process anyway. That sizzling as the meat hits the pan or the grill is the sound of water, instantly vaporising; the high temperature, not the salt, is responsible for that. When the meat rests after cooking it exudes more juices, whether it is salted or not.

Salt added to meat before cooking will not penetrate

much, but will add savour to the browned crust. It's an effect worth having, in my opinion.

Marinades

So, yes, you can add salt to a marinade (see above).

Books on barbecuing and grilling can lead you to believe that, in order to be interesting, grilled meat must first be bathed in some exotic compound, for at least six hours. I find the Hugh Fearnley-Whittingstall argument persuasive. In essence, it's this: the acid in marinades will mess with your meat; if you've got a decent piece of meat, why would you want that to happen? If you want a lemony, or vinegary, taste, marinate with lemon or vinegar just before you start grilling.

Without acid, however, marinades scarcely penetrate the surface of the meat. Punctilious cooks use syringes to inject flavoursome compounds, but that kind of technique is not for you and me. We're happy if our marinades give a coating of flavour, enhancing the finished dish; and therefore we need apply them only when we're ready to cook.

Here are various types of marinade you can rub over your meat. Use some oil with all of them: it provides lubrication, flavour and a certain amount of protection, both for the dry ingredients of a marinade and for the meat – oil gets very hot, but not as hot as a naked flame.

Herbs: thyme, rosemary and oregano are good; also, for pork, sage.

Spices: see **Curry** on page 247. Mix these with oil

before coating the meat (you could do the same with the herb marinade). They are less likely to burn with an oil coating. An alternative is to mix the spices with yoghurt. A yoghurt marinade, if given time, will work on the meat, which in this case you want to be imbued with as much spiciness as possible.

I give a cheat's jerk marinade under **Chillis** on page 150. **Harissa** (page 129), thinned with oil (olive, sunflower or vegetable), is an alternative fiery coating.

Garlic: crush it with some salt and rub this paste over the meat.

Barbecue marinade: it might consist of tomato ketchup, soy sauce, mustard, vinegar, crushed garlic, salt, pepper and oil. Honey or brown sugar is optional; but you may find, if you use either of these, that the outside of your meat gets charred. As I said in the introduction (page 17), you can also use this marinade to coat slow-cooked meat, such as spare rib chops or belly pork (or chicken wings from a stock – see page 57). Poach the meat, very gently, for an hour, or until tender; drain, coat in marinade, and put on the barbecue or in a gas mark 6/200°C oven until the marinade becomes pleasingly sticky – five to 10 minutes (or perhaps 15 to 20 if the meat is heating up again from cold). What you hope is that the marinade will protect the meat enough to stop it drying out. This technique also works with spare ribs; but you can cook them from raw as well, barbecuing them or roasting them in 15 to 20 minutes in a 200°C oven.

Frying and grilling steak

I warm the frying pan (my heavy cast-iron one), over a medium to high flame, before I add the oil; if you put the oil in a cold pan and then give it a blast of heat, you're more likely to burn it. Use just 1 dstsp of sunflower, vegetable or groundnut oil (which withstand higher temperatures than does olive oil) – enough to provide a very thin layer in the pan. When the oil is hot but not smoking, salt the steak and put it in. Don't crowd the pan with steaks: you'll lower the temperature, halting the browning reactions (see page 229). After one minute, turn over the steak, which should have browned. (If it is brown in much less than that time, you're probably cooking it too fast; if it's not brown, the heat is too low.) After another 60 seconds, turn it over again.

Now, how thick is your steak? Hugh Fearnley-Whittingstall says that a 3 cm thick steak will be rare in three to four minutes, and medium rare in five to six.

The problem is that your steak is already browned after two minutes; leave it for another minute on each side, and the surface meat will burn and dry out. Turn down the dial, and you may find water entering the pan: the meat, which the browning has not sealed (see page 229), continues to expel its moisture, which the pan is not hot enough to vaporise. When the meat stews, it dries out very rapidly: water has this paradoxical effect, because it is such an efficient cooking medium.

One answer is, once the initial browning has taken place, to turn the meat very regularly – every 20 seconds or so, until it is done to your liking. It gets enough heat to continue cooking, but not enough to cause it to burn. Or put it in a gas mark 6/200°C oven for the remainder of the cooking time. To judge whether it's done, you might have to dig into it and have a look.

Put the steak on a warm plate to rest for a few minutes (see page 205). It will exude some moisture, but will nevertheless be juicier and more tender.

You could make a simple sauce, as you would with a **chicken sauté** (see page 259). To grill, rub the steak with a little oil and seasonings before putting it on a barbecue or ridged grill pan. Follow the frying procedure, above.

Lamb

I prefer to fry steak, but to grill lamb, perhaps because lamb is often fattier; also, the grilling flavours complement the meat particularly well. Thicker cutlets or lamb steaks may require five to 10 minutes of cooking to get to medium rare; but you can turn down the heat under your pan without risk of the stewing that steaks suffer under the same treatment. On the barbecue, start the cutlets in a place of high heat, turn over after a minute, brown the other side, then move them to a place where the embers are less fierce.

Chicken

You can fry or grill any parts of a chicken. But the legs take about 25 minutes to cook; they are quite difficult to manage on a barbecue, and almost impossible to grill successfully on a ridged pan: the skin and outer flesh burn before the heat penetrates the interior. You could use an overhead grill, which cooks chicken much more satisfactorily than it does other meats; or you could bone the legs, creating a thinner cut. Make an incision starting from the thin end of the leg, and follow the line of the bone to the thigh end; prise away the flesh, and chop off the tendons. The absence of bone will not cause the chicken to be less tender, unless you overcook it. (It's worth boning thighs, but not drumsticks.)

Thick pieces of chicken breast on the grill or barbecue may develop on overcooked outside and a rare interior. Finish them in the oven; or (my preferred option), cut them into thinner pieces before cooking; or cube and skewer them, then grill.

The easiest way to cook chicken wings, unless you're happy fiddling about with 20 pieces of meat or more on your grill, is in the oven. I like to get them very tender. Try mixing the wings with a barbecue sauce (see above) and baking them for 30 to 40 minutes at gas mark 5/190°C, turning once. They respond well to slow cooking too: 75 to 90 minutes at gas mark 2/150°C.

You can pan-fry chicken legs (or just thighs) slowly (see **Chicken sauté**, page 259). Or make a seasoned crust: mix flour with cayenne pepper and salt, dip the chicken in egg, then in the flour, and put on a rack (such as the one from the pan in the overhead grill); repeat the egging and flouring, in order to get a thicker crust, and fry. You need a medium heat, to crisp the crust; so perhaps it's a good idea to bone the chicken first.

Pork

A pork chop is the cut of meat for non-cooks. All you do is shove it under the grill, turn it once, and it's ready in 15 minutes. Serve with plenty of mustard or bottled sauce, to compensate for the dryness of the meat.

The Food Standards Agency advises that pork, along with chicken, be cooked through. We shouldn't, according to that official advice, leave in it the pink centre that in beef or lamb represents tenderness and juiciness. But a pork chop is particularly lean: it lacks the fatty lubrication that will give an impression of tenderness even when the muscle fibres are dry. An overcooked chop is an uningratiating meal.

The best way I have found to retain some tenderness in a chop is to fry or grill it for a minute on each side (see steaks, above), and then give it a further 15 to 20 minutes, depending on thickness, in the oven (gas mark 6/200°C). Hugh Fearnley-Whittingstall has a nice recipe (for four): fry a whole head of separated, unpeeled garlic cloves in a layer of olive oil in a large pan for a few minutes; add the chops and brown for a minute on each side; remove the chops and garlic, and place in a pre-heated oven dish, with the thinner ends of the chops pointing upwards to expose the fat; throw away the oil; deglaze the pan (see page 61) with a glass of wine or cider, reduce the liquid by half, and pour it over the chops; season, and put in the oven.

Sausages

They may be an unassuming foodstuff, but sausages are difficult to cook well. The challenge is to get them nicely browned without causing them to burst and lose their juices.

HOW TO COOK THEM

Melt a small knob of butter in a heavy frying pan. Put the pan on a heat disperser on one of the back rings of your hob, and place the sausages in it. The heat should be so low that, after 25 minutes, it has just begun to brown the undersides of the sausages. Turn them; the other side will brown more quickly – perhaps in 15 minutes. Turn again. And, after another few minutes, again. And so on (see *Frying and grilling steak*, **page 267). At this heat, it may take an hour to cook through the sausages properly.**[1 – see WHY YOU DO IT] **If the browning is progressing faster than the cooking, you'll need to turn the sausages frequently from the moment the browning process starts.**[2]

You might also grill or bake them.[3]

WHY YOU DO IT

1) *An hour to cook a sausage?* Even for a sausage sandwich? If you have the time, it's worth taking it. They don't split; they keep their juices; and they remain tender.

2) *Defusing bangers*. Sausages came to be called bangers because many of them had high water contents; as they heated up in the pan, the water would boil and cause them to explode. The preventive measure was to prick the skins, to give outlets to the liquid. We have less need to defuse the better sausages that are more widely available nowadays, and we don't like to encourage the loss of juiciness. But sausages still split quite easily. A gentle heat preserves the succulence.

3) *Grilling and baking*. Among grilling tools, a barbecue works better than an overhead grill. A barbecue's heat may appear to be very fierce, but it is usually less aggressive than a grill flame, which has a tendency to dry out sausages and toughen their skins. Another advantage of the barbecue is that, as fat leaks from the sausages, it spits back at them, forming a tasty crust. Don't put sausages on a ridged grill pan: they'll stick.

The oven has its advocates. I have sometimes produced succulent sausages from the oven; more often, I have got dry ones, and I haven't worked out how to guarantee the best results. The problem, I think, is that the oven's heat is too strong; but, if you turn it down, you don't get much browning. My best advice is to warm a little olive oil or lard in a roasting pan, add the sausages, and put them in a gas mark 5/190°C oven for 15 minutes, then turn them over, and cook them for another 10. If they're already nicely browned when you first look at them, turn down the oven a couple of settings. Don't add the sausages to scorching hot oil: you'll be lucky if they don't split. Olive oil or lard is my preferred fat here: butter will burn in the oven, and I don't like the taste of sausages cooked in sunflower or vegetable oil.

I'll keep trying the oven, because it's often easier to cook sausages that way than to fry them; but gentle frying, in order to retain as many juices as possible, is my preferred method. No, you don't have to spend an hour doing it. But, if you want to cook sausages at a higher heat, turn them regularly, or the skins might char and split before their contents are properly cooked.

Bacon

Cheap bacon is pumped full of water. As you fry or grill it, a slimy brine floods the pan; the meat contracts and curls. A good deal of the salt remains behind in the bacon, too, in concentrated form. You get a piece of meat that is dry, rubbery and salty. You may think that the quality of bacon matters less than that of other meats, because all you want it for is a cheep and cheerful sandwich with lots of ketchup and mustard; but good bacon – which is still pretty cheap – is worth the extra money.

I prefer streaky to back bacon. Back is more expensive, because it is leaner; but because it is leaner, it is inclined to become very dry when you cook it.

I prefer to fry bacon, in a little oil and over a low to medium heat, or to put it on to a ridged grill pan, than to cook it under an overhead grill, which produces a drier and tougher rasher.

FISH

A fishmonger – if you're lucky enough to have one within reach – can be the most daunting of food shops. The conceptual gap between the creature on the slab and a plate of food seems, to the inexperienced cook, too large to bridge. Those scales, fins and gills don't advertise edibility; nor do those shells and pincers.

Fish, with the possible exception of the Japanese ones that kill you if you don't prepare them properly, need not be alarming. They will respond to a brief subjection to one of the basic cooking methods: poaching, steaming, baking, grilling, frying. (Oily fish such as mackerel are not suited to poaching or steaming – that's about the only exception you need to know.) The fancy part of the process is making a sauce, but the home cook may want to leave elaborate sauces to fancy kitchens. It seems pretentious to make something complicated when, cooked simply, it is unimprovable.

You could take home one of those daunting fish, without even knowing what species it was, and simply wash it, season it, brush it with a little oil, and put it in a gas mark 6/200°C oven for 15 minutes or so; it is likely to be delicious. You could put your unnamed fish under the grill. Or you could wrap it in foil, with some chopped shallots, parsley and a few tablespoons of white wine. Or get the fishmonger to fillet it for you. Keep the heads and the bones, and make a stock with them (page 62). Poach the fillets in the stock; then reduce the stock and swirl in some butter and cream to make a sauce. Or fry the fillets, accompanying them with the fish stock sauce.

The biggest headache is the size of the fish. One person will eat an entire sole; how, then, are you going to fry, grill or even bake enough for six? You might manage it for four, using two frying pans, frying a sole in each, and keeping them warm in a low oven while the other two cook. But you'll wish you were serving only two, as you will when cooking many fish dishes. If I have a larger number to feed, I look for fleshy fish that will fit in my oven or under my grill, or I make a **stew** (page 293), or I poach a salmon.

Poaching and steaming

Poached salmon

You need a fish kettle – a long, narrow pan with a lid. Unless you have a long, central ring on your hob, you can put the kettle over two rings. Or, if you have a roasting pan deep enough to contain a salmon and water to cover it, try that.

The traditional fish-poaching liquid is court bouillon – a kind of vegetable stock made with water, aromatic vegetables, vinegar or wine and salt. I have cooked a salmon in court bouillon and in plain, salted water, and cannot say that the latter was less interesting. I suspect that the influence of flavourings in water on a large fish over the course of half an hour's cooking is minimal. Salt, though, does penetrate the flesh, and tenderises it.

Put the salmon in your kettle, cover it with water, add a generous portion of salt, and turn your ring or rings to low/medium. When bubbles start to appear, turn down the heat.[1 – see why you do it] From this point, a 1.5 kg salmon will take 20 minutes to half an hour to cook. Test with a knife at the thickest point. You can look at the flesh, which should have turned opaque; or you might be able to tell by the feel of the fish, which should be flaky rather than firm.

Serve, hot or cold (cold is more common), with boiled new potatoes and **mayonnaise** (page 45).

VARIATIONS

Nigel Slater recommends this method: you bring the fish slowly to a simmer in water containing 50 g of salt for each litre (that's a lot), put on the lid, turn off the heat, and leave overnight to eat for lunch the next day.

For two people you could poach salmon fillets or steaks. Cook them briefly, in hot water: bring enough salted water to cover them to the boil, turn down the heat, and slip in the salmon. Test after three minutes: they'll probably be ready.

1) *Gently does it*. Salmon, being fatty, is a forgiving sort of a fish. Nevertheless, it and other fish require the care you give to meat when cooking, and for the same reason: they dry up and toughen if heated for too long. A poaching liquid will cook a fish most sympathetically if kept at a temperature some way below boiling point.

Poached white fish

By white fish, I mean fillets of such fish as cod, haddock, hake, plaice, sole, turbot, brill and sea bass. You can use any kind of pan, including a frying pan, large enough to hold the fish; and, because they cook so easily, you don't have to cover them completely in liquid. Simply turn them halfway through to immerse the exposed sides. Flat fish fillets can be rolled or folded to fit the pan.

HOW TO COOK IT
For 2

Bring a couple of ladlefuls of fish stock (page 62) to a simmer in a saucepan or frying pan. Turn down the heat to the gentlest simmer. Slide in the fish and cook until the flesh becomes milky, turning halfway through if the slices are not completely immersed. Even a chunky piece of cod or haddock won't take more than five minutes in total. Lift out the fish using a slotted

spoon, transfer to a warm plate, and put it in the lowest part of a warm oven.

Turn up the heat under the stock, and boil until you have just a few tablespoons of syrupy liquid. Throw in a small pot (142 ml) of double cream, and bubble until thickened. Add 1 tbsp of chopped parsley and, away from the heat, a walnut-sized knob of butter. Check the seasoning, and serve the fish with the sauce.

VARIATIONS

You could poach the fish in milk, and use that as the basis for the sauce. Many parsley sauces are **béchamels** (see page 50), so you could use the poaching liquid to make one of them (if you use stock, the sauce is called a velouté); but I find a flour-based sauce a bit heavy as an accompaniment to delicate-fleshed fish.

Leave out the cream; just enrich the reduced stock with a little butter, added away from the heat to prevent splitting.

Sauté some mushrooms, with a little garlic if you like (see page 157), and add them to the reduced stock. Sharpen the sauce with a squirt or two of lemon juice.

Steamed fish

You can steam a fish or a fish fillet – the same kinds of fish that you would poach (see above) – as you would vegetables, in a **steaming basket** (see page 29) placed above salted boiling water in a saucepan. Or you could put a rack inside a roasting pan, and steam your fish, covered tightly with foil, either on the hob or in the oven. A whole fish may take 12 to 15 minutes; a fillet may be ready in less than three minutes. The flesh turns white, and acquires a flaky, rather than taut, texture.

There, you have a steamed fish. Even I, an advocate of simplicity, can see that it needs a little embellishment. An eggy sauce, such as **mayonnaise** (see page 45) or **aioli** (page 46) or **hollandaise** (page 48), might suit. Or try an oriental theme.

For 2
1 clove garlic, finely chopped
2 spring onions, coursest green parts removed, finely sliced
1 tsp ginger, finely chopped
1 dstsp sunflower, groundnut or vegetable oil
1 dstsp vinegar
1 dstsp soy sauce
1 dstsp sesame oil

Here's the schedule for a very quick meal: put a steaming basket in a saucepan, pour in water beneath it, add salt, put a lid on the pan, and put the pan on the heat.

Cut up the garlic, spring onions and ginger, and get ready the other sauce ingredients. By this time, the water should be boiling; place a couple of fish fillets in the basket, and cover.

Warm a frying pan or saucepan over a medium to high heat.[1 – see WHY YOU DO IT] **Add the oil, and when**

it is hot (but before it smokes), add the garlic, spring onions and ginger, and stir them around quickly until the onion wilts a little – no more than 30 seconds.

Add the vinegar, and let it evaporate for a minute.[2] Remove from the heat, and stir in the soy sauce and sesame oil.[3]

By this time, the fish may be ready; remove the fillets to warm plates, and pour the sauce over each.

WHY YOU DO IT

1) *Warming the pan first*. Or else you might overheat the oil. See page 125.

2) *Evaporate the vinegar*. Reducing vinegar – and alcohol – removes some of its harsh notes. See page 39.

3) *Delicate sesame*. You have to be very careful if you fry with sesame oil – it burns at a low temperature. Here, you're using it as a flavouring rather than as a frying aid.

You can also half-poach, half-steam fish in milk in the oven. It's a useful method for preparing the fish for a fish pie: the milk doesn't boil too rapidly, as it might do in a covered pan on the hob, and then provides the basis for the sauce.

Fish pie

HOW TO MAKE IT

For 4

650 g smoked haddock

560 ml milk

10 black peppercorns

1 bay leaf

57 g plain flour

57 g butter

Handful of parsley, chopped

900 g maincrop potatoes (King Edward,

Maris Piper or Desirée, for example)

50 g more butter

Put the haddock fillets in an ovenproof dish, and set the oven at gas mark 4/180°C. Heat the milk gently in a saucepan with the peppercorns and bay leaf; when it starts to bubble, pour it over the haddock, cover the dish with foil, and put it in the oven for five to 10 minutes. The fish has got more cooking to come, so it doesn't need to be cooked through; all you need now is to get it to a stage at which you can flake it.[1 – see WHY YOU DO IT]

Or: put the haddock into a saucepan, cover with the milk, peppercorns and bay leaf, bring gently to the boil, turn off the heat, cover the pan, and leave for five to 10 minutes.

Peel the potatoes, cut them into slices about 1.5 cm thick, cover with cold water, bring to a gentle simmer, and cook until tender. Drain them, and return them to the hot saucepan to dry. Mash them; as when making shepherd's pie (see page 254), you may not feel that a perfect purée is essential, so use a hand-held masher if you like. Season. (No milk and no butter at this stage.)

Lift the fish out of the milk, which you should strain and reserve.

Melt the butter in a non-stick saucepan, add the flour to make a roux, cook it gently for a couple of minutes until sandy (but don't let it darken), and gradually add the strained milk to make a béchamel (see page 50), stirring continuously. Let the sauce bubble for a minute or so, then throw in the parsley. Check the seasoning; you may not need any salt, because the fish is salty. The sauce should be thick enough to coat the back of a spoon.[2]

Pull the fish off its skin, separating it into decent-sized flakes (it's easiest to do this by hand). Stir the flakes gently into the sauce. Then pour this mixture into a pie dish, and cover it with the mash. Cut the butter into little pieces, and dot them on top.

Bake the pie in a gas mark 6/200°C oven for about 30 minutes, or until the surface of the mash is golden.

VARIATIONS

You don't have to use smoked haddock. Any fish (including salmon, but not including mackerel and sardines) will do; but smoked fish works particularly well.

Add sautéed mushrooms to the sauce (see page 157). Or stewed leeks (page 155). Or cooked, peeled prawns.

Hard-boiled eggs are nice in a fish pie. The problem is that they are usually hard-boiled before they go in; then they get half an hour in the oven, and overcook. Try this: boil the eggs (one for each person) for six minutes; drain them and cover in cold water (to arrest the cooking). Peel them, and bury them gently, whole, in the fish and sauce mixture just before you cover the whole lot with mash. They should finish cooking with the pie. If they're still a little soft, will you mind?

WHY YOU DO IT

1) *Pre-cooking the fish.* The fish is about to be immersed in sauce and put in the oven for half an hour – plenty of time to cook it. But if you simply added skinned, raw, chopped-up fish to your béchamel, it would exude a good deal of its own liquid and thin the sauce to a probably disastrous extent. The pre-cooking allows it to shed some of its liquid, flavouring the milk; it also enables you to skin and flake the fish more easily. But it does mean that the fish in a fish pie is cooked for longer than is ideal.

2) *Thick sauce.* The sauce will undergo conflicting processes in the oven. The further cooking will thicken and concentrate it; but any further liquid from the fish will thin it. A sauce that's too thick is preferable to a runny one, so err on the side of thickness.

283

Pan-fried fish

I sympathise with Elizabeth David in her dislike of the term "pan-fried". It seems factitious, created because chefs think that "fried" sounds a bit downmarket – just as executives think that they appear more dynamic if they "head up" rather than simply "head" an organisation. "Waiter, is this fish fried?" "No sir: it is *pan-fried*."

Having got that off my chest, I have to admit that the term creates a useful distinction between fish that is fried in a thin layer of fat, and fish that is immersed in fat completely, usually with the protection of a coating such as batter.

Pan-fried sole or plaice fillets

HOW TO COOK THEM
For 2

Your largest, 28 cm frying pan may just be able to contain four fillets of fish. Season them on both sides with salt, and pepper if you like, and dredge the flesh sides in a plate of flour, to give them a light dusting.[1 – see WHY YOU DO IT] Put the pan on a medium heat, and add enough butter to provide a generous coating to the surface, with 1 dstsp or so of sunflower or olive oil.[2] When the butter is foaming, slip in the fish, skin side down.[3]

The fish won't take long to cook. You might turn a thin fillet after a minute, and give it no longer than 30 seconds on the flesh side.

Lift the fillets, skin side up,[4] on to warm plates. Pour away the butter and fat. Add more butter – 50 g, say – to the pan, and swirl it around until it's melted. Throw in a chopped handful of parsley, and squeeze over the sauce 1 tbsp of lemon juice. Pour the sauce on to the plates with the fish.

Spinach (see page 189) is an ideal accompaniment; boiled new potatoes, too (page 172).

VARIATIONS

Any fish fillets, provided they are not very thick, will be good when given this treatment.

I think that sole, plaice and other delicate white fish need no further embellishment. Salmon, though, will take the addition of strong extra flavourings. Try Nigel Slater's idea: fry the salmon as you would the sole or plaice (see above – the salmon will need longer in the pan), discard the butter, add more, then add a tablespoon or two of rinsed capers, and 1 tbsp of red or white wine vinegar. Bubble this sauce for a minute or so to soften the raw, vinegary taste.

You can cook whole flatfish or mackerel in this way, too. There's no point in flouring them first (see WHY YOU DO IT, below). Cook them on a moderate heat, to avoid scorching the skin before the inside of the fish is tender. You can fit several mackerel into a large frying pan, but only one flatfish, which one person will happily consume. So you'll need either to cook one sole or plaice at a time, keeping the first one warm in a low oven while you tackle the second, or to use two pans – if your hob is large enough to accommodate them.

285

1) *Dredging*. Cooks give fish a light dusting of flour in order to protect the tender flesh, and to provide a crispy surface. I'm not sure that the flour does much protecting: Tom Stobart (*The Cook's Encyclopaedia*) insists that it doesn't. So this stage is optional.

2) *Oil with the butter*. Elizabeth David tells us that the fish in sole meunière – the proper name for the recipe above – should be fried in clarified butter, which doesn't burn as readily as does the normal stuff. A simpler way to avoid burning is to add oil to the butter. When butter is alone in the pan, the liquid evaporates from it; the solid material in the remaining butter gets very hot, and burns. The addition of oil, which retains its liquid consistency on heating, thins out the butter, and makes burning less likely. The oil will have only a small influence on the flavour, because your sauce will be based entirely on butter.

3) *Skin side down*. The skin protects the delicate flesh, and crisps as it fries. Fry the fish on the skin side until only a brief cooking on the flesh side will bring it to readiness.

4) *Skin side up*. Is serving fish with the skin confronting the diner a ridiculous restaurant affectation? Not entirely. The skin will go soggy if the fish is turned over. But if you don't want to eat the skin anyway, this serving method is redundant. If you do want to eat the skin, don't pour the sauce over it – unless you like your fish skin soggy.

Fry and bake

Chunky steaks of cod or other fish will spend too long in the pan, and dry out, if you try to cook them through by frying. Instead, you start them on the top of the stove, to crisp the skin, and complete the cooking in the oven.

Melt a layer of butter and oil in a roasting pan, or any other pan that will go in your oven, until the butter starts foaming.

Put in the fish, seasoned with salt and pepper if you like, skin side down. Fry it for a minute or so until the skin starts to crisp, then turn it flesh side down and put the pan in a gas mark 6/200°C oven. The fish may take eight to 10 minutes to cook; you'll be able to see that all the flesh has turned milky white.

Once you've removed the fish from the pan, you can follow the meunière method above: pour away the cooking fat, and melt more butter in the pan (which will be hot, so you probably won't need to return it to the hob), along with lemon and parsley if you like. A tablespoon of rinsed capers would be nice, too.

The flesh side of the fish will have more protection in the oven if facing downwards than if facing upwards, when it would be exposed to the radiant heat.

You may not want to throw away the butter and oil in which the fish has cooked. As long as they haven't burned, they'll make a fine sauce themselves.

Fish in batter

When I have made battered cod, I've infected the air of the house for several days. The fish has tasted great, though.

Make a batter (according to the recipe on page 218) with beer (any kind) as your liquid, but use half the amount that you would in the normal recipe: in other words, 224 g of flour, one egg and 280 ml beer. That should be plenty for two decent-sized fillets. The liquid is meant to be so thick that only a little of it falls off when you move the fish from batter to oil.

Pudding and pancake batters benefit from a rest before cooking. However, Harold McGee tells us that coating batters for frying will be crisper if used immediately.

Heat, in a fryer or deep saucepan, enough sunflower or vegetable oil to cover the fish, to 175°C. If you don't have a thermometer, drop in a small piece of bread, which should sizzle vigorously.

Salt your fish fillets; that will make their surfaces sticky. Then dredge them in flour, which will help the batter to adhere. Dip the fillets in the batter, holding them at their thinnest points. Quickly, so that not too much batter falls off, transfer them to the hot oil; but submerge them gradually. They may rise to the surface; if they do, turn them halfway through cooking. An average-sized fillet will take about 10 minutes to cook. The batter should be puffed and crispy; the fish, which has steamed inside its coating, moist and tender. Serve immediately, before the batter goes soggy.

The ideal accompaniments are, of course, **chips** (see

page 182), made first and held spread out on a baking tray in a warm oven, and **tartare sauce** (page 47). What a lot of rather scary work. But only a select few chippies, along with some quite expensive restaurants, will make fish and chips as well as you can.

Grilled or baked fish

I treat them together because many recipes are inter-changeable: you coat the fish with a marinade of some sort before putting it under or on the grill, or in the oven.

I was a bit sniffy about overhead grills in the **Meat** chapter (page 264), but I like them for fish: they cook quick-ly enough to keep the fish tender, but not so fiercely that they scorch it. Even better is a barbecue. If you're going to use it a lot, you might invest in a fish-shaped, long-handled grilling basket, to which your fish won't stick as eagerly as it will to a grill rack.

You shouldn't go wrong if you bake fish at gas mark 6/ 200°C. Put it in a roasting tray or baking dish, and cover it with your marinade (see below). It's impossible to give accurate cooking times: the best I can manage is to tell you that a 500 g fish might take 15 to 20 minutes. You'll have to stick a knife into the thickest part to see if the flesh is opaque and flaky.

Another way of baking fish is to enclose it in a loose parcel of foil. Lay it on the foil, sprinkle over some salt, pepper, herbs (chives, parsley or thyme, say) and a couple of tablespoons of white wine. Bring up the sides of the foil to make a tent, and scrunch the edges together. Marinade 2 (from Nigel Slater): for each fish, a couple of chopped chillis (with seeds if you want them fiery), a couple of smashed pieces of lemon grass, a couple of tablespoons of rice wine (or juice of a lime or ¼ lemon), a few sprigs of coriander, some salt.

A grilled fish will take less time to cook than will a baked one. Line your grill pan with foil, place your fish in it, and cover with marinade. Turn it halfway through cooking; the operation requires some care.

2 marinades for a 500 g grilled or baked fish

HOW TO MAKE THEM
1 tbsp olive oil
1 clove garlic, finely chopped
1 shallot, finely chopped
1 dstsp herbs: parsley, chives, rosemary, thyme, oregano
Juice of ¼ or ½ lemon, to taste
Salt

You can scatter these ingredients separately over the fish.

1 tbsp olive oil
1 clove garlic, finely chopped
1 tsp coriander seeds
1 tsp cumin seeds

½ *tsp cayenne pepper*
Salt

Put the coriander and cumin into a small saucepan, and place over a medium heat, shaking the
pan until the spices give off a toasted aroma.
Grind them in a mortar, or in a small electric mill
or coffee grinder. Mix with the olive oil, garlic,
cayenne pepper and salt, and pour over the fish.

Fish cakes

Restaurant fish cakes come covered in golden, unbroken
casings of breadcrumbs. I do not kid myself that I can repro-
duce that effect at home, satisfying myself merely with egg
and flour.

HOW TO MAKE THEM
For 2
250 g fish (any you like – smoked is good)
250 g maincrop potatoes (King Edward,
Maris Piper or Desirée, for example)
250 ml milk
1 tbsp chopped parsley
1 tbsp chopped chives
1 egg, beaten
Flour on a plate
Oil and butter, for frying

Cook the fish (in the milk) and potatoes as
described in the fish pie recipe (see page 281),

flaking the fish and mashing the potatoes. Stir the herbs, with salt (remember that smoked fish is salty), and pepper if you like, into the mash; gently blend in the flaked fish.

Mould the fishy mash into four patties (or two large ones if you like; or six small ones). You won't be able to get them perfectly formed; not to worry. Dip them in the egg, and roll them in the flour.

Warm a frying pan over a medium heat; add enough oil (you choose what kind) and butter to coat the surface with a little to spare; when the butter is sizzling, slide in the fish cakes. (If the butter and oil mixture is not hot, the fish cakes will absorb more of it.) When you think the undersides are brown (probably after a couple of minutes), turn the cakes over gently. The other sides will brown faster.

It would be a shame to waste the milk. Make a béchamel with it (see page 50; with 250 ml of milk, you probably need about 25 g each of butter and flour).

If you find you've used too much flour for the milk you have, you'll have to thin the sauce with more milk from the fridge. Season with nutmeg and salt; pepper too, if you like. Cook quickly 400 g of spinach (see page 188); drain it in a colander, pushing out the excess liquid with a wooden spoon. Stir the spinach into the béchamel. You could chop it first.

Divide the sauced spinach between two warm plates, and lay the fish cakes on top.

Fish soup, or stew

As Richard Olney puts it, inimitably: "The line dividing a soup from a stew is often infirm." With both, you may get bowls full of chunky bits of fish and vegetables, sitting in quite a lot of liquid, and you need a spoon among your cutlery.

The following recipe will make a soup or a stew; if you want a smooth soup, it will make that too.

HOW TO MAKE IT

For 6

1 kg mixed fish, including whole ones (but not
oily ones), cleaned and gutted[1 – see why you do it]

2 onions, chopped

2 leeks, chopped

1 bulb fennel, chopped

4 cloves garlic, chopped

2 tbsps olive oil

1 400 g can tomatoes; or 6 medium-sized fresh ones,
chopped (don't worry about the skins);
or 1 500 g carton passata

2 medium potatoes, peeled and quartered

Zest of 1 orange

1 sachet saffron, or ½ tsp strands, dissolved in warm water

Rouille (see below)

1 baguette, for croutons

Warm the oil in a heavy, large saucepan or casse-
role. Add the onions, leeks, fennel and garlic, and
cook gently until they are soft – maybe 15 minutes

or so. Chop up the fish, heads and all, into 5 cm pieces, and add them, along with the tomatoes, potatoes, orange zest and some salt; pour in enough cold water just to cover the ingredients, bring to the boil, skim any scum from the surface, and simmer with the pan uncovered for 20 to 30 minutes, or until the potatoes are soft.

You have a stew, or a soup if you prefer to call it that. Add the saffron, check the seasoning, and serve in bowls.

However, you can go on to make a smooth soup. It's one of my favourite things.

Place a food mill, with the coarse mesh attached, over another pan, and pass the soup through it, pushing down on the fish with a wooden spoon and grinding as much of it through the disc as possible. Or: pour the soup into another pan through a colander, again pushing down on the ingredients with a wooden spoon.

Now refine the soup further: strain it into another pan (back into the first one, perhaps) through a sieve, pushing down on the pulp with the back of the ladle; discard the pulp that won't go through the mesh.[2]

If, before you strain the soup, you think that it is likely to be too watery, pour it through a colander into another pan, reserving the solid ingredients left behind. Boil the liquid until you think it has reduced sufficiently, then process it with the fish and vegetables as above.

Rouille is a fiery mayonnaise. Make a mayonnaise with two egg yolks, 300 ml of oil and three crushed garlic cloves (see page 45); add to it ½ tsp of cayenne pepper or 1 tsp of **harissa** (page 129). (Best add a little cayenne or harissa at first, and then taste before adding more.) You could put a little cayenne into the soup, too.

Cut the baguette into rounds, then into spoon-sized halves or quarters. Lay them on a baking tray, and put them in a gas mark 6/200°C oven until lightly toasted.

When you're ready to serve, add the saffron (with its soaking liquid if you've used threads) and reheat the soup gently without boiling; check the seasoning. Place a bowl of croutons and a bowl of rouille on the table; guests dollop the rouille on to the croutons, which they float in their soup.

Soupe de poisson, as I just about dare to call this recipe, often comes with bowls of grated Gruyère to go with the croutons and rouille. As served in most restaurants, the cheese is sweaty and unappetising, having been grated too far in advance. Even when it's in tip-top condition, I'm happy to leave it.

I don't dare to call the stew version of this dish a bouillabaisse, although it resembles it in composition. Bouillabaisse, the Marseillais fish stew, includes a more generous portion of olive oil, and is moistened with boiling water and kept at a rapid boil, so that the oil and water amalgamate and the stew thickens. Elizabeth David absolves me from giving further advice: "It is useless attempting to make a bouillabaisse away from the shores of the Mediterranean," she warns.

1) *What fish?* I ask the fishmonger. The last time I made a soup, he gave me a snapper (which I chopped into three pieces), the tail of a coley and a cod fillet.

2) *Double straining.* This process is fun, provided you're not in a hurry. The point is to get every last bit of liquid from the solid material.

A food mill will make the first round a lot easier than will a colander. Put the soup into it a portion at a time; use a wooden spoon to force the fish and vegetables between the metal attachment and the disc. Brief anti-clockwise turns of the handle can help the stuff to go through.

Sieve the pulp a portion at a time as well. The back of a ladle will help you to force the liquid through the mesh; throw away the dried pulp, and repeat.

Mussels

Mussels are enjoyable to cook: you get, as you lift the lid of the cooking vessel, the small miracle of the opened shells, as well as the wonderful briny, winey aroma. But preparing them is a little tedious.

HOW TO PREPARE THEM

Put them in a bowl of cold water. If any float, or are broken, throw them away. Drain them in a colander. Wash them again under running water, pulling off the beards if they have them. Look

out for the following, and throw them away: any mussels that are open and do not close with a sharp tap on the side of the sink, or when you give them a little squeeze with your thumb and forefinger;[1] – see why you do it any with shells that you can slide sideways with your thumb and forefinger (they will be gritty).

Phew. Now the more enjoyable bit.

HOW TO COOK THEM

As a starter, for 2 – double the quantities for a main course

500 g mussels
2 shallots or one onion, finely sliced
1 clove garlic, finely chopped
1 tbsp olive oil
1 glass white wine
1 tbsp chopped parsley

Warm the oil over a medium heat in a heavy casserole or saucepan. Add the shallots or onion, and the garlic. Fry, stirring, for just a minute or two, or for three or four if you're using onion; a slightly raw taste is fine in this context. Throw in the wine, and let it bubble (you shouldn't need salt – the mussel liquor is salty); tip in the mussels, and clamp on the lid. Shake the pan a few times while the mussels are cooking. Check after three minutes: a good many of them should be open. If not many are, they obviously need longer. If most are, put the lid back on for another minute to give the closed ones the benefit of the doubt;[2] if a few still refuse to co-operate, throw them away. (Don't try to prise them open to eat them – they'll probably poison you.) Scatter over the parsley.

Serve from their cooking vessel: eat the mussels from bowls, with spoons for the sauce, and bread to mop it up. If you're worried about grittiness in the sauce, scoop the mussels from the cooking vessel into a warm bowl, and strain the sauce over them through a sieve. Scatter on the parsley. You'll lose any shallot or onion you didn't pick up with the mussels, unfortunately.

You could add a couple of tablespoons of double cream to the cooking liquid at the end.

WHY YOU DO IT

1) *Alive, alive-o*. Mussels, as you probably know, are alive – or should be – when you put them in the pot. If they don't close when you tap them, or open when you cook them, they are probably dead, not worth eating, and potentially harmful.

2) *Quick cooking*. Mussels toughen, as do all protein-rich foods, if overcooked. It's a lot easier to deal with a moderate quantity of them: they should be ready at the same time. Crowded in a huge pile, they get varying access to the heat. When you cook more than a kilo of mussels, you may need to remove to a warm bowl the ones that open first; you'll protect them from toughening, and hasten the opening of the others.

PUDDINGS

Puddings sit a little oddly in this book. I've been trying to show you why, for the cook operating informally at home, recipes for most savoury dishes – certainly for most of the ones here – are merely templates, guides to the kinds of things that produce good results. We shouldn't need to get out a recipe book or the scales every time we make a pasta sauce or marinate a piece of chicken. If we know what works and why, we can save ourselves the effort and anxiety of feeling that we need to follow, to the letter, what the experts tell us to do. However, in the world of puddings, recipes rule. A certain number of eggs will set a certain amount of liquid; a certain proportion of flour, eggs and liquid will make a batter. You cannot improvise your way around those determinants.

I take a recipe to be something that you attempt to follow with accuracy. In that sense, there haven't been many recipes in this book so far. But there are a few in the following pages.

I'm not saying that you have to obey them to the letter. You may prefer more sugar than I suggest, or less. I've left up to you the quantities you use of flavourings such as cinnamon. But I wouldn't advise you, for example, to be too liberal in your interpretation of the proportion of milk to eggs in the custard.

Custard puddings

Custard

HOW TO MAKE IT
As an accompaniment to puddings for 4 to 6 people
3 egg yolks[1 – see WHY YOU DO IT]
150 ml milk
150 ml double cream
½ vanilla pod, or 1 tsp vanilla essence
2 tbsps, or about 30 g, caster sugar[2]

Slit the vanilla pod lengthways with a sharp knife; scrape the seeds into the milk and cream. Warm the milk and cream with the pod and seeds in a saucepan until bubbles appear; turn off the heat, cover the pan, and leave for 20 minutes.[3] Lift out the pod. Return the pan to a simmer.

Or, if using vanilla essence: bring the milk/cream and vanilla essence to a simmer.

Beat the egg yolks and the sugar. Pour a little hot milk into the mixture, whisking;[4] then a little more; then tip this mixture back into the saucepan. Over the gentlest heat, stir the custard until it starts to thicken; remove it from the heat immediately, and pour into a warm, but not hot, jug.[5]

Serve right away, or keep the custard covered in the fridge, where it will thicken, to serve cold.

WHY YOU DO IT

1) *Yolks only*. They will produce a richer custard than would whole eggs – in part because of the richness of the yolks, and in part because you'll need more eggs to thicken the liquid. Two whole eggs would produce as thick a custard as would three yolks. Thicker, probably.

2) *How much sugar?* Recipes vary wildly. Of course, it's a matter of taste.

3) *Infusion time*. To let the vanilla flavour the milk and cream. If you want a milder vanilla flavour, without the seeds in the milk, drop in the whole pod without slitting it; you'll probably be able to use it again. If you don't want vanilla seeds in your custard, pour the milk and cream – after the infusion process – into another pan through a sieve.

4) *Milk into eggs*. Put the hot liquid into the cold liquid, so that the volume of the cold liquid is greater, and whisk all the time to distribute the heat. That way, you avoid making runny scrambled egg rather than custard. If you put the eggs into the simmering milk, they will get a sudden

exposure to boiling heat, and curdle. (Similar considerations – along with ones of social status – inform the decision about whether to put milk or tea into your cup first. But let's not go there.)

5) *Don't boil*. Your safest bet is to warm the custard in a double boiler above simmering water. Or put it into a bowl – a glass one will do – that fits inside a saucepan. The bowl shouldn't touch the water. But you can get away with stirring the custard vigorously in a heavy-bottomed pan above a very gentle flame, perhaps with a heat disperser between flame and pan. To be thorough, clean any scorched milk from the bottom of the pan before returning the custard to it.

If bits of custard stick to the bottom of the pan, they will curdle – the egg will scramble, in other words. The egg will also scramble if the liquid approaches boiling point. Heat the custard gently, and stop heating it, despite the temptation to get it just a bit thicker, as soon as it has the consistency of a pouring cream.

Baked custard

HOW TO MAKE IT
For 6
4 whole eggs
300 ml milk
300 ml double cream
(Rich version:
6 egg yolks

150 ml milk
450 ml double cream[1 – see WHY YOU DO IT])
1 vanilla pod, split lengthways, or 2 tsps vanilla essence
50 g caster sugar, or 1 tbsp (about 50 g) honey
A little butter

Make the custard as you would the pouring version, above. (If you use honey, you can beat it with the eggs – thick honey will go runny.) Pour it into an ovenproof dish, lightly greased with the butter, and put the dish inside a pan – a roasting pan, say. Pour hot water into the pan to come halfway up the sides of the custard dish.[2] Bake at gas mark 3/160°C for about 35 to 45 minutes, or until the custard is set. Serve hot or cold.

WHY YOU DO IT

1) *How rich is your taste?* I sometimes prefer the lighter, less unctuous texture of the custard made with whole eggs.

More egg yolks, and more cream, are required to set the richer version. Of course, you could perm these ingredients: use two whole eggs and three yolks, for example; or, in the yolk-only version, use less cream and another egg yolk (making seven).

2) *The bain-marie.* The temperature of your oven is 160°C – high enough to curdle the custard in contact with the sides of the cooking vessel. The water in the bain-marie – the bath in which the cooking vessel sits – cannot of course get hotter than 100°C, and protects the

custard from the oven heat. Don't allow the water to come too high up the sides of the custard dish, or it might bubble over.

Panettone bread and butter pudding

HOW TO MAKE IT

For 6

6 slices panettone[1 – see WHY YOU DO IT]

Butter

Ingredients for 600 ml baked custard (see above)

Lightly butter, to grease the surface, an oven dish. Butter the panettone slices (on one side only, if you want to make a token concession to protecting everyone's hearts), and place them in the dish, as evenly as possible.

Make the custard according to the baked custard recipe, and pour it over the panettone. It should cover the slices, but not swamp them; add another slice or two of cake if you think there's too much liquid.

On the other hand, you might find that the panettone is quite bulky; if so, start with fewer slices, pour on the custard, and then add more cake if there's room.

Place in a bain-marie (see "Baked custard", above), and bake in a gas mark 3/160°C oven for 45 minutes, or until the custard is set.

This recipe is itself a variation, on traditional bread and butter pudding made with sliced white bread. One reason why I like it is that the cake provides the fruit and spice that you would otherwise have to supply yourself.

For the traditional version, use about eight thin slices, crusts removed, of white loaf, again buttered on one side. If you want fruit, scatter about 20 g each of raisins and sultanas over the bread slices; you could soak them first for 20 minutes in a few teaspoons of brandy or liqueur (pouring the alcohol over the bread with the fruit). If you want spice, flavour the custard with a pinch or two of grated nutmeg and cinnamon.

WHY YOU DO IT

1) *How much cake?* As I imply in the recipe, I cannot give precise quantities. I don't know how big your panettone is, or how thickly you've cut your slices. What I do know is that most bread and butter pudding recipes give too high a proportion of bread for my taste: I think that bread and butter pudding should consist of bread (or cake) with a liberal lubrication of custard, rather than simply of eggy bread. For this reason, I don't leave the bread (or cake) to soak up the custard before baking it, as some recipes advise. It absorbs plenty of liquid while baking, anyway.

Rice pudding

This is a Heston Blumenthal recipe – rice pudding meets

risotto. I've reduced the quantity of milk he gives, because I didn't need so much. Perhaps your rice will absorb more; you can add it during cooking.

HOW TO MAKE IT

For 6

600 ml milk

1 vanilla pod, or 2 tsps vanilla essence

135 g arborio or carnaroli rice

110 g caster sugar

1 pinch nutmeg

150 ml double cream

2 egg yolks

Split the vanilla pod lengthways; put it, with scraped-out seeds, in the milk, bring the milk to a simmer, cover and turn off the heat. Leave for 20 minutes.

If you don't want the seeds, sieve the milk into another pan.

Bring a pan of water to the boil, throw in the rice, bring back to the boil, simmer for three minutes, and drain.[1 – see WHY YOU DO IT]

Add the sugar and nutmeg to the milk, and return to a simmer (if you're using vanilla essence, you'll have started here). Add the rice and simmer it, stirring. It should take 20 to 30 minutes to become tender.

If the rice is still drowned in liquid, strain some milk into another pan and simmer it until it reduces, before returning it to the main dish.

A certain amount of runniness is fine, particularly if you're going to serve the pudding cold: it will thicken as it cools.

Add the double cream; cook for a couple of minutes longer. Remove from the heat, add the egg yolks, and stir. Blumenthal tells you to stir the pudding for three minutes, perhaps because there's a danger that the egg will curdle; but you can probably get away with being a little less assiduous.

Serve hot or cold.

WHY YOU DO IT

1) *Blanching the rice*. To blanch is to part-cook something in boiling water. In this case, you do it to lessen the starchiness of the rice.

Lemon surprise pudding

This is a lemony sponge on top of a lemony custard. Nigel Slater, with credit to Margaret Costa's classic *Four Seasons Cookery Book*, reproduces it in *Real Cooking*, but includes an egg too few and a lemon too many for my taste: I find the custard too thin, and sharp.

In *Appetite*, he offers an updated version, with orange and lemon, and gives the same number of eggs but less milk and flour.

The following recipe is halfway between the two.

HOW TO MAKE IT

For 6

100 g butter

175 g caster sugar

2 lemons – their zest and juice[1] – see WHY YOU DO IT

Yolks of 5 (or 6, for a thicker custard) eggs, whites of 4[2]

50 g plain flour

500 ml milk

Cream the butter and sugar.[3] Beat in the egg yolks, and add the lemon zest and juice. The mixture won't look too good, but don't worry: it's going to look even worse in a minute. Pour in the milk, and gradually whisk in the flour (see the batter recipe, page 218).

Beat the egg whites with a balloon whisk – use an electric beater if you prefer (see page 34) – until you can make firm, snowy peaks with them.[4] Fold them gently into the batter. Pour the mixture into a buttered oven dish; it should come halfway up the sides.

Put the dish into a roasting pan or other vessel, and pour in hot water to come halfway up the sides of the pudding dish (see *The bain-marie*, page 303). Bake in a gas mark 4/180°C oven for about 50 minutes, or until the sponge is golden and, well, spongy.

VARIATIONS

You could try an orange surprise pudding, with the zest and juice of two oranges; or use one orange and one lemon.

1) *Zesting*. I scrape the lemon against the finest mesh on my cheese grater, and try to grate only the skin: the white pith underneath is bitter.

2) *Separating*. Crack the egg, and allow the white to pour into the bowl. Hold half the egg shell upside down over the bowl, with your finger keeping back the yolk. Transfer the yolk to the other half of egg shell, and hold it upside down too, allowing the remaining white to drip out.

3) *Creaming*. This is what you do when you make cakes: it aerates the fat/sugar combination. It's a lot easier if the butter is at room temperature. Squash the butter into the sugar with a wooden spoon; as you work away, the mixture will become creamier, until you can whip it with a balloon whisk. Keep going until it's light and fluffy.

4) *Whisking*. Egg whites need to be free of contamination — traces of yolk, or extraneous material in the bowl or on the whisk — to become foams. Don't add salt (you don't want it in this recipe, but you might if you're making a savoury soufflé) until the white is beaten. Harold McGee tells us that sugar (not needed in this recipe, because it's already in the batter) helps to firm the whites, but lengthens the firming process; if you're using an electric whisk, you might not mind. Otherwise, add sugar at the end. However, a squirt of lemon juice, or a drop of vinegar, will help.

Use a large bowl, and tip it towards you, so that the

whisk gets access to as much egg white as possible.

For your lemon surprise pudding, you should stop whisking the egg whites when the whisk, lifted from the foam, creates peaks, which do not subside. As when making a pouring **custard** (see page 300), it's tempting to carry on, just to make sure you've got the right consistency. Resist. Further beating causes the firm peak stage rapidly to be succeeded by collapse.

Stir ("fold" is the term writers like) the foam into the batter gently, in order to retain as much of its airiness as possible.

Fruit puddings

Fruits in syrup

Try this ratio: 1 g of sugar – it doesn't matter whether it's caster or granulated, but remember that caster sugar will have a more concentrated sweetness – to each 2.5 ml of water. So your syrup might be 100 g of sugar and 250 ml of water; put them in a pan, and bring to the boil, to dissolve the sugar. You might add the following flavourings: a cinnamon stick or pinch of cinnamon; a pinch of nutmeg; a vanilla pod or teaspoon of vanilla essence.

You can poach any number of fruits in this syrup. For example: apricots, halved and stoned; plums, likewise; peaches; nectarines; strawberries; raspberries; blackberries; blackcurrants; any more you can think of. Put them into the pan with the hot syrup and simmer gently, until

310

tender. Use a pan that's wide enough to allow all the fruit to get a bath. If you need more liquid, simply add more water and sugar; but 250 ml should be plenty for about 600 g of fruit – you don't need to drown it, and you can use just enough syrup to come halfway up the fruit, which you turn halfway through cooking. Cover the pan; but make sure that the contents don't boil too vigorously, or catch and burn on the bottom.

When the fruit is tender, remove it with a slotted spoon. (Plums, turned halfway through cooking, might be ready in no more than six minutes. Blackberries, which should acquire a melting texture, will take longer.) Turn up the heat under the pan to reduce the liquid to a syrupy consistency. Pour it back over the fruit.

Serve hot or cold, with cream or **custard** (see page 300).

Rhubarb

It's not a fruit, of course, but a vegetable – a leaf stalk. But we eat it sweetened, as a pudding. You can poach it, as above; but I prefer to cook it in a minimal amount of liquid. Wash the stems, and cut them into short (3 cm, say) pieces. Melt enough butter in a saucepan to coat the bottom; add the damp rhubarb, and warm, with the pan covered, over a gentle heat. The rhubarb will throw off liquid. Now you can turn up the heat a little, and add sugar. You can uncover the pan too, because you want the liquid to evaporate, and because with stirring you can give all the rhubarb access to the heat. Simmer until tender. Tip the rhubarb into a sieve, allowing the liquid to pour into another pan; boil the liquid to thicken it. Re-combine it with the rhubarb; check for sweetness, adding more sugar if necessary. Serve hot or cold, with cream or **custard** (see page 300). Or use it in a **crumble** (see opposite).

Sorry to be vague about the quantity of sugar. Say you have 600 g of rhubarb (by the way, get rid of the leaves, which are reputed to be poisonous): add 2 tbsps of sugar. It probably won't be enough. But it's better to start with too little, and to add more as your taste dictates, than to start with too much, when your only way of tempering the sweetness will be to add more rhubarb.

Fruit fools

Stew rhubarb or gooseberries as in the basic rhubarb recipe (above), but without the butter. Drain off the liquid into a pan; put the rhubarb or gooseberries into a sieve held over the same pan, and crush them with a wooden spoon. Boil all the liquid in the pan until it is thick; re-combine it with the rhubarb or gooseberries. Check for sweetness. Put the fruit into the fridge, to acquire a holding, slushy consistency.

You can give the same treatment to redcurrants and blackcurrants.

About 600 g of fruit (for stoned fruit, that's the weight when the stones are removed) should be good for six people. How much cream you use is a matter of taste; I suggest a similar volume to that of the fruit – 400 ml, say. Pour the cream – double or whipping – into a bowl, and whisk with a balloon whisk, until it thickens but before it goes firm. It should have a coating, but still liquid, consistency. Combine it with the fruit, and chill again.

Strawberries and raspberries don't want cooking. Pour sugar on them, bash them up with a fork, check the sweetness, and combine with the thickened cream. Chill.

Fruit crumble

HOW TO MAKE IT
For 6
200 g plain flour
125 g butter
75 g caster or demerara sugar
More sugar for the fruit
600 g fruit (if you're using plums or damsons,
you'll probably need about 1 kg; if you're using apples
such as Bramleys, about 900 g)

This is one job for which I always use a food processor. Cut the butter into pieces, and whizz them with the flour briefly; the mixture should resemble fine breadcrumbs. Then stir in the sugar.

Or: work the butter into the flour with your fingertips. Some people find it satisfying.

Apple crumble. Most crumble recipes under-estimate the amount of softening you need to give to the fruit before you bury it in crumble. If fruit goes into the oven crunchy, it will probably emerge crunchy.

Peel the apples, halve and quarter them, take out the cores, and cut the flesh into wedges. You can stop them going brown if you drop them in water into which you've squeezed some lemon juice. In a heavy saucepan, melt enough butter to coat the pan bottom, add the apples (damp from their soaking), and cook them gently, with the pan covered.

When there's a bit of liquid in the pan, you can add some sugar – start with a tablespoon, and then taste – without fear of caramelising it.

You may find that your apples give off a good deal of liquid; uncover the pan to allow it to evaporate, and continue to cook, stirring regularly. But others may need the help of a little additional water. They'll take 15 to 20 minutes to soften. You could add a little cinnamon and nutmeg.

If you can't find Bramleys, try other varieties with a bit of acidic character to them: Cox's, for example.

Apple and blackberry is good. Poach the blackberries (see page 310), and add them, with a reduced and thickened syrup, to the cooked apples.

Or apple and rhubarb; again, cooked separately (see "Rhubarb", page 311). Try equal volumes of each fruit, weighing about 900 g in total.

Tip the cooked apples, having checked that they're sweet enough, into a pie dish or other ovenproof dish. Cover with the crumble. The quantity of flour, butter and sugar given above is only a guide, and may be over-generous; don't use it all if it threatens to overwhelm the fruit. You want a light, buttery layer of crunchy crumbs, not a thick, dry layer of compacted stodge.

Put into a gas mark 5/190°C oven for about 30 minutes, or until the top of the crumble is golden.

Plum crumble. Cut 1 kg of plums – or more if you like – in half, and remove the stones. Simmer in syrup (see page 310), in a wide, covered pan, for about two minutes on each side; they should just be starting to tenderise.

Transfer them in a slotted spoon to an oven dish; reduce the syrup to a thick liquid, and pour it over the fruit. Cover with the crumble, and bake as above. You don't need much syrup: just enough, say, to come a third of the way up the stoned and halved fruit.

Blackcurrant and/or redcurrant crumble. Simply mix 600 g of them in an oven dish with 3 tbsps of sugar, cover with crumble, and bake.

Plum clafoutis

Is it a custard? Is it a batter? Recipes disagree. The one I like best, of which the following is an adaptation, is quite a custardy one; it comes from Raymond Blanc's *Blanc Mange*. My version never resembles the one on the cover of the book – but then, you don't expect that to happen, do you? It tastes pretty good, nonetheless.

HOW TO MAKE IT
For 6
12 plums, halved, stones removed
Syrup: 150 ml water, 50 g caster sugar
55 ml milk
55 ml double or whipping cream
3 eggs
90 g caster sugar
20 g plain flour
½ vanilla pod or 1 tsp vanilla essence

In a wide saucepan, warm the syrup; when it's
simmering, add the plums (which should all have
access to the water), and cook for about five
minutes, turning them halfway through. You don't
need to put the lid on the pan. Check to see that
the plums are soft, but not mushy. You can let
them cool in the saucepan, covered.

Slit the vanilla pod lengthways, add it, with
scraped-out seeds, to the milk and cream in a
saucepan, and bring to a simmer. Turn off the
heat, cover the pan, and let the vanilla flavour
infuse for 20 minutes. Remove the pod.

You want to get air into the eggs. Whisk them,
with the sugar, until you can see that they have
expanded considerably in volume. Stir in the flour,
and then the milk and cream, which – if you want to
lose the vanilla seeds – you can pour on to the mixture through a sieve. (If you're using vanilla essence,
you won't need to have heated the milk and
cream beforehand. Simply add the vanilla now.)

I use a flan dish with a diameter of about 23 cm.

**Grease it with a little butter; lay the plums in it;
pour over the batter; bake in a gas mark 4/180°C
oven, for about 30 to 35 minutes, until just set.
You could boil down the syrup to use as a sauce.**

You're supposed to wait until the clafoutis is tepid; but I don't
see why you shouldn't eat it hot. That's how some like it.

VARIATIONS
Raymond Blanc's recipe is for apricot clafoutis; the apricots
are prepared as above. He also includes some alcohol: for
the recipe above, you'd want about a tablespoon of amaret-
to liqueur, poured into the custard/batter mixture. A classic
clafoutis involves cherries, which don't require pre-cooking
and are simply mixed with the custard/batter. Guests have
to pick out the stones themselves, while eating. How many
would you like? About 36 in total, I'd suggest.

Two chocolate puddings

Chocolate mousse

HOW TO MAKE IT
For 6
*200 g dark chocolate (with at least 70% cocoa solids –
Green & Black's organic makes a fine mousse)*
4 eggs, separated[1] – see WHY YOU DO IT
200 ml whipping or double cream
25 g butter, cut into pieces

317

Whip the cream until it thickens, but not until it goes stiff. It should still be liquid (or the mousse will be too solid). In a separate bowl, beat the egg yolks.

Melt the chocolate in a saucepan over a very gentle heat, or in a bowl resting in a saucepan above simmering water. Keep stirring, to encourage it to melt quickly. Overcooked, the chocolate will go grainy. Remove from the heat, and stir in the butter.

Whisk the egg whites until they form stiff peaks.[2] Stir the egg yolks and the cream into the chocolate; fold in the whites, gently turning them through the mixture in order not to bash the air out of them.

Divide the mousse between six bowls, and refrigerate for at least a couple of hours.

VARIATIONS

You could leave out the cream. Or – particularly if you're nervous about raw eggs (see page 81) – make an egg-less mousse. Mix 200 g of melted chocolate with 400 ml of whipped cream. Refrigerate. That's it.

Elizabeth David says that "Nearly everyone knows and appreciates the old reliable formula for a chocolate mousse – 4 yolks beaten into 4 oz [113 g] of melted bitter chocolate, and the 4 whipped whites folded in." Nowadays, most recipes include, as does mine above, roughly double that quantity of chocolate. But the old reliable formula works well too, giving a mousse with a more airy texture. Airy, you may feel, is what a mousse should be.

Include in the mousse the grated zest of an orange.

This mousse is meant to be bitter. I think that it would be a shame to sweeten it.

WHY YOU DO IT

1) *Separating eggs*. See page 309.

2) *Whisking whites*. See page 309.

Baked chocolate pudding

Not much different from a mousse – only baked. Actually, it is sweeter, and has a cakey texture.

HOW TO MAKE IT
For 6
200 g dark chocolate (with at least 70% cocoa solids)
100 g butter, cut into pieces
50 g caster sugar
50 g plain flour
4 eggs, separated

Melt the chocolate as in the chocolate mousse recipe (page 318). Away from the heat, stir in the butter, sugar and flour.

Separate the eggs (see *Separating*, page 309). Beat the yolks. The chocolate mixture should be cool by now; stir in the egg yolks.

Whisk the egg whites until they form stiff peaks (see *Whisking*, page 309). Fold the whites gently into the chocolate mixture.

Butter an ovenproof dish – a soufflé dish, say. Pour in the mixture. Put the dish inside a roasting pan, and surround it with hot water, which should not come further than halfway up the side of the dish (see *The bain-marie*, page 303). Bake in a gas mark 4/180°C oven for about 30 minutes, or until set.

A flan dish would work but, having low sides, cannot sit in a water bath. Cook the mousse instead in a low oven: gas mark 1/140°C.

Serve hot or cold.

Cheesecake

Most of the recipes in this book have some relationship to classic dishes. Not this one. It belongs to the cooking league inhabited by the likes of chicken nuggets, Hawaiian pizza, and pasta and tuna surprise.

I don't care. I much prefer it to those gooey, mouth-coating, stomach-sinking, baked cheesecakes.

HOW TO MAKE IT

For 6

150 g digestive biscuits
75 g butter
200 g full-fat cream cheese

397 g can condensed milk
142 ml double cream
Juice and zest of 1 lemon
Juice of 2 limes, zest of one

Blitz the biscuits to crumbs in a food processor; or put them in a plastic bag and set about them with a rolling pin. Melt the butter in a saucepan; stir in the crumbs, or pour the melted butter into the food processor and blitz, briefly, again. Tip the melted crumbs into a 20 cm flan dish, and compact them with the back of a spoon. Put the dish into the freezer for 30 minutes.[1 – see WHY YOU DO IT]

Meanwhile, whisk the cream until it thickens, but not until it goes stiff; it should be thick but still fluid. Combine the cheese and the condensed milk, and whisk them until they have the same consistency as the cream. Stir in the cream, along with the juice and zest of the citrus fruits. (You could of course use just lemon, or just lime.) Pour the mixture over the biscuit base in the flan dish, and chill in the fridge for three hours, or overnight.

WHY YOU DO IT

1) *Firming the base*. The contrast between the light, creamy, tangy filling and the crunchy base is what makes a cheesecake so pleasurable. Too often, the filling is poured straight on to the crumbs, which go soggy. A blast of freezing air firms them up.

Bibliography

Top three

For the cooking we do every day, recipes are less useful than is a set of principles, techniques and templates, on which we can create our own recipes. Here are the three books that are the best I know at inspiring that improvisational confidence.

Simple French Food by Richard Olney (Grub Street). "It ought to be called *Incredibly Complicated French Food*," someone once said to me. "Simple", in this context, does not mean "basic", but indicates that Olney is dealing with regional cooking rather than with high gastronomy. Actually, there are plenty of recipes here that are far from complicated; but only the most dedicated reader is likely to follow Olney every step of the way in his "Sauté-type" stew, or in his fish terrine with whipped tomato cream. The real genius of *Simple French Food*, though, is in the prose. Olney, who died in 1999, was an American who lived in France, and he wrote with a patrician fastidiousness reminiscent of another American expat, Henry James. *Simple French Food* is about the principles and, it is not going too far to say, philosophy underlying the preparation of classic dishes. "By knowing and accepting rules, one frees oneself of rules," he summarised. Even if you never cook a recipe from this book, you'll find it a revelation.

Real Fast Food by Nigel Slater (Penguin). What Olney

does for classic French cuisine, Slater does, in an appropriately chattier style, for the kind of cooking most of us do after a trip to the deli and a raid on the store cupboard. Again, it's not the recipes that make this book stand out, although they are worth more than the cover price, but the emphasis on improvisation. That is the guiding principle of all Slater's books, particularly *Appetite* (Fourth Estate), with its series of recipe templates.

McGee on Food and Cooking by Harold McGee (Hodder & Stoughton). This is an 850-page book on the science, history and culture of the kitchen. Don't be daunted: Harold McGee is a most engaging, companionable guide to these topics. After reading him, you'll know why a sauce thickens, what happens when you make a mayonnaise, how vegetables lose colour, whether flash-frying seals meat. It will put you in a better position to assess the recipes of others; and it will give you confidence to adopt your own techniques, based on the soundest principles.

Some more books I like

The Pedant in the Kitchen by Julian Barnes (Atlantic)
The Science of Cooking by Peter Barham (Springer) – aimed
    at schoolchildren, but of interest to anyone.
Classic Turkish Cookery by Ghillie and Jonathan Basan
    (I B Tauris)
The Gastronomy of Italy by Anna del Conte (Pavilion)
French Provincial Cooking by Elizabeth David (Penguin)
The Perfect . . . by Richard Ehrlich (Grub Street)

The River Cottage Meat Book by Hugh Fearnley-Whittingstall
   (Hodder & Stoughton)
Jane Grigson's Vegetable Book (Penguin)
Marcella's Kitchen by Marcella Hazan (Macmillan)
Nose to Tail Eating by Fergus Henderson (Bloomsbury)
How to Cook Better by Shaun Hill (Mitchell Beazley)
How to Eat by Nigella Lawson (Chatto & Windus)
Keep It Simple by Alastair Little and Richard Whittington
   (Conran Octopus – but out of print)
The Rice Book by Sri Owen (Frances Lincoln)
The Food of Italy by Claudia Roden (Chatto & Windus)
Sauces by Michel Roux (Quadrille)
How to Cook by Delia Smith (3 volumes, BBC)
The Man Who Ate Everything by Jeffrey Steingarten
   (Headline)
The Cook's Encyclopaedia by Tom Stobart (Grub Street)
Home Cooking by Richard Whittington (Cassell)

Acknowledgements

Emma Hayes of the Food Standards Agency answered all my queries informatively, and with patience. Darren Chant of Basingstoke and Deane Borough Council also gave me useful advice on food safety. Claire Domoney of the John Innes Centre in Norwich furthered my understanding of the cooking of legumes, as did Geoffrey Kite at Kew.

I'd like to thank also Cortina Butler, Anne Dolamore, Fiona Hunter, Gwilym Lewis, Marion Regan and Betsy Tobin.

Index

In case of difficulty in purchasing any Short Books
title through normal channels, please contact
BOOKPOST Tel: 01624 836000
                   Fax: 01624 837033
email: bookshop@enterprise.net
www.bookpost.co.uk
Please quote ref. 'Short Books'